PRODUCTIVITY

A GUIDE ON HOW TO MANAGE YOUR TIME
AND TO STOP PROCRASTINATING. FOLLOW
THESE MENTAL MODELS IF YOU WANT TO
MASTER SELF-DISCIPLINE WHILE STILL
ENJOYING A STRESS-FREE LIFE

Mark Mind

METAL TOUGHNESS

Table of Contents

Introduction 10

Chapter 1 Crucial Tips To Solving Overthinking............................ 16

Chapter 2 The Number One Most Important Thing To Understand If You Want To Be Happy In This World: Mastering Your Mind 24

Chapter 3 How To Improve Your Performance In Work? 30

Chapter 4 How To Increase Your Productivity? 36

Chapter 5 How To Improve Your Mood, No Matter What Are Your Circumstances?... 42

Chapter 6 Simple Steps To Remove Negative Influences From Your Life 46

Chapter 7 How To Develop Self-Confidence 52

Chapter 8 Develop The Habits Of Successful People........................ 56

Chapter 9 Why And How To Stop Procrastination In Your Life........ 62

Chapter 10 Ways To Avoid Decision Fatigue.................................. 68

Chapter 11 Challenging Your Thoughts....................................... 72

Chapter 12 Mental Clutter 78

Chapter 13 Embracing Mindfulness As An Efficient Alternative To Overthinking 86

Chapter 14 Effects Of Overthinking 94

Chapter 15 How To Stop Overthinking With Positive Self-Talk........ 100

Chapter 16 How To Solve Worry Problems? 108

Chapter 17 Reframing Your Negative Thoughts 116

Chapter 18 How To Use Meditation To Deal With Overthinking?.........122

Chapter 19 Returning To Self-Care...128

Chapter 20 The Key To Feeling Good...135

Chapter 21 Self-Discipline..142

Chapter 22 Goal Setting 148

Chapter 23 Forgetting Your Past...154

Chapter 24 Deliberate Thinking 160

Chapter 25 Exercises That Help Positive Thinking 166

Chapter 26 How To Make Important Decisions Today? 170

Conclusion..176

STOP OVERTHINKING

Table of Contents

Introduction 184

Chapter 1 What Is Mental Toughness? 186

Chapter 2 Characteristics Of Mentally Tough People 190

Chapter 3 Assessing Your Mental Strength.................................... 196

Chapter 4 How To Develop Mental Toughness............................... 200

Chapter 5 What Does Habit Have To Do With My Mental Toughness 206

Chapter 6 Controlling Fear Or Failure With Mental Toughness 212

Chapter 7 How To Change Your Mental State And Increase Mental Toughness For Personal Success.. 218

Chapter 8 Using Mental Toughness Or Self-Confidence, Self-Discipline, Willpower And Self-Esteem 222

Chapter 9 Achieve Success Using Mental Toughness 228

Chapter 10 Improving Your Emotional Intelligence Using Mental Toughness ..232

Chapter 11 Leadership Skills And Mental Toughness........................ 238

Chapter 12 Be Spiritually Grounded Using Mental Toughness 246

Chapter 13 Applying Mental Toughness In Different Fields 250

Chapter 14 Improving Your Odds With Mental Toughness............................ 256

Chapter 15 The Secret To Staying Motivated 260

Chapter 16 Improve Focus And Concentration With Mental Toughness 266

Chapter 17 Mental Toughness Techniques That Can Help You Achieve Your Goals And Be Strong In Every Situation.. 270

Chapter 18 Watch The Pros Not The Joes 276

Chapter 19 Time Management Strategies.. 280

Chapter 20 Declutter Your Mind, Body And Environment 286

Chapter 21 Some Apps For Productivity 290

Chapter 22 Improving Family Relationships.. 294

Chapter 23 Myths About The Mentally Strong 298

Chapter 24 The 80/20 Rule 304

Chapter 25 Know The Enemy To Know Victory 308

Chapter 26 How To Accept Things The Way They Are 314

Chapter 27 Habits That Guarantee Our Success In Life 320

Chapter 28 Your Attitude 328

Chapter 29 Strategies To Help Stop Procrastinating.............................. 332

Chapter 30 When Procrastination Is Not The Problem – Other Issues Which Look Like Procrastination 338

Chapter 31 The Principle Of Cause And Effect And How It Controls Everything
.... 340

Chapter 32 Change Your Action 344

Chapter 33 How To Take Your Practice Skills Into The Big Game.................. 350

Chapter 33 Train The Brain 354

Conclusion 360

.

STOP OVERTHINKING

HOW TO OVERCOME NEGATIVE THINKING, PROCRASTINATION, ANXIETY, AND OTHER NEGATIVE EMOTIONS. HOW TO INCREASE SELF-ESTEEM, SELF-CONFIDENCE, EMOTIONAL INTELLIGENCE AND PRODUCTIVITY.

Mark Mind

Introduction

The biggest cause of unhappiness is overthinking.

A big gap exists between deliberating and solving problems. Some often suggest that women are more likely to overthink than men, but the truth is that no one manages to avoid overthinking; it is something everyone does.

A therapist meets with thousands of individuals in their office daily, many of whom are searching for help in dealing with overthinking. Many often complain about their inability to relax. They feel that their brain is constantly preoccupied with worries and negative thoughts, and, as a result, they feel so much anxiety that they can't rest. Some complaint about the fact that they focus excessively on how much better their lives would be without the mistakes they have made.

There is a strong connection between overthinking and mental health problems, such as anxiety and depression. Those suffering from overthinking might not even notice the decline in their mental health because they are so preoccupied and worried; they are not living in the mindfully. Such individuals might feel that their overthinking is healthy and useful, and without it, some horrible calamity might happen.

But the truth is just the opposite. Overthinking increases the chances of feeling lost, anxious, and miserable. It can also lead to resentment and anger that clouds your judgment and makes it hard for you to make the right decisions. This state is often referred to as analysis paralysis.

Overthinking keeps reminding you of things you can't control, such as your failure. There are basically two forms of overthinking, namely: an excessive rumination on the past and worrying excessively about future events. These preoccupations prevent you from making progress in your life. There is a clear difference between overthinking, self-reflection, and problem-solving.

How is overthinking different from problem-solving? There is a clear difference between problem-solving and overthinking. When problem-solving, your goal is to solve an underlying problem. Overthinkers dwell more on the problems themselves than possible solutions to their problems.

How about self-reflection? Is it the same as overthinking? No! Self-reflection has a definite purpose; it helps you discover new things about yourself, your condition, and your situation.

What's the bottom line? While you are overthinking, you're not productive. However, self-reflection and problem-solving help you create solutions and recognize behaviors that may be holding you back.

We all have a tendency to overthink. Being aware of this fact makes it easier to change. And the first step involves identifying the damage caused by overthinking.

The idea that overthinking stops bad things from happening is a subconscious perception nurtured by many; they feel that the failure to ruminate over past events will precipitate some sort of unforeseen calamity. Research indicates that overthinking is not healthy and will impact our lives negatively.

If you notice the tendency to become enmeshed in overthinking, don't despair. You can use the strategies below to get back your energy, time, and brainpower.

From proper time scheduling to thought substitution, here are several exercises that will boost your mental strength and help you stop overthinking everything.

If you are an overthinker, you limit your chances of becoming successful in life. It will prevent you from reaching your goals and make your life miserable.

Why have an uplifting standpoint in life, since you can? Since there's a great deal in it for you. That is the reason. Keep in mind, positive reasoning is believing that is naturally advantageous. This is the thing that makes it 'positive' in any case.

You've just observed the 10,000-foot view perspective on the three essential advantages: positive reasoning causes you to accomplish something you need, encourages you to feel better (or if nothing else better), and it's helpful and quickly improves your life somehow or another.

Be that as it may, you can burrow down further to identify progressively specific advantages that are likewise worth increasing in value. In view of this, here are a few advantages of reasoning all the more emphatically:

More achievement: having more vitality, progressively confidence, and increasingly self-assurance prompts more achievement

Better rest and wellbeing: increasingly quiet, positive feelings imply less unpleasant, negative feelings that can negatively affect your body; the outcome is you appreciate the medical advantages of positive reasoning, including better nature of rest

A progressively beneficial life: the more you increase the value of your life with positive reasoning, the more advantageous life is for you

More noteworthy certainty: the more you trust you can accomplish things (a typical type of positive reasoning), the more self-assurance you have

More satisfaction and happiness: the more positive worth that you find in life, the more joyful you become, and the more you appreciate life

Feeling more grounded: as your certainty and confidence increments because of positive reasoning, you likewise feel more grounded and all the more dominant

More vitality: positive reasoning frequently persuades and stimulates you to accomplish things

More genuine feelings of serenity: the better you feel by and large with positive reasoning, the more significant serenity you have

Higher confidence: the more worth you find in yourself with positive reasoning, the higher your feeling of self-esteem

Increasingly agreeable cooperation with others: the more you appreciate life and worth yourself, the more you will in general appreciate social connections

More noteworthy clearness of brain: since you have a decision, it bodes well to think in legitimate, adequate positive ways that advantage you as opposed to in negative manners that hurt you; this is an advantage of positive reasoning great worth considering

Does thinking positive have any kind of effect?

Completely. You simply figured out how you can profit by positive intuition from numerous points of view, so sure reasoning truly works for improving your life.

The most significant inquiry, at the present time, is this: would you like to think positive contemplations and turned into an increasingly positive scholar?

This is on the grounds that the most significant factor for turning into an increasingly positive mastermind is to just need to think all the more emphatically, and to be definitive about making a move to think progressively positive considerations, paying little mind to whether any other individual needs you to think all the more decidedly or not.

With this lucidity of the brain, you are as of now well on your approach to growing increasingly positive perspectives about things.

Along these lines, if you have just realized what positive reasoning is, your following stage is to study how to think all the more emphatically and how to remain positive regardless of the conditions.

Chapter 1
Crucial Tips to Solving Overthinking

How to form good habits?

Have you, at any point, asked why a few people appear to complete difficult tasks to such a large extent? When the state, "I am going to…" begin working out, eat healthily, get sorted out, read more, and so forth, you realize that they're going to get it going. Be that s it may, when you attempt to follow comparable objectives, it is an alternate story.

You may most likely adhere to them for some time, yet at that point, incidentally, you generally lose your inspiration and quit.

At the point when that happens on enough occasions, it is anything but difficult to get disappointed and debilitated. Be that as it may, making and continuing great habits do not need to be so troublesome and difficult. Actually, it very well may be very simple. Furthermore, even a great deal of fun. Here are the means by which to grow great habits and ensure they remain as such:

1. Observe your small wins

In case you are similar to the vast majority, you are greatly improved at thumping yourself for an awful execution than you are at compensating yourself for a decent one. With regards to overseeing ourselves, for reasons unknown, we appear to favor the carrot. Furthermore, that is a disgrace since research has demonstrated that commending your advancement is significant for your inspiration.

Each time you remunerate yourself for gaining ground, regardless of how little, you enact the reward hardware in your brain. That discharges some key synthetic substances which make you experience sentiments of accomplishment and pride. These feelings, thus, enable you to make a move and make greater triumphs later on. Along these lines, compensate yourself for each positive development, regardless of how little they happen to be.

2. Encircle yourself with supporters

The general population around us has a shockingly enormous effect on our conduct. One investigation demonstrated that on the off chance that you have a companion who winds up fat, your danger of weight increments by in excess of fifty percent regardless of whether your companion lives many miles away.

Other research has demonstrated that we will, in general, feel a similar way, and receive similar objectives, as the general population we invest the most energy with. In this way, one approach to drastically expand your odds of progress is to ensure you have the correct individuals in your corner. On the off chance that you need to make sound propensities, however, the entirety of your companions are undesirable, it is an ideal opportunity to make some new companions.

What's more, on the off chance that you need to make enormous things occur in your life yet you are encompassed with worrywarts who drag you down, it is a great opportunity to make a care group who moves you and lifts you back up when you come up short. You are normal of the five individuals you invest the most energy with, so be particular about them.

3. Get hooked on your habit

Have you, at any point, seeing that it is so difficult to relinquish an undertaking when you have put a great deal of exertion into it? We can utilize this inclination to further our potential benefit by utilizing the "Do not break the chain" methodology.

This is an extremely sharp procedure you can use to make a visual reminder of how much exertion you have put resources into your propensity. You will likely find that the more extended the chain develops, the harder you will battle to prop it up. In this way, get a schedule, put a marker by it, and get the opportunity to chip away at your propensity. Your solitary employment next is to not break the chain.

4. Structure your environment

From various perspectives, your condition drives your conduct. Have you at any point strolled into your kitchen, detected a plate of treats on the counter, and eaten them since they were before you? The thought is that every single one of your propensities requires a specific measure of vitality to complete. Furthermore, the more enactment vitality it needs, the more uncertain you will be to finish and do it.

Suppose you need to peruse more books; however, you more often than not end up sitting in front of the TV. What you have to do is:

• Increase the enactment vitality of your undesired propensity (sitting in front of the TV). For instance, taking the TV remote in the next room.

• Decrease the enactment vitality of your ideal propensity (perusing books). For instance, putting an incredible book beside your lounge love seat.

5. Change your mindset

At whatever point you are making another propensity, receive a researcher and subject mindset. Consider all that you complete a social examination where every mishap gives important information to your subsequent stage. Move your consideration away from the long-haul objective and rather center around appearing and doing your propensity each and every day.

6. Pre-commit to your habit

Envision it is 5:00 am, and your caution goes off. Inside seconds, your arrangement of setting off to the exercise center before work is in peril as your brain begins to think.

"Well, I'm quite drained. I wonder if it is even beneficial to work out when I'm this worn out. I could go to the rec. center after work. Or then again, I could go to the rec. center tomorrow first thing. Definitely, I'll hit the rest catch."

Abruptly, returning to rest won't be such an engaging choice. By pre-submitting thusly, you can include an additional layer of responsibility that makes you push through notwithstanding when it is hard.

How to prevent yourself from falling into the trap of overthinking

Here are practices to help you stop overthinking.

Become aware of your inclination to overthinking

Before one can address or cope with her habit of overthinking, they need to be aware of when they are doing so. They will become aware of it when they pick up on the signs. Even a person's lips signal the person when they are buried in thoughts because the lips will tend to feel dry. Anytime when a person finds themselves doubting or feeling stressed or anxious, they can step back and look at the situation, and how they are responding to it.

Think of what can go right instead of what can go wrong

What? Is it good to prepare yourself for anything by imagining the worst-case scenarios? That may work in the movies, but it is not a philosophy for a meaningful life. In most cases, emotions of fear bring about overthinking. When a person focuses on all the things that could go wrong, they may become paralyzed in their thinking. As soon as a person senses that they are going down an overthinking spiral, they need to stop. Instead, they can visualize all the things that can go right and maintain that pattern of thinking.

Dive into pleasure and happiness

Sometimes it is helpful for a person to have a way to distract themselves with happy, positive, and healthy alternatives. Any experience that can bring happy thoughts is worth spending time on. Activities like meditation, dancing, exercise, how to play a musical instrument, drawing, painting, and knitting can distract a person from overthinking.

Similarly, a person can opt to go on nature walks, take a swim, create a new recipe, bake, eat out with friends, or watch a movie. A person can find happiness in the simplest pleasures. Just be happy, and you can live to a hundred!

Stop expecting, or waiting for perfection

For overthinkers who are waiting to see perfection in the world around them, they should stop doing so. Every person has their idea of what perfection looks like. Therefore, perfection will never be a blueprint for anyone or anything. Being ambitious is a great thing, but aiming for perfection is impractical, incapacitating, and unrealistic. That is because it simply does not exist in the real world.

The moment a person starts to think that certain things need to be perfect that is the moment they should remind themselves that waiting for perfection is not as constructive as making progress.

Change how you view fear

Often a person is afraid because they have failed in the past, or they are fearful of trying or is overanalyzing some other failure. If anything, failure is not a stop sign. Instead, it is merely a way of telling someone to look to the other side.

In such cases, a person needs to remind themselves that just because things did not work the first time, it does not mean that things will not work a second time.

A person should remember that each opportunity is a different chance to have a new beginning.

Put things into perspective

It is always easy for one to make issues more significant and more harmful than necessary.

Just because your workmate did not say hello to you when you greeted them in the morning, does not mean that they are mad at you, or are putting you off. Maybe if you looked at your colleague more intently, you would notice that they were wearing their earphones!

The next time a person catches themselves making a mountain out of a molehill, they should ask themselves whether the issue will matter in five years, or a week.

Realize that you cannot predict the future

No one can. Therefore, all the time a person has is the present time. Sometimes people become bent on living their present time in view of their future. The truth is, no one can predict how things will happen in the next hour, let alone in the future. People can have ideas, but no one can know for sure.

When a person spends her present time worrying about the future, they are robbing themselves of the present time. Spending time thinking of one's future is not productive. Instead, they should spend that time on things that bring them joy.

Appreciate your best

The fear that holds overthinking is often based on the feeling that one is not good, smart, diligent, or dedicated enough. In life, there never comes a time when people feel that they have reached their full potential.

Therefore, people learn to give their best effort to the tasks that they have to do at each level. In other words, being the best person one can be is a matter of choice and effort. Once a person gives their best effort, they should accept it and know that while success may depend in part on some things that they cannot control, they did the best that they could.

Be grateful

A person cannot have a grateful and regretful thought simultaneously. Therefore, why should they not choose to spend the time positively?

Consequently, every evening, one should create a habit of listing down all the things that they are grateful for. The person should then find a friend with whom they can share the list. In that way, both people can learn how to share and be grateful for positive things and experiences around them.

One needs to form a habit of appreciating the good, however small that may be. Little good things eventually become great things!

Chapter 2
The Number One Most Important Thing to Understand If You Want To Be Happy in This World: Mastering Your Mind

You may struggle with your thoughts. Often, we let our thoughts control us, choose our actions, and bring us down. However, you must be able to control your thoughts if you want to be happy. Mastering your mind will help you to become the leader of your emotions instead of feeling the need to react to and follow them. You will be able to focus more clearly on what matters to you instead of being swayed by your current thoughts. When you become a master of your mind, you will be able to face any situation that comes with you, and you will be much stronger overall.

To master your mind, you must learn how to control your thoughts. You must be able to take control of your thinking instead of letting it take control of you. You must also learn how to ride your emotional waves. Instead of letting your emotions control your actions, you must allow your emotions to happen naturally. Manipulating your mindset can also help you, as it will allow you to control the way you think. It's critical for you to not allow outside influences to destroy your thoughts. You are the one and only master of your mind. Don't let others bring you down.

Controlling your thinking

You are constantly thinking. Your brain is always shifting to a new subject; there's always something new to be thinking about. Often, our minds wander to places that we wish they wouldn't. It would make it so much easier if you were just able to control how you thought, right? Well, it's possible. Instead of dwelling on our worries, overthinking every situation, and wasting our time on thoughts that we wish we wouldn't, we may practice taking control over our thoughts. With time and practice, you can easily shift your thinking to more pleasant and productive thoughts. You may find yourself becoming stressed out as a result of your thoughts. However, you can help shift that so that you think better. You may shift your thinking to more important and meaningful thoughts as well. Instead of letting your mind wander, you can control where your mind goes. You may think about what you want to so that you have the desired reaction to your thoughts.

To control your thoughts, you must be able to stop unwanted thoughts. Perhaps you are thinking something that stresses you out, makes you sad or causes frustration. To do so, you must catch yourself when you are thinking one of these thoughts and realize what the thought is and what effect it is having on you. When you feel yourself becoming upset, take a moment to reflect on yourself. What are you feeling at the moment? Are you stressed, mad, frustrated, sad, disappointed, anxious, or something else? Every feeling that you experience is caused by a thought that you have. Take a step back and identify what is causing that specific feeling. You may have to write down every single thought that you have or really scan your brain to determine what you're thinking.

After this, identify the further causes and effects. Why does that make you feel that way? Is it because of a negative event that happened similar to that? Did somebody else give you a bad feeling about an upcoming event? Determine why exactly you feel that way about whatever it is. There is almost always more than just the surface-level emotion and reasoning that is affecting you.

Once you have identified what caused this emotion, let it out. You may rant inside your head. You may choose to write it all down. You may even talk to somebody that you trust. Regardless, you should let out the emotion somehow; it is healthier to do so than to suppress your emotions. If you haven't dealt with a former problem, you will need to now. Perhaps you are nervous about an upcoming interview because the last one you went to didn't work out well. Your brain will return to that disappointment until you have dealt with it and moved on. You must be able to separate the new situation from the old one. Those negative thoughts should not interfere with that. By dealing with the negative thoughts associated with that, you will remove yourself from that and be able to move on from the pain. You will also be able to get this mental image out of your mind.

Riding your emotional waves

Emotions are just like waves. They come and go, and they're always changing. They go in different directions, have different intensities, and can be very powerful. Waves can be dangerous. If you go against the wave, you can be pushed against, pulled down, and even drown. This is similar to your emotions. If you try to suppress them or fight against them, you will not win. The emotions will take over and leave you feeling overwhelmed and defeated. However, it's possible for you to learn how to "surf" your emotions and use them to your advantage. Riding your waves instead of fighting against them can prove highly beneficial to you.

You must be able to anticipate the waves. Recognize that they will always come, and there is nothing that you can do to stop them. However, you may deal with them differently. A wave doesn't seem as overwhelming if you learn how to ride it. It only seems massive when you are about to be overcome by it. Understand that emotions will come and go and develop an appreciation for your emotions. This is what makes you yourself. There will be different emotions at different times and with different intensities.

You must be able to observe the wave before it comes. Acknowledge its existence and what type of wave it is. There will be different waves, and you must be able to identify them and differentiate them. Recognize what type of emotion you are feeling. Do this without adding in your judgment. You must recognize that it is a part of who you are, but it doesn't define who you are. Every wave will be different, and you must be able to realize that. Determine how intense the wave is, as that will determine how you may best ride it.

You must be willing to ride the wave. Instead of letting it drown you, simply experience it. Realize that the wave will come and go. Just let it happen. Experience the emotion. Don't let it overpower you. If you fight against the emotion, you will only feel like you are drowning. Instead, let the wave happen. Realize that it won't last forever and riding it out will really help you. You may let yourself go through the stages of the wave so that you can experience it. You may just take some time to let it happen and do whatever feels natural.

Remember that there are always new waves coming. The wave that you are currently experiencing will not last forever. It will be replaced by a new wave. You will not be stuck on the same wave for the rest of your life. It will, in fact, make it easier for you to move onto the next wave if you learn to ride the current wave out. You may start to develop an excitement for the waves that you experience. It can be like a game for you. There is always a new wave coming; what will the next one be? Develop an excitement and appreciation for the variety of emotions that you experience. Don't view your emotions as either positive or negative. They are all part of the experience of life. You will have an emotion that you are riding right now, but that doesn't mean that you will be riding the same one next week, tomorrow, or even an hour from now. Be open to all of the emotions that you experience, as they will all be temporary. Experiencing one emotion may give you an even greater appreciation for another. Accept the wide variety of emotional waves that you ride.

Manipulating your mindset

Your mindset makes a huge difference in your way of thinking, your amount of motivation, your productivity, and your emotions. When you are able to shift your mindset to the one that you desire, you will be able to accomplish more and feel better. It is necessary for you to reframe your mindset so that you can accomplish your goals. Instead of reacting to everything, you must shift your way to respond to life. Obstacles are not what define you; it is how you overcome those obstacles that make you who you are and define how successful you will be.

One way to shift your mindset is to alter the way you view yourself. Instead of letting your mistakes define you, focus on your success and your potential for greater success. You must be able to be positive with yourself. Recognize that there is always room for improvement, and mistakes will always occur. New opportunities will always arise, and not every opportunity is meant for you. Realize that some missed opportunities will allow you the chance to experience others that you wouldn't have been able to otherwise. In general, you must shift your mindset regarding yourself. Remind yourself that you are capable of anything that you set your mind to, and you will be able to accomplish your goals.

You must also shift your mindset pertaining to outside situations. You may be unhappy with your current life at the moment, but you must be able to appreciate all of life: the good and bad. Shift your mindset to a growth mindset. There is always room for improvement, and you can make changes to your life to improve it. Never sell yourself short, as you always have the potential to make your life closer to the ideal image that you have for yourself.

Control your own thoughts

We often let others control our thoughts. We can allow others to change our way of viewing the world and have them alter our emotions. You may be in a good mood, and one person may completely change your day (for better or for worse). It's important to not allow this to happen. You must be able to take full responsibility for your thoughts and emotions, and you shouldn't let others change that. Stay in control of your own thoughts. Although it's important to allow yourself to learn and grow from others, you must be able to still remain the ultimate master of your thoughts.

Regularly check in with yourself. Determine if how you are feeling is the result of someone else. If so, take a moment to separate yourself from the situation and reflect. Remember that everyone is entitled to their own thoughts. If someone tries to bring you down, respect that they may not be having the best day and handle your own emotions yourself. Stand up for yourself and your emotions. Avoid those who tend to focus on negative thoughts, drama, or the like. Stand up for your own beliefs and don't let others change those or bring you down.

Chapter 3
How to Improve Your Performance in Work?

Stress and work

Stress and productivity affect each other. When one suffers, the other one also suffers. This can have a huge impact on you at work. You can find it difficult to accomplish what you need when you have stress bringing you down. You may also find it difficult to not feel stressed when you are having an unproductive day. Because of this, you must learn how to properly deal with stress at work so that you can remain productive and accomplish what you need to throughout your day at work, reducing stress.

When you're at home, it may be a bit easier to manage your stress. You may have loved ones (people or pets) around, and they can support you. There is food available, and you can relax in an area that you choose. You may not have to worry as much about anybody needing you to do anything, and it can be easier to destress. At work, however, there are others around that will need help from you. You will have a boss supervising you (or you'll have to set a good example for those that you are the boss of). There are others around you that may not be your favorite people. You may also be unsatisfied with your job. There are a lot of possible ways that you may become stressed out at work. You must know how to manage this stress to make your workday better for yourself.

When you feel stressed at work, you may start becoming overwhelmed, anxious, irritable, unmotivated, or fatigued. It may become hard for you to focus on your work. When this happens, it's important to take a small break if possible. If it is possible, you may take a few minutes to go to the bathroom just so that you may take a bit of time away from your current task. You may even walk around or do something for a bit to distract yourself. If you can't take a break, at least take a few breaths. Distract yourself by thinking of something that calms you down and makes you happy. You may try to talk to others, whether those are customers or coworkers. Try to reach out to others at work so that you have people to support you and to socialize with. By having people at work that you enjoy talking to, you can enjoy your job much more.

Remember to take care of your body. When you don't sleep properly, you will lack the energy you need to stay focused. Always eat a good breakfast and remember to pack food for work. If you eat your meals at work, pack something nutritious and filling. Don't forget to have snacks and water available to you, too.

You may also leave earlier in the mornings. This will give you some extra time to get there in case there is traffic or anything else. It will also give you a bit of time to mentally prepare before work. You may make any plans for the day and schedule what needs to be scheduled. This is also a time to plan your breaks and what you'll do during your breaks. Remember not to over-commit yourself, as it will only wear you down.

Habits for increasing productivity

As you've learned, increasing your productivity is crucial to your success. It's necessary for reducing stress and getting more done at work. You'll feel much better when you increase your productivity. You'll also be able to get more done in a smaller amount of time. This means that you can meet more people, go to more places, make more money, accomplish more goals, and achieve more of what you want. What's to lose? Of course, you may lose out on some of life's distractions and wasted moments. But what are you waiting for? Tomorrow never comes, and it's important to live in the moment and enjoy it as much as you possibly can instead of letting life pass before your eyes. The following are some helpful habits that you can implement so that you can increase your productivity.

One way is to track yourself. On your phone, you may be able to track how often you use certain apps. However, you should be able to do this in real life. Often, we don't even realize how we're spending our time. By scrupulously tracking your time, even if it's only for a bit, you'll learn how to better gauge the passing of time. For a week, have a clock ready and write down every single thing that you do. You may try this at work. Set up a place to write, and track everything you do. You may even do this for every hour of work that you do. However, the more detailed it is, the more that you'll learn from yourself and understand your habits. Instead of having a specific time to write down what you're doing, you may just write down whenever you change what you're doing. The example shows the tasks completed every hour, which can help you to understand how much you truly accomplish in a day.

By doing this, you may realize that you accomplish more in a day than you think you do. If this is the case, you can celebrate your success and work on improving yourself even more. Is there room for more improvement? If you find yourself accomplishing less than you thought you did or know that is possible for yourself, work on fixing one area at a time.

Eliminating distractions

From the notes about yourself that you made, you may identify what distracts you. By writing down what you get distracted by, you can make it much easier for yourself. Recognizing what distracts you is the first step to eliminating distractions from your life. When you can recognize what distracts you and catch yourself when you get distracted, you can reduce and eliminate distractions from your life, helping you to accomplish more instead of getting caught up in the distractions.

You should work in an environment that helps you to get more done, not one that distracts you. If you can eliminate what physically distracts you, it can be easier to get work done. At the end of each day, make sure that you clean up after yourself so that you don't have a huge pile of clutter to greet you at the beginning of each day. Staying organized and having a system for your items can help you to feel less overwhelmed. You'll also be able to focus on what matters. Turn off notifications from your phone, computer, and other devices that will distract you. You may even uninstall apps or put a block on them so that you aren't tempted to use them during work. Get rid of any distracting items that you may have. Typically, bright colors can be distracting and will catch your attention. By working in a place that you can focus on, you'll feel much better.

Eliminate potential bodily distractions. Keep snacks and water handy in case you get hungry and thirsty. This will save you the time that it takes to go get these items. Remember to get a proper amount of sleep so that you aren't tired. When you're tired, you won't have the energy to focus and be productive. Go to the bathroom before starting tasks and while on breaks. If you have to use the bathroom in the middle of working, remind yourself to get back on task instead of prolonging your break. You must take breaks, but it's also important to be able to regain your focus after taking a break. Otherwise, you can spend more of your time taking breaks instead of working. This is not a good way to be productive and accomplish what you want to.

Priorities and procrastination

To be productive, you need to eliminate procrastination and learn how to prioritize. Procrastination can really get you down and stop you from achieving your goals. However, you can eliminate procrastination by implementing a few habits into your life. You may also cut out some bad habits that serve as aids of procrastination. Prioritizing your tasks will also really help you to get done what you need to first. You will be able to focus on accomplishing what matters first instead of letting yourself get distracted by what doesn't. For this reason, procrastination and prioritizing go hand-in-hand. When you learn to prioritize, you are eliminating your procrastination.

Often, we tend to procrastinate without even realizing it. You may complete tasks that aren't as important or urgent instead of completing tasks that are more important and need to get done quicker. For instance, you may need to work on cleaning the house and scheduling a doctor's appointment for your medical issue. The house is important, as it needs to be clean so that you're healthy and happy. The doctor's appointment is urgent, as you must go to take care of your health. Instead of doing these tasks, which are the most important to you, you may find yourself doing everything but these tasks. You may go to the post office, shop for things you don't need, talk to friends and family, and do other unimportant tasks. When you look back at it, you had a productive day! You accomplished a lot and were able to get a lot done. However, you weren't accomplishing what you were supposed to be doing. It's important to realize that priorities only matter if you stick to them. It's possible to procrastinate and still get things done. You must learn how to truly avoid procrastination and follow your priorities.

The best way to do so is by utilizing to-do lists. Make a to-do list for the next day every night. This way, you'll focus on what actually needs to get done instead of what you want to get done. Come up with 1-3 IBU (important, big, and urgent) items for your list. These are the super important tasks for yourself. If you only accomplish these and absolutely nothing else, you'll be happy with your day. You can then jot down other, less-important tasks as well. These tasks, however, you can only work on if you've already accomplished your IBU tasks. This will help you to focus on what matters instead of getting caught up in what doesn't. It can also help you to split up the bigger tasks. If you find yourself becoming overwhelmed by everything you need to do, split up your tasks into smaller tasks.

You may also put yourself on a timer. Give yourself a set amount of time to work and a set amount of time for a break. Perhaps you work for 45 minutes and take 15-minute breaks. This means that you're working for 75% of each hour. Experiment and see what works.

Stress has a huge impact on your life. It can especially have an impact on your productivity. It can be really difficult to get things done when you're feeling stressed, which is why it's so important to learn how to properly manage your stress. When you're stressed, your productivity decreases. When your productivity decreases, your stress will increase. They have an inverse effect on each other. It's important to become more productive so that you may prevent and reduce stress for yourself.

Chapter 4
How to Increase Your Productivity?

One of the biggest problems with overthinking is that it leads to procrastination. In fact, the whole point of the brain for causing anxiety is to push you into inactivity. It wants you to stick to a corner so that the risk can be minimized It is no way to live in this world where your contribution matters.

Procrastination is one of the most common side-effects of overthinking. It keeps you in a never-ending loop of thinking that has no scope of action. Your mind can keep forming strategies and then discarding them after a point to form newer and better ones. This process can be continued until the end of time.

What you really need is a plan to break the chain of thoughts and get into action. The longer you keep thinking, the harder it will get to stop overthinking about it. Even the best strategies in the world can get washed down the drain if they are not put into action.

Procrastination can be one of the biggest negative traits of an overthinking person, and it would also support your habit of not taking action on time.

Given below are 5 strategies that can help you in ditching the thinking mode and taking action. You can pick any of these as per the situation and break the deadlock. Remember, the longer you remain in the deadlock, the harder it will become for you to get out of it.

The 5 second rule

Fear has a very deep-rooted relationship with postponing things. When you are afraid of doing something, its results, or have a distaste for it, the mind automatically starts overthinking about it. It makes you think about the consequences if things go wrong and would also make you believe that things would go wrong. Many a time, if you don't act on time, the mind will be able to convince you that the time has passed and there is going to be no use of taking the action then.

The mind likes to keep you sitting tied to thoughts. That's the safest playing ground as per the mind.

We only postpone things for the future that we don't like to do. The things for which we don't feel that passionately or the things that have been forced upon us. The things about which we feel passionate, we prepone them. People don't want to get up in the morning even though the alarm clock rings several times and gets snoozed. The reason is their dispassion for getting up. They don't feel excited about the prospects of the day.

The same people would get up hours early if they have to do something about which they are really passionate.

However, you can't be passionate about everything you need to do. Especially not about the things you fear or loath. Yet, inaction will only push you into overthinking.

Make it a rule to get into action within 5 seconds of having the thought. It is a very short window. But you don't need to finish the job in 5 seconds. You simply need to initiate.

For instance, if you need to go to the office, within 5 minutes of the ringing of the alarm clock, you must be off the bed. Any longer you stay there, and your first preference would be to snooze it one last time.

Once you cross the 5 seconds window, your mind would start overthinking the whole process and would surely find things to prove the futility of the whole process.

Get into action before it is too late. This is a great way to break the shackles of procrastination.

Ditching the autopilot

Most of the decisions taken by us are not conscious decisions. They are the decisions taken on instinct. We really don't put much thought into them. This happens because our mind remains on an autopilot mode most of the time.

If you have not been taxing it much about making real decisions, it likes to make decisions based on references. The things you did in similar situations earlier. Did they lead to any negative outcome? What probability of success does it see of for the actions in this attempt?

Your actions are guided by the autopilot in your mind on the basis of such questions. The situations are never judged on their merit. The mind doesn't like to see the probability of the success this time and the conditions that might lead it to the result. It wants to maintain inertia. This is the reason most people procrastinate and never take action. Their mind easily disqualifies most of the possibilities without even considering them a little. The remaining time you'll have at hand now will get utilized for overthinking.

If you want to ditch this trap of overthinking, you must ditch the autopilot. Look at the things mindfully. Take all the decisions consciously. Look at the merit of every situation, and don't try to assume things a lot. This will prepare a better ground for action, and it will also spare you from overthinking when you stop assuming a lot.

Starting positively

One of the biggest reasons for our backing down from taking any kind of action is our tendency to look at things pessimistically. We begin on a negative note and then expect things to end positively. This almost never works.

The negative thought process is disheartening, and it is bad for the initiative. Chiding your own mind will not pump you up; it will push you into inaction.

Try to start anything new, even a day with positive intent. Don't weigh it down with expectations as that may also fill you with worries. Simply set out with a positive note that things would get better from where you start.

If you feel that looking at things in a positive manner from your perspective is not possible due to your limited view, try changing your perspective. Put yourself into the shoes of someone else you could imagine doing a better job at it. Think it through with a different perspective. Sometimes, changing the perspective can bring all the change in the work. The same things that may look very challenging from your angel maybe a piece of cake for others.

Once a man was looking for a famous church in a village. He had come walking from far and was getting grumpy. He saw a boy paying in the way and asked him the distance of the church. The boy thought for a few seconds and said 24,858 miles. The man was awestruck in disbelief. He said that the church couldn't be that far. I have come looking for it from so far.

The boy said that it was 24,858 miles as per the path he had taken; however, it was only 2 miles if he walked in the opposite direction.

Sometimes we simply look at things from a very difficult angle. Looking at it through someone else's perspective can change the whole story.

It can make the work easy and interesting. If you feel stuck at some work and feel that you don't have a going there, try thinking differently from the angle of someone else.

Acknowledging the fears

Fears can push us into inaction. It has a very strong impact on our decision-making skills. If we don't address our fears, it will keep cornering us. Even if we keep avoiding the fears, our mind doesn't sit silently; it makes you think all the time only about those fears and consequences of the actions.

There is no escape from this cycle. If you want to avoid it, the only effective way is to acknowledge your fears.

The moment you acknowledge the fears, they lose the deadly impact they have. You are able to clearly understand the kind of impact they'll have. You also get a chance to look beyond the fears and assess the chances of success clearly.

This is a good way to break the deadlock and come out of the habit of procrastination led by fear.

Learning the Art of Setting Milestones

Our mind is constantly looking for the avenues to push us into inactivity. It seeks ways to push you into inaction, as that is the safest approach.

Many people who began working ambitiously at one point end up in failures not because they had put in the poor effort but because their mind was able to convince them of the futility of their actions.

For instance, you aim to lose 30 pounds and get slim. Your aspirations, external motivations, and inspirations can energize you to begin work in that direction. But it is a task that requires constant motivation as you will be working against your own body. The body would make your work difficult. The mind would assist the body in it.

This means that after a few days, maintaining that motivation can get very difficult. The task of 30 pounds is not something that you are going to get within a few days or weeks, and hence there is a high probability that you'll surrender.

Many people surrender even before they have begun as their mind starts overthinking about the probabilities of success and find none.

Now, think if you had defined your goal in a more accurate way and broken it down into smaller milestones.

You'll lose 30 pounds in 6 months looks like a much well-defined goal. There is a target timeline so that you can't keep postponing it further. This is your first challenge to procrastination.

However, 6 months is a very long period, and maintaining motivation, even with a defined goal, can be difficult.

You also need milestones to help you in your pursuit.

Milestones help you in staging the results in smaller compartments so that you can track your progress.

You need to lose 30 pounds in 6 months means that you have 24 weeks to lose 30 pounds. It brings us to 1.25 pounds per week.

You will have a weekly target, and that can act as your constant motivator. You will have some weeks in which the weight loss would be slower. The milestones would push you to work harder the following week for making up for the deficit.

There will be weeks when your achievements will be higher, and the milestones will pump up to work harder for achieving the final goal faster.

Setting clear goals, dividing them into smaller milestones, and getting into action immediately can help you in breaking the chains of procrastination and inactivity.

Chapter 5
How to Improve Your Mood, No Matter What Are Your Circumstances?

Manage your mind

Taking control of your thoughts and emotions is an important and necessary tool to manage your mind. In reality, if you're not in control of your mind then it is most certainly going to be in control of you. This effective control leads to healthier, more positive choices and habits that can reduce stress and overcome anxiety and depression. It provides you with a framework and the right tools to keep your thoughts from spiraling out of control.

One of the most important keys to managing your mind is understanding that you have the capacity and ability to change. Too often people remain in the same old routine and rut because they don't believe they're capable or worthy of change. Change is inevitable and being ready and willing to embrace change is where the sound, healthy mind comes into play.

Some other ways to manage your mind more effectively could be by filling it with wholesome and positive information. There are many ways this can be achieved - from reading a good book, listening to motivational audiobooks, or even something as simple as a basic daily exercise routine.

Daily habits to manage your mind

There are a number of ways to help you gain better control of your thoughts daily. According to experts, habits are the result of repetitive learning and can be both good and bad. In an article published in Psychology Today, entitled "The Habit Replacement Loop," Dr.

Bernard J. Luskin describes three primary characteristics necessary for forming beneficial habits as follows:

1.   Attention

2.   Focus

3.   Purposeful repetition

Some examples of good habits would include things like meditation, reading, writing and exercise. Each of these habits has been known to help manage an overactive mind. Development begins with the decision to make a change, and committing to see that change through. This means learning to manage your time effectively by setting aside the amount of time necessary for each of these practices and making sure you stick to it. You can begin by allocating 15 to 30 minutes daily, which you can also split throughout the day, or between the morning and night. Here are some examples of how to do this:

Daily meditation

Start your day with five to 10 minutes of meditation. Combined with mindfulness and breathing exercises this will help return your body to its natural balance (homeostasis) and a place of relaxation and acceptance of new ideas. It's emptying your head of unwanted thoughts about your day and replacing them with a clear, focused mind instead.

In an article published in the Harvard Gazette, entitled "Meditation study shows changes associated with awareness, stress," affiliate Harvard University students in conjunction with Massachusetts General Hospital (MGH), discovered that by using this form of meditation over a period of only eight weeks of mindfulness meditation training, physical differences to the brain were observed, such as thickening of the hippocampus (responsible for memory and learning) and other changes appeared to the amygdala, which controls anxiety, fear, and stress. Participants of this study confirmed that they felt as though they were more in control of their emotions and mental state.

Positive affirmations

The concept of positive affirmations has been around for a long time. Napoleon Hill introduced them in 1937 in his best-selling book, Think and Grow Rich. They are a set of positive statements structured to reinforce a positive belief system. Most effective when they can be seen or heard several times a day. Repetition at various times of the day can eliminate any negative thought patterns and replace them with positive affirmations.

Positive affirmations must be realistic and something that resonates with you. They should speak to goals you've set for yourself or ways to overcome limiting belief systems. Commit to writing between 10 to 15 positive affirmations and say them at least three times a day for a month.

- "Mistakes are just stepping stones to success. They are the path I must walk to achieve my goals."

- "Every day, I get one step closer to the life of my dreams."

- "I release all negative thoughts about myself and accept myself as I am."

- "I have the power and ability to control my weight through regular exercise and eating healthy."

- "I deserve to be successful and happy."

These are just a few ideas to get you started. There are affirmations you can create to associate with every aspect of your life and give you the necessary boost. Make each one personal, and believable as they are just meant for you.

Practice gratitude

In an article entitled "Giving Thanks Can Make You Happier," (n.d.), published by Harvard University, confirms that a joint psychology study between the University of California and the University of Miami was conducted on the impact of practicing gratitude. Divided into three groups, participants were asked to write a few brief sentences each week on specifically assigned topics. One group was asked to focus on things they were grateful for; another group had to write about things that annoyed them throughout the week; the final group could write about anything that influenced them within the same time frame.

At the end of this 10-week study, those who had focused on gratitude were more optimistic and felt better about themselves. In addition to this, they were more inclined towards incorporating some form of physical exercise into their daily routine and did not visit physicians as often as the group that was asked to write about those things that annoyed them.

End your day with the same routine, but add another exercise where you mentally run through your day. Keep a small notebook or journal next to your bed and before going to sleep, list five things you're grateful for that happened to you that day. They don't need to be big things, but they need to mean something to you. Try not to be repetitive with what you write down, this will challenge your brain to come up with new ideas, breaking down some of the walls of overthinking.

By practicing each of these daily habits and developing a routine, you'll slowly begin to notice that you're moving your mind away from the way you once were. It will take persistence, perseverance, and effort, but remember that it is possible. Repetitive learning is the key to breaking free from the compelling habits of overthinking. You'll start to shift your focus slowly into the present moment, which is exactly where you want it to be.

Chapter 6
Simple Steps to Remove Negative Influences from Your Life

Negativity is a way that we view the world, which is marked by the thoughts and feelings a person expresses toward reality. Negative thinking comes from within a person. Whenever you think negatively, you will only focus on the bad in life and don't reflect enough positivity. As a result, you will think of the worst possible results of an action or decision. Negative people tend to be skeptical of any advice that is given to them, and they don't trust people because of their past experiences.

Even though a person might adopt a negative mindset, it is not healthy, and it hinders your ability to form meaningful connections with other people. Do you tend to look on the bright side, or do you always find things to gripe and complain about? If you are optimistic, you will see things on the bright side. However, if you are a negative person, you will only see the dark side of every kind of situation.

When a negative person is faced with a challenge or difficulty, he or she will automatically default to a negative prediction of what might happen in a given situation.

Where do you get negative thoughts from?

The negative thoughts that arise in our minds come from many places, including the patterns of belief that we develop over time. Our values may include our money, job, relationships, jobs, and other things. If you want to know where your negative thoughts seem to be coming from, then you should ask yourself some questions.

1. Do you find yourself complaining about everything?

2. Do you blame others before yourself?

3. Do you like to predict a negative outcome in any given situation?

In addition to these basic questions, you also should think about things that contribute to your negative thinking, including criticism of people, feeling victimized by different situations, experiencing depression, and always predicting an emergency. As you think about these ideas, then you realize how quickly negative thoughts can spread like wildfire. Whenever you are in the company of people who always think negatively, you will be prone to thinking that way. The more that you hang out with people who have a pessimistic view on life, the more negative you will become. Therefore, it is crucial to find friends you can be with who can build you up instead of those who constantly tear other people down.

Having negative thoughts in your life

When you have negative thoughts, you experience a severe impact on your overall health. Your pessimistic ideas will make your brain go into survival mode, which will be stressed about all situations that arise. When a person experiences chronic stress, they will feel the effects psychologically. Whether you are aware of it or not, you will see that those negative thoughts will affect your ability to function, and they lead to long-term consequences that can jeopardize your well-being. You may find yourself unable to eat a lot, or you may stress eat in order to deal with the situation. When you lose or gain weight, you are likely dealing with negative thoughts as a result of stress on your body.

Negativity can cause you relational difficulties with family members, colleagues, and other people in your circle. When you choose to stay in the negative areas of your life, other people will follow you, and they will be judgmental and critical of different folks that they might come across. Soon, everything rolls over like a domino, bringing you into a lot of stress and anxiety.

In addition to the relational difficulties, negativity almost inevitably results in depression, and depression affects the health and well-being of people. Furthermore, if you are with people who love to tear others down, you would not want to be with them and would rather prefer to go on your own. It is vital to find people who can be an encouraging presence in your life and give you a better influence.

How to remove negative influences from your life?

Now that we have looked at the causes of negativity, we can look at ways to stop being so negative and start living a life that is joyful and positive.

1. Distance yourself from the negative people in your life.

Think of a person that you know who is always negative. Avoid talking to them. Put some distance between you and them. Do not spend too much time with them because if you do, you might get hurt or experience some hard times. It is better if you stop interacting with them at all.

2. Do not feel bad about cutting ties with people who bring you down.

If you have entered into relationships with negative people, you should cut ties with them as soon as possible. Do not forge a relationship with someone who is always negative. You should find people who will build you up and not tear you down. Prioritize building relationships with this latter type of person.

3. Don't get into an argument with a negative person.

If you engage in an argument with a negative person, you will not win. It will be like a drama from a movie or something, and you don't want to see Mount Vesuvius erupt in front of you. Instead of engaging, you should simply walk away from the situation and come back to the person when they are ready to talk. Give that person some space to get over whatever it is that is ailing them.

4. Surround yourself with positive people.

By surrounding yourself with positive people, you will feel more positive and less gloomy. You will feel good to be around this type of people. You will experience a positive outcome, as well.

5. Replace negative thoughts with positive ones.

It is easy for us to get into negative thought patterns, which cause us stress and anxiety. We have to learn to replace negative thoughts with positive ones. We should not let ourselves get into a whirlwind of negative thoughts. Fill your mind with positive thoughts. Experience the amazing power of positive thinking. It will affect your whole day and make you feel much better as a result. For example, maybe you hate going into work on Mondays, and you dread it like the plague. Instead of dwelling on a potentially negative situation, you can say, "I'm excited about going into work today because I can have my coffee, do my work, and spend time with my favorite colleague." When you can have one positive thought, it will make a great difference in your overall outlook.

6. Stop yourself whenever you see yourself spiraling off into negative territory.

The next thing you should do is to notice when you feel that you are slipping into negative territory. Watch yourself lest you get into the pattern of thinking about the negative things in your life. For instance, you may find yourself getting depressed because you watch the news all the time and see the next disaster happen. After seeing this kind of event, your mind defaults to a pessimistic mindset, and you think that a disastrous situation is looming around the corner.

7. Don't complain.

Whenever you find yourself always complaining about whatever is going wrong, you should stop yourself. Hold the thought and then move on with your life. You should not dwell on the negative and think about all the things that are wrong with your life. The truth of the matter is that complaining will do nothing to benefit your life. It will only bring you down. Complaining pushes you away from the things that you want.

8. Don't gossip with other colleagues at the office.

Many of us gossip with other people. It is a contagious thing, and unfortunately, it affects workplaces and schools. It is not helpful to you or anyone in your life. You should avoid it as much as possible. Gossip can tear down communities, and it can result in distrust and many other things.

9. Do not try to read others' minds.

Many times, we might find ourselves wanting to read other people's minds to know what they genuinely think about us. However, we also expect the worst from their thoughts. It is best to stop thinking that people around you have some kind of bad feelings toward you. This will only bring about more stress and anxiety in your life. Moreover, you should stop thinking negatively. Do not jump into conclusions right away; instead, you should keep calm and relax.

10. Stop watching the news or your facebook account

The news feed is one of the most depressing sources of information in our lives, but we always seem to consume a lot of information this way. We go online on the BBC and learn about the latest attack in Somalia or other things that are going on in the world. Bad news can cause us to worry and have bad feelings toward things, and it affects our health. We would do well if we avoid interacting with media that have particularly disastrous consequences for our mental health. The same could be said for Facebook, which advertises fake news, as well as news stories that make us envious of other people and wanting what they have. These sources of information seem to give us more stress and cause us to worry more. The best piece of advice is simply to avoid hanging out in these places. Stop watching the news and endlessly scrolling through your Facebook newsfeed, which only leads to your own unhappiness and dissatisfaction in life. Better yet, simply get rid of Facebook.

Deactivate your account and only use Messenger to communicate with your friends.

Chapter 7
How to Develop Self-Confidence

Many people are not born confident. You might be one of them. Fortunately, this value can be worked in various ways to a degree of perfection. When achieved, confidence shall improve the quality of your life immensely.

Think positively

Reality is what you perceive. If you think you feel confident, then you are. Relive your happier situations. Thinking positively is not tricking or kidding yourself but taking control. Do not allow yourself to live on negative thoughts. Learn to stop yourself upon such realization or find a way of reframing them positively. Do not be hard on yourself. When you think positively, you also tend to be more confident with yourself in multiple ways.

Be grateful

The more you think and really affirm that things are working out for you in ways, the more you assert that you are good at what you do and that you have every backing with you. You have the skill, talent, mindset, your loved ones, and a future to go for. That is all you need to get going, and it means a great deal.

Smile

Smile and you will be happier. Do not wait to be happy to smile. Smile and be happy. Smile and notice your stress levels and blood pressure down. A smile is a wall of immunity against disease and negativity. Smile and look more attractive. Be happy and build your confidence. When it all depends on you and you make it look good, then you have no reason to worry.

Speak yourself up

Tell yourself how authentic you are like and your brilliance is unparalleled because you exist in your own right. You owe nothing to anyone. Speak to yourself in the mirror and urge yourself to go out for what you must get, everything and everybody notwithstanding. Speak strength, speak speed, speak accuracy and precision, and speak outcomes because you deserve no less than you want in values, actions, and returns.

Dress intently

When you think you look good for the event, you are more confident about it and yourself. Take the shower, wear clean and on purpose, do the deodorant and just feel collected and put together. Modesty is good but the intent is great and powerful. It is a language encoded and decoded with a pleasure and measure of precision.

Mind your posture

Keep your chin up, your shoulders back, and walk like you own the place. Occupy enough space for you. Look unapologetic. Be flexible, relaxed but stable and fearless. Look confident and so be it.

Work out

Work out to look better. Looking better makes you feel better. What's more, working will make you feel more productive, energized, as well as add vigor and dimension in your moves and activity. Working out makes you feel like you contain yourself and are better able to handle what comes your way.

Wear color

In humans, color has something to do with mood. When you look just bright, it is likely that is how you expect things to go. If you wear a dull color, well that's the kind of reception you anticipate too. The little spike in pizzazz could be all your confidence needs. You may be advised by your friend or stylist early about what colors and garment details to go for during specific events.

Speak with everyone and compliment where due

Contrarian, you may think. When you understand people, you will know how to carry yourself assuredly around them. Simply, do talk to everyone even for a few seconds. People are friendly and will not try to catch or judge you by your statements. Rather the benefits are mutual. People like being approached for conversation and appreciate it when you break the ice for them. And that is a plus for you.

Chapter 8
Develop the Habits of Successful People

The life you live today is contributed by the habits you have. Habits results to all the success you have achieved. For example, your health, moods, and achievements have been successful because of habits. The activities you take part in shape your life. If, for instance, you engage in bad habits continuously, the bad habits will destroy your life. If you decide to implement good habits, this can change your life forever. It depends on one if he chooses to change his life, then he will make the changes unbeneficial behaviors and replace them with what will benefit him in terms of behaviors. Don't despise the small changes that may take part because they make a great difference in the life of somebody.

Establishing good habits and behaviors takes time to implement; it is not something that will happen in seconds. There methods that can help you to implement the desired behaviors. The following method can be used to help one build new habits:

Setting a trigger

This is having intentions to change the habits and increasing the likelihood of forming a new habit and implementing it. For instance, if you are used to eating chocolates daily, then you can change that habit by saying this to yourself, that when you feel like eating chocolate, then eat the vegetable snack first then chocolate later. You will be building your habits by replacing the bad ones with the good habit. For the new habits to survive, you will need repetition so that they can stick to your mind. Below is the list of the good habits that can be picked by individuals and if they implement them, then they will transform their habits and life completely.

Waking up early

Waking up early will increase productivity because it contributes greatly to the accomplishment of the goals but also brings balance in their lives. You will only get up early if you had enough sleep. This can be achieved if you get to bed early or at a reasonable time and wake up early. You will enjoy life and see the benefits of greater concentrations. You will concentrate if you had enough sleep.

Be ready to learn

 Be that person who will be curious to know something, and above all, will be willing to learn that particular thing. If this will continue, then you are going to be a great person sooner than later. Developing the habit of exploring new habits and strengthening existing knowledge can bring a great improvement in your life. What it takes to accomplish all this is the urge to be ready to learn, and you will be boosting your learning curve. Doing this will not take much of your time if you will be more than willing.

Setting priorities

You have several tasks, and you are trying to tackle them at the same time, will you succeed in handling all the tasks? The answer is no, and you need to prioritize the responsibility. Try to see which one has to be done with urgency. It is also good to prioritize your leisure activities and your goals. For example, watching television is of lesser priority than accomplishing tasks that will contribute to your goal. Don't prioritize things that don't contribute to your goals. If they don't add value to your life and goal, exclude them in your priorities.

Have resilience

This will be of great help if stricken by disaster, you easily step up and try to reorganize things before you lose everything. You will have built your mind in a way that it will cope easily and find a solution to the problem you will be encountering. The only way to strengthen resilience is by believing in your abilities. When faced with tribulations, don't give up, but you should keep moving. Move out of a problem by re-organizing things one by one.

Motivating yourself

If you have the habit of motivating yourself whenever you accomplish anything, then forever, that habit will be part of you. This habit will be instilled by yourself. No one else can ignite such a habit in your own life. People may try and motivate you, but with time, you will find that they got tired on the way. You can look for effective ways to do motivation. Keep practicing it each day so that you will keep the fire burning.

Be positive

The way to think can either build you or destroy your life. if you are that person who will always think of failure, then it will happen. You will find that in everything that you try doing then failure becomes part of instead of success. Having positive thinking will act as fuel to your problem. No matter how hard it can be to find a solution to your problem but the positivity you will easily find a solution to the challenge. Being positive has an impact on your life and health. It will help one to live a life with no stress at all.

Have a vision

Are you that person who sees himself or herself succeeding in one way or the other? If you visualize yourself, then it can give positive results. By having a positive vision, then the brain will help you to look into steps in which you will take so that you can accomplish. The main reason why visualization is important is that the mind will be used, and it is hard for the mind to differentiate reality from what it has set to accomplish.

Setting goals

Do you have goals in life? a life without a goal is like going hiking without a map. You will be wandering in the forest, but you will not have the right route out of the forest. Same case in life, no set goals, then no direction in life. You will be wandering doing other things but, in the end, it will not add value to your life. a goal gives you direction, gives the necessary focus to overcome the necessary obstacles in life. You can do this by writing your goals down, then make it a habit of rereading them daily.

Have room for improvement

It gets to some point in life when you get to abandon the old way and get to create some room for something new. The rule does not only limit us to the old ways but something that will bring a difference to our achievements. It got to bring positive achievement. By doing that, you are creating room for improvement and letting go of things that don't add value.

Make and meet the decisions

The decisions you make can either build or destroy. Be careful when it comes to deciding because the moment they are made, no reverse gear. If planning to change the decision, it may cost you a lot of things. Your success depends greatly on the decision you make. To some other individuals, they spend more time overthinking a problem. By doing that, they will be wasting time on one problem. People don't want to make the wrong decision; that is the reason they will take long before making one. They don't know that deciding whether right or wrong is much better than not making one. Instead of wasting time and you are there, marking your plan and remarking. Act upon what you have at that particular time and will only make adjustments as you move instead of letting indecision to kill your productivity.

Meditation

If you want to change many aspects of your life, then you should start meditating on what you are planning to change. This habit has not been valued by many, and the reason are they see it as a useless habit that cannot help one. In the real sense, this is the habit in which it relieves stress and at the same time, will reduce depression. Those who fear to think, then this can be the best habit for them.

Do physical exercise

When you have regular activities, then you are on the right track of living a healthy life. Regular exercise improves your mental health. By doing regular exercises, then you will be boosting your energy and your mood as well. Once you have, it has a habit, and then you will never be tempted to push it to the next day.

Have little Breaks in life

We have become so busy with life, and we forget to enjoy the little breaks that we get. Nowadays we spend more time on social media forgetting that is depriving us of the times having leisure time. We have many distracters, but if we can slot in time for taking a break, then it will become a habit. At your break, lean back, relax and don't do anything that should take a couple of minutes. The little breaks are effective because, after the break, you will feel refreshed.

Make new friends

When it becomes a habit of meeting someone new every day, it can refresh your mind. You will end up having a different discussion from what you had the preceding day. The different people you will meet will challenge you in different ways. From that, you will be built in all aspects. What is important of all is that you get to meet the right kind of people who will share their private lives stories and professional stories as well. Such people can be a blessing to you.

Learn from those who have made it

When you meet up with new people, you will be able to learn new things from them. It may be hard to meet with those who are experts in a particular field. But you will find that some have written books, others have blog or documentations. Knowing the lives of these experts will act as inspiration on your side. You get to know how they achieved in life, and this will motivate you to do more than what they accomplished.

Listening to others

It is great when people pay attention when you are talking, it is a sign of respect, and it means that you are following what you are saying. But nowadays, what has happened to our conversations? We have people who like to dominate in a conversation. At that particular time, you will find that those who were listening are now thinking about how they will get that chance to also conveyor say whatever idea they may be having. We should be ready to listen to others because by doing that, we will be improving the relationship. It also helps us to be a better negotiator.

In conclusion, it can be hard to have new habits.

You will have many challenges in that journey as you try and getting new habits. At some point in life, you will find that old habits will keep appearing. That should not be the reason for giving up because of the challenges. You should be patient and stick to the new behavior you have acquired for a longer time. After that, you will cross the line, and the new habit will be part of you, and you will engage in it automatically.

Chapter 9
Why and How to Stop Procrastination In Your Life

When talking about procrastination, everyone might relate to it because there isn't anyone who could deny it. At least, once or twice in your life, procrastination would have played its role. Whenever you miss your deadlines, the level of anxiety rises above your head and you are forced to complete the project as soon as possible. But deep down, you know it is impossible to complete because there is so much to do. Yet, you try! Procrastination will make your life miserable, so try not to make it a habit.

Some people want to stop procrastinating, but they are unable to because they don't know how to do it. Or sometimes, they might be missing the motivation they need. And it can be frustrating, I know. You must understand the fact that procrastinating factors differ from one individual to another:

The following are practices that will help you beat procrastination even if you are feeling lazy or unmotivated:

Find solutions to potential emergencies

Procrastination is not just simply a bad habit; rather it is a dangerous one. It will have a huge impact on your health. Sometimes, you might even lose the great bonds that you shared with your family members. They might even come to a point where they assume that you no longer care. There will be situations in life where you have to deal with unexpected priorities such as death, sickness, and much more. Such situations can't wait because you will have to address them immediately. In such an instance, you would have to drop all the scheduled tasks. Some other times, great family events might turn into dreadful situations, and you can't avoid them and get back to your work. Emergencies don't come with a warning, so you have to put up with the obstacles they create. How can you avoid emergencies? Are you going to stop everything and address the issue? Or if you have already delayed the work and then, something urgent comes up, how are you planning to handle it? What might happen when you ignore the emergencies?

To handle emergencies, you have to have a clear picture of the type of emergencies that you are dealing with. You can think about the aftereffects of avoiding the emergency. Or think about the people who are related to the emergency, how will they feel if you ignore it? What are the actions that you can take to solve this sudden issue so that you can get back to work? Or can you put off the emergency issue because it is not life-threatening?

Before you dig in further, let me tell you. If you are working so hard that you don't even have time for your family, it means you are losing a lot of good things in life, there is a lack of balance. You are not living your life — this where the concept of smart working comes into the picture.

Carry out daily evaluations

Another excellent way to avoid procrastination is through daily evaluates. If you allocate ten minutes from your day, you can assess how things are going. When you are doing the evaluate, you will be able to find the priorities of your day. Then, you can analyze the tasks that will have a huge impact on your short-term goals. To make this evaluate session simpler, consider carrying out a Q&A format. What are the scheduled meetings that you need to attend? Are there any emails that you must reply to today? Are there any documents that need to be edited today? Are there any appointments that will take more time than you allocated? What are the tasks that require more attention?

Likewise, you should do a Q&A to find out the layout of the day. But you don't have to stick to the questions that I have mentioned. Instead, you can prepare your own Q&A and follow it. If you do this daily evaluate, you will be able to understand the layout for the day. When you have your layout, you will be able to stay on the track. You will have proper knowledge of the tasks that need more time or a quick response. Hence, you will not procrastinate because you are aware that it will impact your goals negatively.

MIT's or the most important tasks

It's tough to beat procrastination if you begin your day with a to-do-list that bursts with tasks. You must have a simplified to-do-list if you want to get things done on time and correctly. How can you simplify your to-do-list? It is pretty simple if you focus on MIT's - most important tasks. You have to settle for the tasks that will have a considerable impact on your long-term goals. This is recommended by many experts who focus on productivity.

My tips are to select the top three important tasks that need to be handled by the end of the day. It is better to pick two important tasks that have tight deadlines and another that will impact your long-term career goal. If you keep an eye on MIT's concept, you will be able to curb procrastination. Once you complete the two most important activities, you will be interested in doing the other activities by the end of the day. And that motivation is very much needed if you want to succeed in beating procrastination.

The Eisenhower matrix

If you want to make a quick decision, you need the support from the Eisenhower Matrix. The founder of this concept, Dwight Davis Eisenhower, was a general in the army. It was the reason why he invented this concept. It's not always possible to work according to the plan when you are in an army. There will be sudden and important changes. In such an instance, the Eisenhower Matrix concept was the guideline.

If Eisenhower utilized this in the army, there is no reason why we can't utilize this in our lives to avoid procrastination! When you are dealing with this concept, you shouldn't forget the four quadrants related to it. By focusing on the four quadrants, you will be able to approach your day-to-day tasks accordingly. Let me mention the four quadrants in detail:

Quadrant 1: Urgent plus important

These are the tasks that need to be completed first because they are way more important than any other tasks and they directly deal with your career goals. Plus, you must complete the tasks right away because they are urgent. If you complete these tasks, you will be able to avoid negative consequences. Once you get your Q1 tasks completed, you will be able to focus on other tasks. For example, if you have to submit a project by the end of the day, your complete attention should be given to that project because it is both urgent and important.

Quadrant 2: Important yet not urgent

The tasks under Q2 are important, but they are not urgent. Even though they might have a huge impact, they are not as time-sensitive as Q1. Compare Q2 to Q1, and then, you will understand the difference clearly. Typically, Q2 tasks will include the ones that have a huge impact on your long-term career or life goals. Yes, you need to allocate more time and attention to these tasks. But you seldom do it because your mind knows that the tasks in Q2 can wait.

Quadrant 3: Urgent yet not important

The tasks under Q3 are urgent, but you don't necessarily have to spend your time on them. You can either automate or delegate tasks to someone who can handle the work. These tasks are not so important, so it is okay to delegate them. These tasks often come from a third party and the tasks under Q3 will not have a direct influence on your career goals. But when you are handling Q3 tasks, you must note down the tasks that you delegate. For example, if you are working on a time-sensitive project and the phone rings, you might get distracted answering it. Or sometimes, it might not even be an important call. For such activities, you can assign someone. Even if it's an urgent call, you can still assign it to a person who can handle it. Through this, you will be able to manage your day!

Quadrant 4: Not important plus not urgent

The tasks under Q4 include the tasks that need to be avoided. These tasks waste your time unnecessarily. If you don't spend ANY time on Q4 tasks, you will be able to spend more time on the tasks under Q2. By now, you'll know what Q4 tasks consist of. Anyway, they are activities like watching TV, surfing the Internet, playing games, and much more. So, should you eliminate Q4? Well, no! You shouldn't. If you don't have a balanced lifestyle, you might even struggle to protect your job. The tasks in Q4 will help you whenever you take a 5-minute break or whenever you want to step away from work. These tasks shouldn't even be in your mind when you are trying to be productive.

To apply the Eisenhower Matrix to your life, start by drawing a table on a piece of paper or your journal. Then, divide the table into four columns and seven rows. Divide the rows according to the days and add the quadrants to the columns. When your table is ready, analyze your week. But don't write anything down yet. Before you start the day, think, analyze again and allocate the tasks as per the matrix. If something else comes up, you must take some time to analyze the nature of the task, and then classify it in the right quadrant.

5. Do it quickly

Sometimes you come across tasks that don't need a lot of time, not even five minutes, yet you delay it. For example, cleaning after having dinner, sending an email, or even changing into your PJs (this is laziness). Even though these tasks don't take much time, you don't do them because you consider yourself too busy.

Your way of ignoring quick or minor tasks is by telling yourself you have too much to do. But the problem is whenever you delay minor tasks, it builds up into a pile, and you might have to deal with huge tasks at the end. If you don't act immediately, you will have a lot to do when you take days off. Also, if you complete the minor tasks quickly, you will be able to avoid them from accumulating into bigger tasks. There are two practices that you should consider if you want to get minor tasks done.

The Two-Minute Rule is one of the practices that you must follow. If you think that the task will only take two minutes or less, you can do it instead of putting it off, can't you? So, whenever you come across any minor tasks, think whether it will take longer to finish those. If they don't, why not get them done? Also, if you follow this habit throughout, you will feel that you are removing a lot of negativity and you have more time to spend on important tasks. Besides, you'll feel that you are more organized and then you have achieved more than before.

Chapter 10
Ways to Avoid Decision Fatigue

On an average, we make 35,000 conscious or unconscious decisions every day. Most decisions do not need your active involvement. However, even some simple decisions can cost you a lot of time and cause stress. A quick glance at an online sale can cost you an hour. Making the choice of breakfast can be tough for some people. To sleep or to go for a walk can be a harassing dilemma. These decisions can cause decision fatigue. They can make you feel exhausted, spent, or apathetic.

The best way to avoid facing decision fatigue is to follow some simple steps:

Build habits into your schedule

Bringing habits into your schedule is the best way to avoid such decision-making points. If you have a fixed schedule that you follow, then such worries wouldn't arise. Fix a time for daily activities. Following a schedule keeps you sharp and makes you more efficient. It also eliminates the chances of procrastination from your life.

Be firm

The dilemma of whether you are choosing the best or not can be crunching. However, most of the time it is a baseless debate. If there is a product, it is made for the consumption of someone. Do not look for the best qualities in the products, look for the qualities that you desire and once you find them, stick to your decision. Indecisive people radiate a lot of negativity.

Make joy and happiness the parameter for your decisions

The final deciding parameter of most of the things should be the amount of joy it would bring in life. We all have this as the end goal behind all our decisions. However, mostly this is hidden behind riders. If I buy a bigger TV than John, I would have an edge and that would make me happy. This is a bad decision process. John can buy an even bigger TV at any point and then my same TV would start making me feel miserable. If you are going to buy a TV, then the only correct question is the kind of TV that would make you really happy. The kind of viewing experience you would want. The amount of clarity you are looking for. The size that would fit your wall and suit your room size. Your joy and happiness should be directly behind your decisions and not some hidden agenda. It would take away the decision fatigue.

Choose a role model

Following a role model is always easy when you are picking such habits. It makes your choices simple. If you have a role model then put them in your place for easy and stress-free decision making. Imitating their decisions will absolve you of all the responsibility and fatigue. The ultimate goal of the practice is to ensure that you have to make a fewer number of such decisions on a daily basis.

You do not have to lose your identity. It is only for taking decisions that have no effect on the course of your life. In fact, easy decision-making process frees up a lot of time for you. You will be in a better position to ponder over the larger problems in a relaxed manner.

Learn to say 'No'

Being resolute is very important for the success of any such exercise. Despite your efforts, there will be times when you'll be standing at the crossroads. You'll have to learn to firmly make a decision and go with it. You may not have the clarity but if you keep fighting with the idea, it will lead to stress. Learn to live by your decisions.

Some simple stress saving habits

Eating similar food

Food is an important choice that we make every day. You have several meals a day. If you start spending 10-15 minutes before every meal to decide the menu, you are doing a great disservice to yourself and humanity. You are only useful for the food-producing industry. The best way to expedite the process, or to make it simple is to either plan in advance for the week or month or eat similar food daily. You can have minute variations but stick to the same script. This will save a lot of time and effort.

Have a smaller wardrobe

Trim your wardrobe as much as possible. The lower the number of choices in clothes you have, the shorter you'll take to get ready. It will save time and you wouldn't have to ponder about your shining armor daily. Limited choice of clothes is a strategy adopted by some of the most successful people in the world.

Follow daily routines

Follow daily routines like a clockwork. If you are being lenient about your routines then you are cheating yourself. Stick to the routines as they help in the formation of rigid habits. Look at the people retiring from military service. They need to train daily in the morning for around two decades. It is a compulsion in the beginning. But they find it hard to shun the habit even after they have retired. The routine becomes a part of their life. It keeps them fit and functioning.

Have fixed corners in your schedule

Do not compromise with the time of separate activities. Everything has a definite importance in life. If you have designated a specific time of the day to one activity, do not try to fit the other into it. This adjustment trains your mind to make a compromise. It also has to make an unnecessary decision. Strictly avoid it in all circumstances.

If something makes you feel anxious, drop it

Do not do things that cause stress. Modern life mandates us to do several things in peer pressure. This is tiring and uninspiring. If you do not like anything, learn to stay away from it. It will cause unnecessary levels of stress and anxiety which you had been trying to avoid in the first place.

Do not fall in the trap of problem of choice

Economists say that the biggest problem of this world is not poverty or hunger; it is the problem of choice. Rich or poor, man or woman, healthy or sick, we all have to face this problem. We have to make numerous decisions on a daily basis. Some decisions make you feel liberated and others crush you down. The marketing industry has perfected the art of using the problem of choice to its advantage. They put you in the trap of choosing between better and worse, small and big, cheap and costly, bright or dull, light or heavy and in the process, you end up making choices that were not even required. Keep your choices simple if you want to remain happy and stress-free for the whole of your life.

Chapter 11
Challenging Your Thoughts

To stop overthinking, you need to first retrain your brain. Fortunately, there are many exercises and activities that you can use to reshape the way you think.

Now that you know a little about overthinking, and you also know when you are on the verge of dropping into that deep whirlpool of infinite negative emotions, you can start getting rid of it entirely, and you can start by challenging your thoughts before they run out of control.

Before you begin

Here are some of the things that you need to know before you start challenging your negative thoughts so you will not get too surprised and overwhelmed with everything that is happening.

1.   You need to know that challenging your thoughts might feel unnatural, sometimes even forced at first. But with a bit of practice, it will start to feel natural and believable.

2.   To build up your confidence for thought challenging, you should practice them on thoughts that are not as upsetting and provides a bit more flexibility. It is also a good idea to practice this technique when you are still feeling a bit neutral and not too overwhelmed by your thoughts. Trying to practice thought challenging after a particularly rough and problematic day would be asking too much from yourself.

3.   The first couple of times you try thought challenging it would be best if you jot down your responses. Often, when beginners try doing it in their heads, they end up with their thoughts going around in circles, which makes their thoughts all the more intense, and might cause them to spiral into overthinking.

4.   Another benefit of taking down notes is that if a similar thought pops up in the future, you can refer to your notes and find out how you reacted to it.

5.   You can practice with a family member or a friend whom you know will not judge you. Practicing with another person might help you by shedding light on the blind spots of your thinking, or they can offer you different viewpoints that you might find useful.

6.   When you are first practicing thought challenging, you should focus on a single thought instead of a series of them this early in the game. For instance, instead of thinking "It's pretty obvious that my bosses thought I messed up the project" you should break down your thoughts into smaller, simpler sentences, and then challenge these thoughts one by one. You will only be confusing yourself if you start challenging a pile of thoughts at the same time.

7.   Do something that will distract yourself once you finish working through a couple of thought challenging questions. This will give you some time for your mind to settle down.

Now that you know what you should expect, here are some of the most popular thought challenging exercise that you can try now.

Step back and assess the situation

Here's a scenario that you might have experienced: you feel as if your boss is constantly and intentionally ignoring you. You think that the reason why your boss did not greet you this morning is because you somehow messed up something and that he is contemplating firing you very soon. Usually, this kind of thought will cause your mind to overthink and cause you to lose sleep, thus causing you to not be as efficient at work, which therefore leads to you getting fired; in short, overthinking problems turns them into self-fulfilling prophecies.

On the other hand, if you just step back and analyze your thoughts before your overactive brain blows it way out of proportion, you can control it better. Next, think about what you could do in order to not get fired, like increasing your productivity, or maybe learn a new skill that can help you do your job better.

In just a couple of minutes, you have derailed your train of negative thought before it even gets a chance to gain momentum.

Write them all down

Another way to challenge your negative thoughts before they trigger you to overthink is to write them all down on a piece of paper. When you write down the things that are bothering you, it gives them a somewhat tangible form, which actually helps you reanalyze them in a more rational manner. If you want to take this to the next level, you can start making a thought journal.

What is a thought journal/diary?

A thought diary is different from the traditional form of journaling, it has a structure that you have to follow to make analyzing your thoughts much easier. For instance, in a thought diary, you do not start an entry with a "Dear Diary" or any form of it, the entries look more like a ledger if anything.

You make a thought diary by making a couple of columns on the page and then you title them as follows:

Antecedent – These are the things that triggered you during the day.

Beliefs – These are your thoughts about the things that you listed in the first column.

Consequences – These are the things that happened because of your thoughts.

This is why a thought journal is called an ABC journal.

Here is an example of how you write an entry in your thought journal. You suddenly start worrying because you have an upcoming bill that you have to pay, this is your consequence. In the second column, you write that you were worried because you might not be able to make your due date.

After some time of writing in your thoughts journal, you might start noticing that the triggers are usually not related to the thoughts that made you worry. Thoughts just occur, and the triggers that caused them to surface might be related to them at all; thoughts are fickle in that way.

In the consequence's column, you then might write down something like, "I took an aspirin to get rid of the headache that I felt was coming."

Every Sunday evening you could evaluate your entries and then think of the things that you could have done better. For instance, for the entry above, instead of taking an aspirin, you could have just walked around the park to clear your mind, or at the very least you could have eaten an apple or something just so your headache will not get any worse. Or you could call your utility company and inform them that you might be a little late on the payment, but you will be paying, and ask if it is possible for them to waive the late fees. Your thought diary will help you make sense of your muddled thoughts by laying them out on paper for you to easily analyze. This tool can help you understand your less-than-ideal coping skills and why you end up making choices that lead to consequences that are not really best for you. With the help of a thought journal you can change your future consequences by restating and reanalyzing your past thoughts and making the necessary adjustments.

Benefits of a thought diary

Writing in a thought journal/diary helps you identify the things that trigger you into overthinking. When you write down your thoughts, you will easily see if they are actually legitimate concerns, or if they are just irrational. Thought journals help you recall how you behaved during the time you were triggered into overthinking, and in time you will start to notice the patterns in the way you think.

When you recognize your existing thought patterns, it will be possible for you to change not only your behavior but also your thoughts. When you notice evil thoughts start to creep in, you can practice mindfulness and just observe and acknowledge them so they will go away. You actually do not need to behave according to your thoughts, you can actually ignore them and just continue living your own life. It is much better to write down "I ignored the thought of..." instead of "I went to the pub and drank a few pints to make myself forget," and if you notice that you are doing basically the same thing almost every day then your thought diary is actually working.

Make a habit of writing a thought journal

You can use a small notebook, a stack of papers, anything that you can write on and keep confidential. No one else aside from you and your therapist (if you are seeing one) must know about the existence of this journal; no one else should have access to your inner thoughts.

If you do not want to use the traditional method, you can also use your smartphone or laptop to create a secret document. Gradually over time, you will start noticing when you are starting to spiral into overthinking and then stop yourself from going any further.

Negative emotions, like those that shatter your confidence to pieces, can usually lead to clinical depression, which makes you feel irrationally lonely, hopeless, and they will break you apart from the inside. Writing helps you get rid of your self-destructive thoughts. It is an art that can help you share your innermost feelings and your deepest thoughts.

Writing down your feelings onto paper is a way for you to freely express your views and opinions on the things that happened during the day, and what effect they had on your life. You are not just writing words on paper, you are effectively eliminating all these negative thoughts from your mind, and with them goes all that negativity that came with them.

Get a hobby

Have you always wanted to learn to play the piano, the guitar, ukulele, or any other kind of musical instrument, why not try learning today? Do you want to get good at drawing, calligraphy, or painting? Attend classes or watch online video tutorials. You can also play your favorite video games for an hour or so. Having a hobby not only gives you a creative outlet, but they also provide you with a way to create something with your hands, it also allows you to think individually, and most importantly, hobbies provide you with an escape from your negative thoughts.

Whenever you feel as if your thoughts are starting to overwhelming you, whip out your hobby kit, and immerse yourself in the activity. Lose yourself in the skills, coordination, concentration, and repetition that your hobby requires you to do. Focus your mind on the comfort or challenge brought about by your chosen hobby, and allow it to chase away all of the worries that used to trigger your overthinking.

Chapter 12
Mental Clutter

What is mental clutter?

What comes into your mind when you hear of mental clutter? Do you visualize a physical clutter that you know of? Mental clutter simply means mental overload, mental stress or mental fatigue. This is anything that gives you anxiety, depression, frustration, sense of overwhelm, and anger. This clutter comes in the form of:

- Regrets for past failures and regret for not doing some things that you should have done

- Too many bills to pay and increasing debts as well as unfinished projects

- Worries and insecurities

- Inner critic

- Feeling bad for failing to achieve something

What causes mental clutter?

Worry

When we encounter challenges in our daily activities, our brains naturally go to a state of worry. Although it is a natural reaction, we can always control it because it will not solve any of our problems. Instead, worrying will worsen the situation. Worrying will take away your peace of mind and it will stress you. Worrying is a waste of energy.

The best thing you can do is to stop worrying. Find something to do that will divert your thoughts to something better like going for a walk, dancing, cooking or anything that interests you. You can also write down those things that are robbing you of your peace of mind and write how you are going to solve them.

Regret

Gee whiz! "I wish I worked hard in school my life could be better!" Such remarks are common when having a conversation with friends or family members. We all have those things we wish we had done or not done in our lives! Sometimes our minds can focus on those things but we should not allow it. Focusing your minds on regrets will rob you of your happiness and cause you mental fatigue and stress. You cannot change the past so put your energy into creating a better vision for your life.

Fear

Fear is an enemy of progress! You should not allow fear to hinder you from taking chances and chasing after your dreams and enjoying life. Do you dream of owning a business but you are afraid that it might not take off if you start? Start it anyway and silence the fear that you have.

Guilt and shame

We should take responsibility for our wrongdoings and learn some lessons from it. Never allow yourself to be a prisoner of guilt and shame because it will cause you to have resentment self-hate, and even kill your self-esteem. The best way to get rid of guilt and shame is to acknowledge your mistake, forgive yourself and move on. This will empower you, motivate you to become a better person, make you value yourself. You should never repeat the same mistake.

The inner critic

How do you perceive yourself? Do you frequently have negative self-talk dominating your mind? Negative self-talk will limit our mental growth and lower our self-confidence. Remember your brain will believe what you tell it. If you constantly tell yourself that you cannot do it, your brain will act according to that belief.

You need to learn to refuse negative self-talk and replace it with positive talk. If the inner critic is telling you that you cannot do it then do it and you will silence that inner critic that is hindering your progress in life. Talk to yourself positively every day and you will see changes and your self-confidence and esteem will improve making you feel good about yourself.

14 Tips to clear mental clutter

Mental clutter can greatly lower your productivity because you will lose focus and concentration. Assess your life, identify the source of your mental clutter, and try to fix it. Remember, the design of the brain does not allow it to divide its attention in too many directions. That is the reason why it needs to be orderly and peaceful so that it can filter information into the right place and act.

To get your mind in a good state, you need to clear it of any clutter. You should organize your thoughts, worries, and tasks so that your mind can have somewhere for focusing and acting accordingly. The following are some of the tips that can help you to get rid of mental clutter.

Declutter your physical environment

When you sit in an environment that is full of clutter, it will cause your mental clutter. This is because the clutter will keep on telling your mind that it needs to work extra hard to clear the clutter. These excessive stimuli will likely suck your mental energy. If you clear the clutter from your physical environment, you will also be clearing your mind from the mental clutter.

Get rid of the non-essential items and put everything else in its rightful place. The best way to clear your mental clutter is by clearing your environment or workspace every day so that clutter does not pile up. Tidying up your workspace will promote your mental clarity.

Write a "to-do" list

You do not have to overwork your brain by storing so much information in it. Having a "to-do" list where you write all that you have to do will free up your mind. The list should have priorities of tasks and you should check them daily and work on them depending on their priorities on the list. The list can have appointments, projects, bills to pay and so on. You can always tick against a task when you complete it.

This list can help you in collecting your scattered thoughts and tasks. Work on the critical tasks first then you can move to the less critical tasks.

Keep a journal

A journal is almost similar to a "to-do" list, but here you document those things that disturb your peace of mind and give you anxieties and worries. You can write down your worries, plans for achieving certain goals, and even problems in your relationship that are draining your peace of mind.

Commit to remain in the present

You need to let go of your past. Holding on to regrets from past mistakes or missed opportunities, or people who have hurt you, will clutter your mind and rob you of your mental peace. Getting rid of unnecessary thoughts and fears will reduce stress and improve your confidence. These negative memories do not help you at all, so try to delete them in your mind so that you can have a better focus on the things that are more important in your life.

Avoid multitasking

Organize your work well and tackle them on a priority basis. This will prevent you from straining and you will reduce stress and overwhelm. Although multitasking may seem like being counterproductive, it will eventually limit your concentration span and stress you. If you find your home or office is in a mess, start by clearing the clutter before handling any other business. Clear your mind of any other thoughts and focus on clearing the clutter.

Limit the amount of information you consume

The amount of information that we consume can have an impact on our mental health. Too much information from the media, newspapers and the internet can clog our brain causing stress and anxiety. Spending so many hours reading some information on social media, blogs or any other platform can clutter our minds with unnecessary stuff causing mental fatigue and mental stress.

You should limit the amount of time on social media and select only important information to read. You should never allow yourself to consume negative content and cancel any blog subscription that does not help improve your life. Ensure that the information you read is authentic and from a credible source, then store only relevant information while you discard the rest.

Set priorities

What are your goals in life? You should identify which things are most important in your life and which ones are not. Setting priorities can help you in taking control of your life and it can help you in identifying and reaching your goals in life. Having an endless "to-do" list can clutter your mind. You should know that you could not do everything in one go. So, decongest your mind by having a top priorities list.

You can start by writing down a list of what you want to do and achieve based on priorities. The next thing is to plan on how you will do the tasks and how you will achieve your goals. After writing down how you are going to execute your plan, you can now allocate each task the time you will take to finish it. Keep checking and updating your priorities to ensure that they remain relevant because they can change over time.

Make decisions on time

Postponing decision making will clutter your mind with pending decisions. So, act right away and avoid procrastination. However, remember to evaluate your decisions first before implementing them. Therefore, if you delay decisions, you are simply cluttering your mind. Check your emails, letters, bills, requests and respond to them accordingly so that they do not pile up giving you mental clutter.

Put your decisions on autopilot

Daily tasks that require decision-making can clutter your mind. Examples of these daily tasks that require daily decision-making include:

- Deciding on what to cook for breakfast, lunch or dinner
- Deciding on what you will wear to work
- Deciding on which TV channel to watch the news

You should prevent your mind from cluttering with these daily tasks for example:

- You can design a weekly schedule for meals indicating which food for each day and meal
- You can watch specific TV channels at specific times
- Set specific clothes that will take you through the week
- Set specific days' tasks like doing the laundry on Saturday

Practice meditation

Meditation is a great way of relaxing your mind and clearing it of any stressful thoughts. You need to make it a daily practice to help you eliminate any unnecessary thoughts and to calm your mind.

Take some time to unwind

Take a break from your busy schedules and stressful situations. Take a walk in the park, go swimming, go to social events, and go for hikes or anything that will calm you and make you happy. Give your mind rest and let it recharge so that you can improve your focus and mental clarity.

Share your thoughts

Sometimes talking to someone eases the emotional burden and clutter in our minds. You can share your thoughts with a trusted friend or a family member. This can help you to see things differently and make sound decisions.

Practice breathing exercises

Taking a deep breath and exhaling slowly can work magic by calming your mind and relaxing your nerves. Deep breathing can also clear your mind giving you a calm mood. It is also helpful in reducing stress and promoting concentration.

Eat healthily and get enough sleep

A good diet and good sleep are essential to your mental health. Getting enough sleep will help your mind to rest and recharge. This is also the best remedy for reducing stress and fighting depression and anxiety.

Chapter 13
Embracing Mindfulness as an Efficient Alternative to Overthinking

Worrying blurs your mind and prevents you from seeing clearly. Instead, embrace mindfulness.

What's mindfulness?

In simple terms, mindfulness is the average ability of a man to be completely conscious of his current location and what he is doing in that location and not being distracted by what goes on within his environment.

Naturally, everyone is blessed with the concept of mindfulness within them; notwithstanding, it can only be accessed when it's consistently used. But how do you know you've become mindful? You become conscious of what is going through your brain. When you consistently teach your mind to be mindful, you redesign your brain.

Further, the aim of mindfulness is to be conscious of their inner operations of the function of the brain, its physical processes, and feelings. If, by chance or knowingly, we lose grip on the critical things in life, life may leave us behind. With mindfulness, we can be more present, more aware, and more capable of dealing with life.

How people define mindfulness

Some have defined mindfulness as a condition of being conscious of one's current situation. They say that individuals who do not judge situations as either good or bad are not being controlled by their thoughts and that these individuals can be tagged as being mindful.

Being mindful is a useful tool to help one understand and control subconscious feelings that may present big problems in both our work and personal relationships. Mindfulness suggests being in the current moment instead of dwelling on the past or peering into an unknown existence. As a tool, mindfulness has been defined by many to be utilized during meditation.

Many see mindfulness as therapeutic. There are a series of advantages to being mindful. Some of these benefits include reducing a person's level of anxiety and depression and boosting a person's general well-being, helping them to combat feelings of isolation and rejection.

The best way to lead a mindful life

A person's emotional condition determines their ability to remain objective in stressful situations. Dwelling on painful memories and past events can haunt people and prevent them from doing their very best within their individual environments.

A man or woman may have, many years ago, doing something wrong, and years after year, the thought will keep returning and haunting him or her. He may want something to happen that will take away the thought of remembering that occasion. But how could that be solved?

This person would need to focus on that reality that is existing within his/her environment, and not let his past regrets disturb his/her present happiness. There is no doubt that the best tool to help a person to be conscious of what happens within his or her environment is mindfulness; it enables us to stop judging whether the situation is good or bad.

If you really want to control your feelings, mindfulness is something you should practice.

Important facts to know about mindfulness

These mindfulness facts are important for you to know. Knowing them will allow you to understand mindfulness and appreciate its functions.

Fact 1: Mindfulness is not a myth or farce.

Developing mindfulness is a scientifically-proven method which will result in improved relationships **with friends, neighbors, families, coworkers, and other individuals.**

Fact 2: You need not alter your personality.

We don't need to change anything about our personality to become capable of being present. Changing who you are will achieve little or no success at all; methods like these are bound to fail. But with mindfulness, you can bring the best out of yourself and become a new, improved you.

Fact 3: Everyone can learn mindfulness.

Mindfulness is gained by learning and practicing. And it is very easy; anyone can learn how to become more mindful.

Fact 4: Mindfulness is a way of life.

Mindfulness is not just common practice; it is a way of life. This way of life helps us to get rid of mindless stress and handle life's challenges more easily.

Fact 5: Evidence supports the benefits of mindfulness.

The effects and benefits of mindfulness have been observed in scientific studies and in the personal experiences of those who practice it. These studies indicate that mindfulness improves health, general well-being, and all other aspects of human lives.

Fact 6: Mindfulness gives birth to innovation.

Mindfulness eliminates mental clutter and frees the mind up for creative and intellectual pursuits. You will find it easier to provide answers to complex situations and problems.

Fact 7: There are some mindfulness practice basics.

With mindfulness, your reaction to daily events becomes more positive. Self-control is improved, making the impact of mindfulness more beautiful.

Wondering how to go about practicing mindfulness? Here are some important steps to follow;

• Set aside time and space for your practice.

For effective mindfulness practice, it is best to schedule a regular time and place. Always set time and space aside for this task.

• Do not pass judgment on your thoughts.

The chances that we will judge our thoughts while practicing mindfulness are high. The right thing to do is to observe such thoughts without passing judgment.

• Have a positive view of the present moment.

The goal of mindfulness is not only to achieve unmatched calmness and quietness; it is actually to increase our attentiveness to each moment, without judging it to be good or bad. Hard as it may be, the goals of mindfulness are achievable.

• Accept each moment as it is.

We might easily get lost in thought. The best way to come back to the present is through mindfulness.

• Stop your mind from wandering mindlessly.

At every moment, numerous thoughts will pop into your head. But never let these thoughts be the basis for your judgment. Identify the point at which your mind starts to wander and refocus it on the present moment.

These following practices will help you achieve mindfulness more easily. They are simple, but you must be dedicated and work hard to bring about positive results.

Mindful practices to help you improve your life

A positive change in attitude and the effectiveness of your activities increase when you can set time aside each week to practice mindfulness or mindful exercise. This exercise will help you to become more patient and better tolerate others. Your mind will worry less about criticism or negative comments. It will result in you socializing more easily and becoming friendly.

The result will definitely affect your sleep. You will get a sound and peaceful night's rest. Overall, your day will be eventful, happy, and you will feel fulfilled long into the evening.

Mindful walking

Think about what you want to do for 15 to 20 minutes each day while walking. This is mindful walking. Since walking helps to keep you refreshed and improve thinking, mindful walking has a definite purpose. To get better results, you have to stick to a particular pattern and method. This will enhance your progress.

You need to be attentive and concentrate well if you are engaging in mindful practices. Endeavor to pay attention to even the littlest of details, such as the people and events around you. Four essential elements will make mindful walking possible: a steady pace, relaxed gaze, straight posture, and good balance.

Posture

The success of mindful walking is influenced by your posture. You need to hit that perfect position while you engage in mindful walking. Getting the right posture involves releasing your body into each moment. Getting rid of stiffness, standing in an upright position, and ensuring that your feet are planted firmly on the ground. This will help you to walk better.

Balance

To avoid distraction while engaging in mindful walking, you need to have the right balance. This balance should be obvious from your finger down to your arms, and even to your tummy.

You may need to do this to be successful; bend the left thumb and wrap the other finger around it. Then place it on your stomach. Now place the right hand on it and let your right thumb rest in-between the left thumb and the index finger.

Gaze

Your gaze level affects your attentiveness to things around you, and how well you concentrate. More success is achieved when you lower your gaze; don't necessarily look at the ground, though. Remove or lower your gaze when you start to become too focused on the things that you see around you.

Pace

During mindful walking, your pace is another thing to consider. Walking too fast will help you achieve nothing. Try a steady pace; walk slowly, or at least below your average walking pace. When your feet touch the ground, it will help you to feel more grounded at the moment and able to concentrate.

Why should you practice mindfulness?

There are many misconceptions about mindfulness. Therefore, people who start engaging in mindfulness often find that the results are very different from what they expect or from what they have been promised.

Below are some of the six most frequent misconceptions about mindfulness:

- The goal of mindfulness is to make you a better person.

- The goal of mindfulness is to halt your ideas.

- Mindfulness is a religious practice.

- Mindfulness will protect you from being affected by real-life conditions.

- Mindfulness will solve all your problems.

- The goal of mindfulness does not go beyond eliminating stress.

Yes! Mindfulness helps people to deal with their stress, but that is not the main objective of mindfulness. What then, is the goal? It is to ensure that you are conscious about what is happening around you: things happening in the physical, mental, and emotional faculties. Start learning mindfulness today for the following reasons:

Train your body to thrive via mindfulness

One thing that has helped athletes to surpass their own expectations, achieve greatness, and rid themselves of negativity is mindfulness. Their training often involves channeling their strength in the best possible way and gaining better control of their breathing.

Athletes can attain full presence and achieve their goals when they work on a mix of mindfulness, which includes tactical breathing, and intellectual, behavioral exercises.

Boosting your creativity via mindfulness

By becoming more mindful, you can clear your mind, freeing yourself up to become more creative in all of your daily tasks or assignments.

Strengthen your neural connection via mindfulness

The development of new neural routes and building new connections in the brain can be made possible through the practice of mindfulness. This improves your abilities and helps you concentrate more on things that are currently happening around you. It also helps you become more flexible and promotes well-being.

Chapter 14
Effects of Overthinking

There is a high possibility of experiencing somatopsychological problems if your vagus nerve is inflamed or damaged. These problems are mostly related to your psychological aspect and can only be noticed through your actions, and they initiated in your head as it depends on how your brain responds to different situations, so you need to understand the two systems of the vagus nerve continuously communicate with the brain, mainly about other body organs. The sympathetic nervous system is responsible for keeping you in action by feeding the cortisol and the adrenaline while the parasympathetic nervous system is reliable while you are relaxed or resting.

In other words, the sympathetic system activates actions while the parasympathetic decelerates actions and keeps you at rest. However, the latter utilizes acetylcholine as neurotransmitters that control the blood pressure and the heart rate to create a perfect condition for relaxation. As a part of the body's autonomous nervous system, the vagus nerve may fail or experience damage hindering its full potential to the body. The most common condition that affects the vagal nerve is inflammation that makes it malfunction. This condition could worsen the functioning of the whole body as the vagal nerve facilitates essential processes that keep the body healthy and kicking. This stage discusses the psychological problems that arise as a result of vagal dysfunction and inflammation as follows:

Chronic stress

The problem is associated with overthinking things that might be beyond your control. Stress can also be a result of issues in your vagal nerve. For instance, when your body is exposed to harmful situations, it releases chemicals that are meant to respond appropriately and avoid injury. As noted, before, the sympathetic nervous system stimulates the response through the fight-or-flight reaction, and it is at this time that your heart rate increases to quickly supply blood to the rushing body parts and muscles. The response likewise enhances the quickened inhalation of oxygen to assist in blood oxygenation. In this case, stress acts as a protective mechanism that your body initiates to keep you alert and out of danger.

There are different perceptions of stress among people. In other words, what causes stress for one person might be of little concern to the other, and people have different ways and potential to deal with it. This means that if stress is meant to prevent you from danger, then it should not be treated as a bad thing. Besides, our bodies have a unique mechanism that is intended to deal with specific doses of stress. However, the body's capabilities could weaken as you may be overwhelmed by chronic stress that could be as a result of vagal nerve inflammation or damage. This type of stress impacts almost every aspect of your life, including physical health and emotions. The chronic stress is also characterized by low esteem where you feel worthless and not comfortable while in public.

If you are suffering from chronic stress, you are likely to feel overwhelmed and easily agitated by others. As a result, you end up avoiding interactions with your peers as you feel they want to control you. Avoiding people and having low self-esteem makes you suffer in isolation as you may not realize the seriousness of the condition. With this in mind, the emotional symptoms of chronic stress could end up being a serious condition if not detected and treated. Consequently, your judgment becomes impaired by the condition as you get prone to the inability to focus and forgetfulness. You also remain pessimistic and unable to view your life positively and exhibit nervousness through behaviors such as fidgeting and nail-biting.

First, people with chronic stress seem to avoid complex responsibilities. They also experience sudden changes in your appetite where they either eat excessively or not eat at all. Second, procrastination is also associated with chronic stress, and you could be at risk of indulging in alcohol and drug abuse. Therefore, you should ask for feedback if you think that you are suffering from stress.

Anxiety and panic attacks

Whenever you come across a stressful situation, the body activates the sympathetic nervous system of the vagus nerve. In most cases, the system is reversed once the situation is over. However, the persistence of the tension would mean that the sensitive effect of the vagus nerve would be prolonged until you are out of harm's way. The effect is usually triggered and ended by a physiological response in your body, but a prolonged fight-or-flight response would cause problems for your body. The situation would lead to the activation of the intestine and the adrenal axis of the brain. As a result, the brain increases the production of hormones that travel through the bloodstream to stimulate the adrenaline and cortisol induction.

The hormones act as inflammatory precursors and immune suppressors, causing the anxiety that could make you ill and depressed, so the chronic anxiety increases the production of glutamate in the brain, which, when combined with cortisol, reduces the hippocampus in charge of memory retention. The worsening of this situation leads to the development of anxiety disorder characterized by panic attacks. The problem is characterized by a sense that you are in an impending danger or your life is at risk. These false signs may be frequent, depending on the seriousness of the condition. With this condition, you feel afraid of losing your valuables or as if you are about to die. In most cases, the effect seems uncontrollable as the panic creates an illusion that it has been decided elsewhere.

At this time, your heart rate is increased due to the tension, making it pound on your chest as your breath goes wild. The blood pressure increases as the body take it as an attack. These panic attacks might confuse your body as they give false alarms making your body sweat as if you are in a serious situation even though you may be lying on your couch. The helplessness associated with anxiety and panic attacks leaves you trembling with fear of imagined imminent danger, and you will realize that your body is shaking uncontrollably due to a perceived situation.

Phobias

Vagal inflammation is known to cause phobias as one of the somatopsychological problems in the human body. Mostly, the problem is characterized by a deep sense of panic and irrational fear reaction. When you are in this condition, you encounter different sources of fear, depending on how you perceive the environment. In some instances, you could be experiencing phobia in specific situations, objects, or places. This form of vagal nerve damage is known to complicate how your brain interprets some aspects of the environment, so you end up feeling insecure in dark or quiet environments, especially if you have had a frightening experience before.

The effects of phobia vary depending on the seriousness as well as the body's mechanism to repair damaged tissues. These conditions determine the impact of phobia in your body as it could only be an annoying experience or build up to a severe and disabling. If you experience phobia, you might be helpless about it as it is caused by other underlying conditions such as vagal nerve inflammation. Therefore, you are prone to stress as you always remain afraid of a possible attack, making you unproductive and unsocial, especially in the workplace. The condition may be different from one person to the other, hence the different categorization according to the trigger and symptoms.

One common type of the condition is known as agoraphobia which is characterized by the panic of situations and places that you cannot escape from. Mostly, people who have an agoraphobia are afraid of being in open places such as outside their houses or in crowded places. People feel uncomfortable while in social areas and like to stay most of their time indoors. The main reason why these people avoid public places is due to the anxiety of experiencing phobia publicly, which might embarrass them and leave them helpless. In some cases, people with an agoraphobia may experience a health emergency, making them remain in places where they could ask for an urgent response.

Social phobia has relatively similar characteristics and is also known as social anxiety disorder when combined with symptoms of anxiety. As the name suggests, the victims of this disorder avoid social places and prefer staying in isolation for fear of humiliation and discrimination in case they become phobic. This type of phobia is as serious as it could be caused by a simple interaction such as answering a phone call or talking to a stranger. It makes the victims go out of their way to avoid these interactions making life hard for them, especially if they are working or attending school. A phobia may be triggered by a specific object with common categories being the environment, medical, situations, or animals.

Bipolar disorder

The problem is also caused by vagal dysfunction and inflammation and was formerly referred to as a manic depression. It is a mental condition that triggers a moody feeling and swinging emotions. When the emotions are high, they are referred to as mania or hypomania, and depression when they are low. If you are depressed, you probably will experience hopelessness, sadness, and lost pleasure and interest. The feeling makes you hate activities that you liked before and lose interest in meeting the people you love. However, the feeling is sometimes short-lived as you may suddenly experience high moods that make you feel euphoric and irritably full of energy.

The drastic changes in mood significantly affect how you behave, judge, or sleep. It also hinders you from clear reasoning and making the right decision. There are numerous episodes of these mood swings that occur several times annually. In some cases, you may experience changes in events and emotional symptoms, while others may not experience them at all. The condition is manageable through the follow up of a treatment plan that includes counseling and medication. When a dysfunctional vagus nerve causes the condition, it could only be treated by healing the nerve. Several types of this disorder include depression and hypomania. These symptoms could cause drastic life effects and significant distress if left unaddressed.

Bipolar disorder is experienced when the condition triggers a break from reality and makes you fear your imagination. It is characterized by a single manic episode and occurs either before or after the incident. Bipolar II is characterized by a major depressive episode that lasts for weeks followed by a hypomanic episode that happens for about a week. The condition is more common in women but is also experienced by men. In cyclothymia, you experience bouts of depression and hypomania, which are relatively shorter than those caused by the last two types. Additionally, the condition is characterized by a month or two for stability when the problem recurs and extends for some weeks. The mania and hypomania episodes are distinct in their symptoms, but the mania episode is more severe and is known to cause problems in public places such as workplaces or schools.

Chapter 15
How to Stop Overthinking with Positive Self-Talk

What Is self-talk?

Self-talk is the inner discussion that you have with yourself. Everybody engages in self-talk. However, the impact of self-talk is only evident when you are using it in a positive way. The power of self-talk can lead to an overall boost in your self-esteem and confidence. Moreover, if you convince your inner-self that you are beyond certain emotions, then you will also find it easy to overcome emotions that seem to weigh you down. If you can master the art of positive self-talk, you will be more confident about yourself and this can transform your life in amazing ways.

You can't be sure that you will always talk to yourself positively. Therefore, it is important to understand that self-talk can go in both directions. At times, you will find yourself reflecting on negative things. In other cases, you will think about the good things that you have achieved. Bearing this in mind, it is imperative that you practice positive self-talk. This can be understood as pushing yourself to think positively even when you are going through challenges.

If your self-talk is always inclined to think negatively, it doesn't mean that there is nothing you can do about it. With regular practice, you can shift your negative thinking into positive thinking. In time, this will transform you into a more optimistic person that is full of life.

Importance of positive self-talk

Research shows that positive self-talk can have a positive impact on your general wellbeing. The following are other benefits that you can get by regularly practicing positive self-talk.

Boosts your confidence

Do you often feel shy when talking to other people? Maybe you don't completely believe in your skills and abilities. Well, positive self-talk can transform the perceptions that you have about yourself and your abilities. Negative self-talk can hold you back from achieving things in life. It can even prevent you from even trying in the first place. Unfortunately, this can drive you to overthink about the things that you feel as though you should do. So, instead of acting, you end up wasting your time overthinking about them.

Positive self-talk lets you put aside any doubts that you could have about accomplishing a particular goal. Therefore, you will be motivated to act without worrying whether you will succeed or not. You're simply optimistic about life. There is nothing that can stop you from trying your best when attending to any activity.

Saves you from depression

Overthinking can make you more susceptible to depression because you garner the perception that you are incapable of performing well.

Frankly, this affects your emotional and physical wellbeing. Some of the effects that you will experience when you're depressed include lack of sleep, lethargy, loss of appetite, nervousness, etc. Positive self-talk has the ability to change all of this. It will fill you with the optimism that you need to see past your challenges. As a result, instead of believing that you can't do it, you will begin to convince yourself that you can do it. Positive self-talk can transform how you feel, it's just a matter of changing how you perceive the world around you.

Eliminates stress

There are many stressors that we have to overcome every day. The truth is that we all go through stress. The only difference is how we deal with stress. Some people allow stress to overwhelm them. Often, you will find such folks with a negative outlook on life. They will have all sorts of negative comments about life. "Life is hard," "I can't take it anymore," "I'm always tired," "Things never get easier," etc. We've heard such comments coming from our friends who have given up on life. The reality is that stress can get the best of you if you surrender. Practicing positive self-talk can help you realize that stress comes and goes. It is a common thing that everybody experiences.

Protects your heart

We all know that stress is not good for our health. Stress leads to many diseases including cardiovascular diseases such as stroke. Therefore, by practicing positive self-talk, you will be protecting your heart.

Boost your performance

Positive self-talk can also help boost your performance in anything that you do. There are times when you find yourself feeling tired and dejected. For instance, when you wake up in the morning feeling as though you ran several kilometers, this can be draining. It affects how you attend to your daily activities. With positive self-talk, you can tap into your energy reserves and boost your performance. It is surprising how you can quickly change how you feel by thinking positively.

How positive self-talk works

Before getting into detail about practicing self-talk, it is important to understand how negative thinking works. There are several ways in which you can think negatively, including:

● Personalizing

This form of negative thinking occurs when you blame yourself for anything bad that happens to you.

● Catastrophizing

If you expect the worst to happen to you, then you are simply catastrophizing everything. The issue here is that you don't allow logic to help you understand that some things are not the way you think.

● Magnifying

Here, you pay more attention to negative things. In most cases, you will block your mind from thinking positively about any situation that you might be going through.

● Polarizing

You look to extremes when it comes to judging the things that are happening around you. From the perceptions that you have developed in your mind, something is either good or bad.

Tips for practicing positive self-talk

Have a purpose

There is a good reason why you will hear most people argue that it is important to live a purposeful life. Undeniably, when you strongly believe that you are here on this earth for a good reason, you will strive to be the best version of yourself. You will be constantly motivated to try to achieve your goals in life. The best part is that you will feel good about your accomplishments. This is because they are an indication that you are heading in the right direction towards your goals. Therefore, when practicing self-talk, always look to a higher purpose that you yearn to achieve. This will keep you on the move without worrying too much about the number of times you stumble.

Get rid of toxic people

It is common to have a bad day. We cannot deny the fact that there are times when life seems difficult. Usually, this happens when our emotions overwhelm us. Despite this fact, there are people who have these bad days every day. They never seem to stop talking about their worst experiences. Unfortunately, this can take a negative toll on your life, especially when interacting with other people. Picture a scenario where you are always told about how life is difficult. Your friend keeps mentioning to you that life has changed and it's impossible for you to realize your dreams. In time, this is the mindset that you will also develop. There is nothing good that you will see in your life since you can't think positively. The interesting thing is that you might actually be making positive changes, but you will unlikely notice.

Never compare yourself to others

It is easy to compare yourself to other people more so when you feel that you lack something. Sadly, such comparisons only push you to look down on yourself. The comparison game will blind you from seeing the valuable qualities that you have. You will develop a negative attitude towards your abilities as you assume that other people are better than you. By expressing how you are thankful for what you have, you can identify the numerous things that make you different from other people. This is a great way of developing your personality and helping you believe in yourself.

Talk positively with other people

Talking positively with other people will have an impact on your self-talk. If you constantly talk about negative things with those around you, then there is a likelihood that you will also engage in negative self-talk. There are probably numerous times where you've heard people say that you become what and how you think. Therefore, if you keep focusing on the negative, expect negativity to flow through your mind. Stop this by trying your best to surround yourself with positivity, starting with the way you talk to other people.

Believe in your success

The best way of propelling yourself to succeed in your endeavors is by believing that you can do it. If you don't believe that you can do it, then this holds you back from trying anything. This should be applied to everything you do. For example, if you are working towards losing weight, you should convince yourself that you can do it. This is the first step that will give you the energy you need to overcome challenges on your way to success.

Overcome the fear of failure

Succeeding in life also demands that you should overcome the fear of failure. You should always bear in mind that your failures are learning lessons. In fact, most people who have succeeded in life have failed at some point. When you overcome the fear of failure, you will be more than willing to try anything without hesitation. This opens doors to plenty of opportunities. The good news is that you will have learned a lot from the experience of failing.

Use positive affirmations

You can also give a positive boost to your self-talk by using positive affirmations. The best way to use these affirmations is by writing them down. Note them somewhere you can easily view them. For instance, you can stick them on your refrigerator or on your vision board, if you have one. The importance of positioning them in a convenient place is to guarantee that you motivate yourself every day. Ideally, this is an effective strategy of training your mind to always think positively. Examples of positive affirmations that you can note down include:

- I am blessed.

- I am a successful person.

- I embrace what life offers me.

- I am happy today.

- I allow myself to be filled with joy.

Avoid dwelling in the past

When you think too much about the past, it will likely be difficult to focus on the present. This will have an impact on your self-talk. If you keep regretting the mistakes that you have made, there is a good chance that you will think negatively. Your emotions will blind you from thinking clearly. As such, this can have an impact on the decisions you make.

It is imperative that you find a balance between thinking about the future and the present. When thinking about your future, focus on the positive. If there is something that you want, think in that direction and convince yourself that you already have it.

Chapter 16
How to Solve Worry Problems?

How much is too much?

It is very normal to experience worries, anxiety and doubts in daily life. It is our reaction to it which makes the greatest difference in our lives. It's very natural to get worked up about a first date, an upcoming interview, or an unpaid bill. Becoming frequently worried becomes overwhelming when it is uncontrollable and persistent. If every day you become worked up by picture all of the negative things that might happen to you, you are letting anxious thoughts interfere with your life and well-being.

Negative thoughts, incessant worrying, and constantly expecting poor outcomes will have a negative effect on your physical and emotional well-being. It gradually weakens you emotionally, taking your strength and leaving you restless and nervous, with headaches, insomnia, muscle tension and stomach problems.

The effect of this on your personal life, your concentration at school and work cannot be overemphasized. For some people, it's easier to take out their frustration on your loved ones and people closest to them, take alcohol or drugs or try to distract themselves by tuning out from everything.

Chronic anxiety and worry is a sign of Generalized Anxiety Disorder (GAD), a disorder that causes restlessness, nervousness and tension, together with a feeling of unease which can take over your life.

If you feel burdened by tension and worries, you can take a few steps to take your mind off anxious thoughts. Over time, worrying constantly becomes a problem. It becomes a mental habit when prolonged and is very difficult to break. Train your brain to be calm and think only positive thoughts, and change your outlook on life to a more relaxed and confident perspective.

How to quit worrying?

Tip 1: Choose a short period each day to worry

It can be quite difficult to be productive when your thoughts are consumed by worry and anxiety, distracting your attention from school, work, or your family. In this case, the strategy of putting off worrying can actually do a lot of good. Instead of getting rid of these thoughts, grant yourself permission to have these thoughts later on in your day.

Dedicate a period for worry each day. Set up a time and place to think of things that bother you. It should be at the same time every day (for example, 6 p.m. to 6:15 p.m. in the bedroom). Choosing a timeframe that won't affect your bedtime and or create additional anxiety in your life. During this period, you can worry about whatever you want. The rest of the day should be classified as worry-free.

Put down your worries in writing. When you find yourself thinking anxious or worrying thoughts, simply note them briefly and continue with your daily activities. Always remind yourself that there's time for you to think about it later; there is no need to get worked up about them now.

Take a look at your worry list during your scheduled worry period. If your thoughts still bother you, let yourself think about those things, but only for your specified worry period. You'll notice that, as you examine your worries in this manner, it's easier to establish a more balanced outlook to worrying. If, at this point, your worries don't seem as important as they used to, simply reduce the length of your worry period and enjoy your day to the fullest.

Tip 2: Challenge anxious thoughts

The way that you look at the world may be altered a bit if you are a chronic worrier and thinker. It changes everything, and you may tend to feel threatened. For instance, you picture only a worst-case scenario, and you assume the worst or handle your anxious thoughts as if they were facts.

As a result, you may not feel secure enough to tackle daily challenges head-on; you may assume that you'll lose it at the slightest sign of trouble. Such thoughts, also known as cognitive distortions, include: "All-or-nothing" thinking, having a black-and-white perspective, concluding that "If it isn't perfect, then I'm a complete failure," or "I wasn't hired for this job; I'll never get any job again." You may make a generalization from just one negative experience and expect it to be true forever. Life doesn't work that way.

You may notice only the things that went wrong in your day, instead of things that went well, resulting in thoughts such as: "I didn't get the last test question; I'm stupid, and I can't do anything right.." You may attribute positive events to sheer luck, rather than your own ability to create positive outcomes.

You may take your assumptions for facts. You may make yourself a mind- reader or fortune teller with thoughts like: "I just know something bad will happen" or "I know she secretly hates me." This creates bad energy. Without faith, your mind may automatically jump to worst-case scenarios, such as: "The plane is experiencing turbulence; it's going to crash." You may take your thoughts for reality: "I feel so stupid; I'm the laughingstock now."

You may make a list of your dos and don'ts and beat yourself up when you default on any of the rules, with thoughts such as, "I shouldn't have gone there. Now I look like such a fool." You may label yourself based on your shortcomings and mistakes, with thoughts such as, "I can't do anything right; I should be a loner." You may take responsibility for things that are beyond your control, thinking: "It's my fault my son died. I shouldn't have left him alone by the pool."

Challenging These Thoughts

Try this out. Challenge these negative thoughts during your worry period, and ask yourself these questions:

- What evidence proves that these thoughts are valid or not?
- Is there a better way to look at this situation? A better and more positive way?
- What are the chances of my fears becoming a reality? What are the probabilities? What are some likely outcomes in this situation?
- Are these thoughts helpful? How do they affect me? Do they help me or hurt me?
- What's my advice to a friend who has been in a similar situation?

Tip 3: Differentiate the solvable worries from the unsolvable worries

Studies have shown that you experience less anxiety when you worry. While you think about the problem in your head, you're distracted from your emotions for a while and feel like you're actually solving a problem; in reality, getting worried and problem-solving are two different things altogether.

By problem-solving, you are examining a situation, thinking of solid ways to deal with it, and putting these plans into action. On the other hand, worrying seldom leads to any solutions. The more time that you spend thinking of worst-case scenarios, the less prepared that you are to handle them if they actually happen. That's the simple truth.

Is your worry solvable?

There are different types of worries; some have solutions, while others don't. Solvable worries are those that you can act to resolve instantly. For instance, when you're preoccupied with your debts, you can call a friend or relative to settle your debts, with the option to repay them later.

This type of worry can also be described as productive worry. On the other hand, those worries that do not have a corresponding action can be characterized as unsolvable problems; for instance, thoughts like: What if I get leukemia someday? What if my family gets involved in an accident?

In a situation where you can take action about the thing getting you worried, begin to look for solutions. Compile a list of all the ways you feel that you can solve your worry. Don't get caught in searching for the one perfect answer to the problem.

Concentrate on those things within your reach that can be changed instead of brooding over situations that are out of reach. After deciding upon the solution that will solve your problem, develop an action plan. Immediately you set out to address your fear; you will be less worried.

On the other hand, when the worry is not something you can solve, make peace with yourself by being at ease with the uncertainty. For people who worry excessively, many of their fears tend to be along these lines. People tend to worry when they are trying to anticipate the future, and this is done to feel more in control and prevent potential problems.

However, the bitter truth is that worrying doesn't solve anything; life is occasionally unpredictable. So why not enjoy your life now instead of being engrossed in unpleasant things that have not taken place?

Most people long for inner peace: the feeling that everything is, and will be, all right. But sometimes, we worry, develop fears, and ponder the same things over and over without finding a way out.

The tragic thing is that, of course, we know rationally that the upcoming test is not a life-and-death situation. Our child is probably not lying in the ditch just because he/she does not call at the agreed-upon time. Our dull headache is probably harmless and not the symptom of a brain tumor.

Tip 4: Interrupt the worry cycle

Answer the following questions:

- What am I worried about?
- What possible solutions exist?
- Which solution should I choose?
- How and when do I implement the solution?

Just writing down your worries can provide you with some relief. If you then also write down different solutions, you will see your fears in a different light. You will adopt the observer perspective and will be able to think more logically about what you can do.

Meditate. Meditation helps to alleviate daily worries by shifting our attention. We focus only on the here and now and can leave the concerns of the past or future behind. Similarly, meditation can also help us observe ourselves and understand our negative thought patterns. We only need to find a comfortable, quiet place and focus carefully on our breathing. Various studies have shown that meditating not only helps to ease worries but can also reduce stress and anxiety.

Practice progressive muscle relaxation. Sports and exercise also promote relaxation and sleep. They also help to distract us from our everyday worries and promote our self-esteem and well-being. This confidence will make it easier for us to address our worries head-on. Also, researchers claim that exercise can reduce not only anxiety but also improve our emotional well-being and energy. Many scientists believe that physical activity can significantly reduce depression.

Tip 5: Talk about your worries.

One way to worry less is to talk to our closest friends about what is bothering us. When we are worried, friends can help us to alleviate our fears and see things from a different perspective. They can help us to look at the problem from the outside. Then, we can often find a solution or come to realize that it's not as bad a problem as we feared. When they listen without judgment or criticism and pay attention to what we say, their empathy can help us to feel calmer and more relaxed.

Having someone listen to us with empathy is essential to make us feel better. Even professional help is very beneficial, in some cases, if you cannot find a way out yourself.

Chapter 17
Reframing Your Negative Thoughts

Like anyone on this planet, there's as much time as you can to be happy. But you still don't have joy as your main priority, like most people. Or maybe you think you do, but in reality, you actively sabotage yourself by falling into depression, misery, remorse and other unproductive negative ideas.

However, it's very easy to fall into depression without joy as a goal and suffer more than you deserve in this lifetime. This is why it is so important if you want to know how to enhance the quality of your life, you'll accept happiness as your first goal and not just as a pleasant idea.

If you genuinely seek joy, you should be able to notice the negative and reframe it, and the right thinking is critical because you have thousands or tens of thousands of negative thoughts a day. You will wake up every day to battle demons—dispute, despair and depression. No other way. It is spiritual warfare and every day you must be prepared to wake up and fight. The positive thing is having the right attitude, and you will start to feel better instantly. Have the right outcome. Better still, everyone can use this technology because it's not based on "objective truth." Reframing negativity does not depend on your wealth, or on your IQ or appearance, or on something else you want. You will make a big difference in the quality of your life from today with the right will and application of your imagination.

How to reframe negative thoughts?

-   AWARENESS

Your awareness is the first thing to concentrate on. In other words, be wary of negative thoughts. If happiness is your first priority, you will take depressing consciousness very seriously, like a gun on your head.

You will be mindful of it and, at least every day, you will have thousands of negative thoughts. It is just a problem to capture them, to admit that you are frustrated and to ask the right questions.

- Ask the right questions

Both combinations of:

- Why am I unhappy?

- What do I do to feel better?

You are the questions you pose, and you know how to make the right questions. This is really necessary. If you ask the right questions, the right reframe is what you want.

- REFRAMING

The correct reframe is the only reframe at the moment. You may not be satisfied, but you can still get out of doubt, frustration and depression—even when it's just optimistic.

The most valuable skill in practice is reframing or state management which is much more successful than any form of therapy. Because counseling deals with the past, the past does not exist anymore. The present is all that is true and policy management regulates the present.

The past, the present and the future are not the way forward. You suffer because you stay trapped in the past.

It's like physical pain, except it's not that bad, from fever to cancer. Once the pain is gone, after you have tried, you can't remember physical pain. However, emotional suffering can be restored, renewed and remembered forever. It is supported by many forms of therapy!

Compare mind to body:

- Therapy is like having a physical wound or injury which causes you to suffer and pick and open and dig into it, thus raising pain so that you recognize pain, and somehow "process it." Compare the mind with the body.

- The reframing, in order to remove the discomfort and feel good at the moment, takes the same actual skull or fracture that causes you pain and takes the right treatment.
- The realization that changes the game comes when you know that you get how you feel.
- Negative thinking will only harm you if you accept it.
- It doesn't matter how bad your feelings are or what has happened to you, you just decide how you feel.
- You can choose positive or negative and you are actually CHOOSING when you are negative.

Different types of reframes

You have to learn two types of reframes to have better positive thinking:

- Unproductive negative thoughts that are pessimistic and purposeless feelings.
- Negative proposals that require practice. These are not even the enemy's negative thoughts. They either alert you to thought changes, or they warn about habits that you have to change.

Reframing unproductive negative thoughts

- IGNORE

For low-level negative feelings, the safest reframe is always to forget it. Forget it. Thoughts like you're a loser or sick of going to work–just like a nervous man at the pub, you talk to them. No or I'm a stupid or distracted.

- Changing focus

Change of emphasis is an ideal way to reframe negativity. The easiest change of focus is about going back to work. When I think negative during the day, my reframe just goes back to my goal. In minutes I'll have totally forgotten the feeling. One perfect way to signal a shift of emphasis is to define and continue thinking as unproductive.

Reframing negative thoughts which requires action

- Positive reframe

For feelings that need a change of mind, it is a positive reframe that your best move is. I hated it every minute when I was in sales from my managers to dealing with rude customers to cold calls to colleagues. That's when I reframed every move and every cold call to make more money, and the money will be saved. And I use this money to fund my enterprises and to avoid wage slavery forever.

If I changed my mind, I could not only excel but turned a big negative into a constructive one. I was actually able to escape, and I was able to monetize my experience by writing a book on how to market it.

One important thing to note is to check the reframes while doing a constructive reframing. Some guys teaching NLP-based pickups teach people to think of themselves as supermen or 10 feet as they approach women. It's not a useful structure, because your subconscious mind would never buy.

Some guys teach the method to approach women in order to make them feel wanted. It is a good thing, and it is a good thing that you can honestly express your purpose but moving around in 2000 is a challenge. Nonetheless, I saw some guys on the pickup boards thinking about their ability and making 2000 females feel desired. This is not a positive reframe.

If you meet a woman, it will be your final game to get this woman and concentrate on the outcome. Under these cases, you have to look at doing something to improve your sexual market interest and make major behavioral improvements.

Ultimately, it's a safe idea to sit down and talk about the most consistent destructive trends. If it is illness, fear of death, or low self-esteem, the development of optimistic reframe can take place. Others will go back and forth when the big negative feedback loops become nasty minds, which they are.

- Behavioral change

The behavioral shift is the perfect reframe for negative thinking about problems in your life, whether they are addictions, unpleasant individuals, or choices in lifestyle or a work you dislike. Such kinds of negative thoughts should be listened to and followed up by your peers. Hearing these kinds of thoughts and applying approaches will be the bulk of your personal development success.

One approach that might be useful when it comes to negative behaviors is to sit down and list the 10 worst recurring issues. From a work you don't want to what your 10 biggest problems are and action-based solutions can be found. I did it myself and it was a huge step forward. I have actually created a system with the Wunderlist task management app to solve those problems by setting my mission, priorities, schedules and tasks.

Chapter 18
How to Use Meditation to Deal with Overthinking?

Meditation is an easy and logical step for any empath. It can be very uncomfortable, at first, to sit quietly all alone with your thoughts. Try to remember that the purpose of meditation is to let those thoughts and emotions come, and then release them. Allow them to wash over you the way waves move over your feet when you walk along the seashore, crashing up and then quickly, gently, fading away.

You can also meditate on specific subjects or questions that you struggle to comprehend. The purpose of meditation is not to stir anxiety, though, so if you note repetitive, obsessive, or negative thought patterns, you may want to change your approach before your next session.

If you are already well-practiced in meditation, you might want to further challenge yourself and awaken your third eye chakra by challenging your thought patterns. Some metaphysical guides suggest using inquisition to aid this process, continually answering each of your thoughts with the question: "Is that true?" If that method feels combative or sparks feelings of internal conflict, you can instead practice disbelieving your thoughts, entertaining the possibility that the truth is the opposite of what you perceive it to be.

Create a safe haven

To ensure that self-care becomes a regular part of your new routine, you'll want to make space for it in your life--literally. Even if it has to be inside a closet, make sure you find some space to create a safe haven for yourself. You could also think of it as a peace bubble, meditation space, or a spiritual altar. The idea is to create an ideal space in which to center yourself whenever life outside this haven starts to feel overwhelming. You may want to fill it with candles and crystals, smudge sticks, plants, cozy pillows, and blankets. If you relish the endless potential of a blank slate, your haven might be completely bare, dark, and quiet. There is no right or wrong way, only the way that feels right for you.

De-Clutter and organize your living space

Now that you've created a safe haven, your next goal should be to arrange the rest of your living space in a way that helps you to feel balanced, organized, efficient, and at peace. Even if you don't consider yourself a visual or materially oriented person, the way your home looks matters; it is the first thing your eyes see every morning when you wake up, and the last thing you see before you fall asleep at night. Its appearance makes a mark on your dreams and subconscious world, as well as on your conscious thought processes. Furthermore, the way it smells, sounds, and feels is important, too.

If you find the theories of Feng Shui resonate with you, then go ahead and evaluate the layout of your home and furniture, and rearrange whatever you have to in order to respect its principles. This is especially recommended for geomantic empaths--Feng Shui is also sometimes called "geomancy," and it addresses the same energetic frequencies that geomantic empaths are attuned to.

If there's no time for a full interior redecoration effort, then instead, you may want to focus on clearing unwanted energy from your living space. Take a mental inventory of the items on display in your home. How many of them were items you chose based on desire? How many did you choose based on necessity? Be on the lookout for gifts you've received, and remind yourself that you are alone and no one is judging you before you ask yourself: how do I really feel about these items that were given to me? Do they have sentimental value and represent a feeling of love and affection for me? Or, were some of them given by people who were trying to manipulate or influence my behaviors? Do some of them remind me that people in my life don't actually get me or understand who I am?

If so, don't feel ashamed for acknowledging it. Sometimes, gifts are not given from a place of generosity, but in an attempt to exert willpower. Recognize these items in your home as centers of negative or stagnant energy, and give yourself permission to dispose of them, give them away, or send them to remote storage.

Yoga, tai chi, and physical mindfulness practice

Exercise is undoubtedly good for the body and soul, but it can be even more effective when combined with mindfulness. Mindfulness is the concept of heightening our awareness of things we usually take for granted or have learned to ignore, like our breathing or thought patterns. Yoga is especially popular, as it addresses the need for physical alignment and mindfulness, promoting focus, relaxation, acceptance, and self-love. It can also be tailored easily to suit many different needs, sometimes fully embracing its spiritual element, or at other times being exclusively concerned with the physical body. You can easily find a yoga class to attend, and there are many schools of yoga to choose from, depending on your desire to enhance strength, find balance, repair injury, or find deeper relaxation. You can also practice alone in your home or outdoors in nature. Tai chi also stimulates mindfulness through a series of slow, controlled physical movements. Generally, yoga can pose more of a physical challenge, whereas Tai chi requires a great deal of patience and focus, so it challenges the mind. It also looks more like a dance form, so those who feel freed by creative expression may prefer tai chi to other similar practices.

Grounding

Grounding is theoretically easy, but will only be as effective as the amount of energy you channel into the practice. All you need to do is remove your shoes and socks, plant your feet on the ground (ideally in a place where you feel a strong connection to nature), and imagine you are growing roots like a tree. Many empaths will close their eyes, breathe deeply, and utilize some form of meditation or affirmation during their grounding practice.

One mantra that you might find useful is the alternating repetition of two phrases: first, "I am one with the universe," where you may substitute the word "universe" with "all things" or the name of a higher power in your faith; and secondly, "I am distinct, unique, powerful and purposeful." These two phrases articulate polarized sentiments that many empaths mentally seesaw back and forth between; the goal here is to honor both ideas as part of the same universal truth. Some empaths find this practice especially powerful near oceans, historical landmarks, or sites of natural phenomena, like volcanoes or earthquakes. Grounding is highly recommended for geomantic and precognitive empaths.

Dietary changes

Every living being, whether plant, animal or human, is made of energy. So, if you are consistently consuming foods that carry forms of negative energy, it can manifest in your body as chronic pain, illness, malnourishment, or even as an emotional symptom, like depression.

An elimination diet is a simple way to effect major change in your personal energy field, and it usually provokes rapid change. You may be very surprised to find aches or points of tension are suddenly released, despite the fact that you never even noticed them before they were flushed away. Intermittent fasting can also be a useful tool to enhance mental clarity, though it should be done with caution. Those who lead highly active lifestyles or suffer from nutritional imbalances may find this practice dangerous.

Affirmations and manifestation exercises

Have you ever had the experience of feeling overwhelmed by a mental to-do list, only to write it out on paper or tell someone else about it, and suddenly realize that it's easily doable, and not worth stressing over?

Or, have you ever felt that a dream or wish was too far out of reach to entertain--but then, by declaring it aloud, you suddenly felt it drawn closer to you, fully within reach?

This is a manifestation in action. Whether you intend to address it or not, the universe is listening to you, so proclaiming your desires and self-esteem clearly can have an amazing ripple effect on your life. It can amplify your confidence, strengthen your resolve, encourage feelings of gratitude, and help you to maintain positive energy. Just be sure to project your truth without distortion, and be careful not to ask the universe for anything you aren't prepared to receive.

Use verbal or written affirmations during any self-love practice (yoga, meditation, bathing, or even while getting dressed in the morning, if you are pressed for time) to encourage self-love, drive motivation, and stay focused on your personal goals and values. Manifestation will be more focused on the future, whereas affirmations influence your current perceptions of reality. Remember that our thoughts shape our realities, so the simple act of reframing negative thoughts through the language of gratitude can change your entire outlook on life.

Journaling

There is no right or wrong way to use this practice. Regular free-writing is a fantastic way to find greater clarity of thought, as well as to self-soothe unexpressed frustrations or concerns. It may also be helpful to read over past entries from time to time, like a detective, whenever you suspect interference from a phantom source of negativity in your energy field. Journaling will help you to note healthy and risky patterns in your own behavior, as well as within the framework of your interpersonal relationships. It will also be cathartic, helping you to let go of negative feelings and leave them sealed in the past.

Chapter 19
Returning to Self-Care

Itis important to take care of yourself while you are trying to recover from overthinking and anxiety. This means you have got to relax. For people with anxiety, it can feel almost impossible because it has probably been a long time since they have felt relaxed. In fact, it can be unsettling to feel relaxed for them because it is unfamiliar. The longer you ignore your need for self-care goes on, the direr it will get. If you don't have the time to relax, you can at least tide yourself over until you can focus on yourself. If you are feeling tired at work, close your eyes for just a few minutes.

Check how you are doing physically because your physical and mental health goes hand in hand. It's easy to not be feeling well for a long time and not realize it or push it to the back of your priority list because you are trying to push through and get through the days.

As an overthinker, you probably spend much of your day grappling with a multitude of worries. Arrange a certain time in the evening where you put away your worries until tomorrow. Save them for a time when you can actually have an impact on them. Also, figure out the ones that are necessary and the ones that do nothing for you but cause you stress.

Overthinkers are masters at borrowing trouble. They can create problems for themselves that do not have to exist. For example, if your car is having trouble, you can give yourself a panic attack thinking of how expensive it could wind up being and worrying about if the car is even fixable. Find out how much the repairs cost first. Go on the assumption that whatever is wrong with the car will be fixable. Think about it this way. If it does turn out to be something serious, by the time you get to the point where you find out this information, you will have worried yourself into a frazzle. This means you will have rendered yourself completely ineffective and unable to figure out how to get yourself out of the situation you have worried so much about. No amount of stressing out can prevent a situation. It only takes energy away from you. If you do not give yourself a panic attack about it, then you will be able to take on the situation while you are still fresh.

You need to redirect your thoughts about the situation. Instead of going to "this is the worst thing that could ever happen" or "this is going to ruin my life," focus on this thought instead: "What is the first step I need to take to get myself out of this situation?" Don't even trouble yourself with the overall solution at first. Just think about how you are going to get through today. Think about paying off the immediate amount.

Let's think about what it means to practice self-care. It could be argued that the root of self-care is getting proper sleep. Every other aspect of your life will take a hit if you are not sleeping well. The timing of your sleep is just as important as the number of hours you get. Let's say you don't fall asleep until 4 in the morning. You probably won't wake up until around noon, so you've already lost half of your day. You will still be groggy, and it'll probably take you longer yet to get out of bed, and even then, you will feel a very low level of energy. It will be all you can do just to get the bare minimum done.

You need to put away your phone before you go to bed. If you don't, there will be a few problems. For one, you will be tempted to play around on your phone and check your social media newsfeeds, and it is easy to lose track of time when you do this. You might look up, and it's 1 in the morning. Then you will need time to fall asleep because no one does the minute they close their eyes.

Do not bring up heavy or upsetting discussion topics late in the evening. If it hasn't come up by then, and no one's life is in danger, it can wait until the morning. Big discussions tend to take an hour to resolve, two if it's a particularly hefty one. If you started it at eight in the evening, you might not be done with it until nine or ten. Then you will have a hard time getting to sleep because when your mind is restless, your sleep will be fitful.

Self-care also means doing things that make you happy. Pick up a hobby. Remember, trying something out doesn't mean you have to stick with it forever. You can take one painting class, decide you don't like it, and never go to another one. Nothing will be lost from trying something.

You often hear "I need a mental health day" as a joke, but there is something to it. Sometimes in our daily lives, with all of our responsibilities, we can become burned out. Just like a cell phone needs its battery recharged, we need our mental battery recharged.

There is no right or wrong way to take a mental health day. It is all about what you want to do. During this type of day, you do not have any responsibilities, and you don't need to think about them. Only do things that make you feel good. It is advisable to avoid too much time on social media during a mental health day.

Establishing good habits for yourself is key to overcoming anxiety and overthinking. If you don't take care of yourself, your defenses are compromised. You are more prone to having physical illnesses, and you will not feel as good about yourself. This means taking pride in your appearance.

Putting effort into your appearance doesn't mean you have to dress in ways that are not you. If you are a woman who doesn't like to wear makeup, you don't have to start doing it. You can look perfectly fine without wearing anything you don't feel comfortable with. In fact, it is cautioned against to try to do that. Then you will feel self-conscious and like everyone is staring at you, which will be the catalyst for an overthinking episode.

What it means to take care of your appearance is to put time and effort into it. When we get into ruts of depression and anxiety, we have a tendency to press the snooze button as many times as possible. Then, when there is no more time to lie in bed, we'll get ready as quickly as we can, and it will be a blur. This means there's no thought put into what you are going to wear, and there's no time to fix your hair other than to run through it a couple of times with a brush. You might not even have time to take a look at yourself in the mirror before you go. This is demoralizing because you know you are not looking for your best and are worried others will notice. It will inhibit your confidence when talking to others and might even prevent you from talking to others.

Some people like to pick out what they are going to wear the next morning. This can help you feel more prepared for the next day and gives you one last thing to think about in the morning. Then you have more time to dedicate to other aspects of your appearance. Create some sort of skin ritual. You will start to see results quickly. Learn about different things you can do with your hair and find out what hairstyles work the best with your face shape and which ones you find appealing.

Taking care of yourself also means taking care of the space around you. It is said that a cluttered room is a sign of a mind that has chaos going on inside of it. That is why de-cluttering your environment is so important. When your house is messy, you will feel uncomfortable inside of it. It can get to a point where you have to go through a lot of trouble to navigate in your own house because of the clutter. You have to walk around and step over things. It will increase your stress to have to go through an obstacle course just to walk around in your own home. It is depressing to look at a messy house because you are living in a space you are not pleased with. Instead of your house being a place to come to at the end of the day and find relief from as you leave your worries behind for the day, you come to see a place that has a chaotic energy and that you are ashamed of. You will avoid having any company over and you will dread when you have to let someone in your house, like a repairman, because you are worried about what they will think when they see the state of your house (this is not good for those who overthink, whose shame about the state of the house will last long beyond when the repairman leaves).

There is an impact the energy in the room can have on you. This does not have to carry a spiritual meaning. Have you ever almost gone to a restaurant, but you looked at the people you were with, and you all decided to leave and find somewhere else to go eat because there was something that felt weird about the place? That is what it means to have positive or negative energy. Sometimes it is called the "vibe" or "juju" a person or place gives off. When you have clutter in your house and have not managed its upkeep in a while, the place you live in will have negative energy. It will not be conducive to living a healthy lifestyle and being productive. The way you keep your house sets a tone for the way you live your life. If you regularly clean the space you live in, you will feel more confident about yourself. You will start to enjoy being at home.

There is something to the phrase "fake it until you make it." Even if you are faking it, you are choosing to dwell on something that is beneficial to you rather than something that is harmful. Have you ever been having a bad day, but one of your friends invited you to go out with them, and you decided to take them up on the offer? At first, it might have felt contrived to go out and pretend to be having fun. There was a part of you that wanted to keep wallowing in your sorrows. However, since you were hanging out with your friend and talking to them about things that were unrelated to whatever was bothering you, you didn't have time to devote all of your time to that. After a while, there came a point where you decided you'd rather have fun with your friend than think about what was upsetting you, most likely something you had little to no control over.

Chapter 20
The Key to Feeling Good

Being happy is so important, yet it's often overlooked. If you don't feel good, you won't feel as motivated to accomplish your goals. It will be harder to be driven and get to where you need to be, as you simply won't feel up to anything. Taking care of yourself is crucial. When you feel good, you may form better relationships with others and have people that can support you and have a good time with you. You can get more done, as you will actually want to improve yourself and succeed. You will be more confident in yourself because you'll be treating yourself the way that you should be and recognizing your worth instead of feeling sorry for yourself. It will be easier to succeed, achieve your goals, and have access to more opportunities.

Improving your mental health

Your mental health is so important, yet most people seem to forget that it even exists. You can go to the gym and eat as healthily as you'd like, yet that won't help you if your mental health is suffering. You must take some time to care for your mental health, as you can't be happy otherwise. There are a few ways that you can make an effort to improve your mental health, and you may incorporate some great habits into your life to better your mental health.

One way to improve your mental health is to practice self-care. Every day, take some time to care for yourself. You may do this a few ways, such as reading a book or relaxing. Find out what works best for you to help you calm down. It's important to make the effort to fully devote some time to yourself. It may even be as simple as lighting a candle and breathing. There are many ways that you can practice self-care, and it's important to find out what works best for you. Maybe you can even practice a new self-care activity every day! You may plan ahead for the upcoming month and pick simple ways for you to practice self-care. Perhaps you can do it for under thirty minutes every weekday and an hour or more on weekends. You may even choose one self-care item for each day of the week. Regardless, it's important to choose an activity that you genuinely enjoy and really go out of your way to take care of yourself. There are so many ways to practice self-care!

Another way to improve your mental health is by treating yourself well. Learn how to master self-compassion and self-esteem. Practice being more understanding with yourself and forgive yourself for making mistakes. Also, remember that you deserve happiness and success. Respect yourself and your decisions, and don't be so hard on yourself.

You may also work on improving your self-confidence. One great way to do this is by building your confidence. Set goals and accomplish them, even if they're small. Successes, no matter how small they are, will help you recognize that you are capable of success.

Practicing mindfulness is a great way to improve your mental health. When you are faced with a difficult situation, learn how to live in the moment. Focus on the present instead of worrying about what will happen in the future or what did happen in the past. If you live your life with regrets, you will never be able to move forward. Wasting your time on worrying will not help solve any of your problems. Instead, take time to appreciate the present for what it is.

Therapy can be a wonderful solution for bettering your mental health. If you have tried to help improve your mental health by yourself but haven't had luck, it may be time for you to seek help from someone else through therapy. Cognitive-behavioral therapy can be a great way to find solutions to your problems. Therapy can be especially helpful if you haven't had luck improving your mental health by yourself or if you feel like you have nobody to talk to. Therapy can give you an outside perspective on you.

Having a positive outlook

Having a positive outlook on life can really help you to be more positive and have an overall greater appreciation for life. You will be able to find joy in life instead of focusing on any negativity. When you can improve your mindset, your whole world will change. Your perspective can turn a bad situation into a good one. Learning to appreciate life can help you to be happier with how everything is going. A negative outlook on life can prevent you from making the most out of your life, and it can cause those around you to be unhappy as well. There are a few simple tips that you can use to change your perspective and have a more positive outlook.

You may start journaling. This can help you to feel like you're in more control of your life, and you may take it any direction that you'd like to. Perhaps you wish to write down what you're grateful for and the good aspects of life. You may also want to write down how you feel so that you can cope with it in a healthier way. Journaling is also great for writing down your goals and your progress toward accomplishing those goals.

Another way to have a more positive outlook is by focusing on the good. For every negative thing that you notice, you must also come up with two positive aspects of it. For instance, you may be stuck in traffic and get upset about being late. However, this can give you some time to call a friend that you haven't gotten the chance to talk to in a while and help you to take time to yourself. There are always positive aspects of every situation. It might just take a bit of effort to find them.

Similarly, you must view challenging situations and mistakes as beneficial to you. If you can learn to view life in the way that everything happens for a reason, you will be much better off. Instead of thinking that your life is ruined because you didn't get the job, know that there is a better job waiting out there for you that will be an even better fit for you. If you can't get past challenges, you'll never grow. You can't let mistakes or failures bring you down, as they are inevitable and will always be a part of your life.

It's important to change your mindset when it comes to change. Without change, you can't grow or improve. Although you may enjoy the risk-free aspect of comfort, it will not get you anywhere. Go for your goals! Chase your dreams! If you don't make the effort to take some risks, you won't get any further in life. Change can be frightening, but it's also very important. You'll never know if you like something until you try it, and it's okay to change your mind. Change is a blessing, not a curse. You must learn how to appreciate change instead of fearing it.

Improving your physical health

Your physical health is also important for your happiness. When your body is healthy, and you take care of it, you will be able to function the best. Taking care of your body can help you to have more energy and feel better overall. It can also help you to do more instead of being held back by your health. Taking care of your body will also help you to feel better about yourself. You will be able to realize that you are capable of taking care of yourself and doing what's best for yourself. You may feel more confident in your body and your ability to accomplish your goals.

First, you must get a proper amount of sleep. This is necessary for allowing you to function at your best and have a proper amount of energy. The amount of sleep that you need will depend on your age and personal preferences. However, it is very helpful to have a sleeping schedule. Going to bed and waking up at the same time every day can help your body to get used to sleeping for the proper amount. You may form routines to perform before going to bed and after waking up to really maximize this effect.

Eating properly is essential for taking care of your mental health. It is important to allow yourself to occasionally eat unhealthy foods, but you should eat an overall healthy diet. Portions are also very important, as eating the proper amount can help you to maintain an ideal weight.

Eating at the same time each day can also improve your metabolic health. Determine when you would like to eat and how often you would like to eat. Making these simple changes can really help you to improve the way you eat.

Staying hydrated is also important for your health. You must get a proper amount of water each day to be at your best. One way to motivate yourself to do so is by getting a water bottle that looks nice. This can encourage you to drink from it more. You may even label the side with the hours of the day as a way to set hydration goals for yourself. Cutting out beverages besides water can really help you, especially since most other drinks contain excessive amounts of sugar. Caffeine and alcohol consumption should also be limited to obtain the best health possible.

Exercising is very important to keep your body healthy. You must choose activities that you enjoy. For some, this may very well be going to the gym. Others don't thrive in that environment and prefer to exercise by themselves. This may be running, swimming, walking, or biking. You may even try at-home workouts. Taking classes or lessons can be a great way to learn how to exercise a certain way. You may also involve yourself in sports or clubs. This is a great way to get out and workout, and you'll be able to meet others with similar interests.

Cultivating positive relationships

To improve your relationships with others, it's very important to surround yourself with the right people. Make sure that you are spending your time with people who motivate, inspire, and encourage you to live your best life possible. It is okay to say no to people, and you must learn to value yourself. Holding on to grudges will not get you anywhere, and it's important to eliminate the conflict that you have. You may also spend more time caring for others. When you put in the effort, others will start doing the same. Work on building positive relationships with those around you.

Feeling good can help you to live your best life. You're at your best when you are happy. It is possible to achieve happiness. You may do this by improving your mental health, which can allow you to think more clearly about the positivity in your life. Similarly, you may have a more positive outlook on life. Improving your physical health can make you feel better, both physically and mentally. You may also work on improving your relationships with others so that you can surround yourself with the right people that can support you and encourage you to be your best.

Chapter 21
Self-Discipline

Self-discipline is important. It can make a huge difference for you, and it can help you to stick to your habits. Instead of giving in to temptation, you will be able to control your actions and make the right choices to take care of yourself. This can be anything from dietary choices to resisting the urge to procrastinate. Although you can't deprive yourself of happiness, it's important to be able to discipline yourself so that you can make the right choices. Often, we get caught up in the domino effect of wrong choices. Once you make one wrong choice, you figure that you've already messed up, so you continue on that path and lose interest in taking care of yourself properly. Although you may allow yourself to give in to temptation every so often, it's important to be able to have an overall sense of self-discipline so that you can live your best life possible. You must learn how to practice self-discipline so that you can begin using it in your life. You may also learn how to control your thoughts and practice self-discipline mentally.

How to practice self-discipline

When you can practice self-discipline and self-control, you'll be much happier. You'll be able to achieve your goals without giving in to temptation. Self-discipline can improve many aspects of your life. You can improve your diet, save money, and accomplish whatever other goals you may have. It will help you to resist the urge to give in to bad habits and focus more on what matters to you in life. You won't be dragged down by certain impulses, feelings, or emotions. Your decision-making skills will improve, and you'll have greater control over your life. Additionally, you'll be happier with yourself and your life because you'll be doing what you want to instead of what others want you to. There are a few ways that you can improve your self-discipline skills and become better at practicing control over yourself. However, it will take practice and patience to master the skill of self-discipline.

First, you must identify and remove your weaknesses. If you are trying to improve your diet and know that your weakness is cookies, you shouldn't have cookies lying around your house within easy reach. Instead of denying what your weaknesses are, or put off getting over them, recognize what you struggle with. You won't be able to overcome your weaknesses until you recognize them. Identify what's getting in the way of achieving your goals. You must then make an effort to remove the temptations from your life. Additionally, you have to commit. You can't remove the chocolate chip cookies and shortly thereafter go to the store and buy sugar cookies. Remove your temptations, and keep them out of your life. You may also develop a further plan for your goals, outlining what you want to do and what you don't want to do. Come up with a path for you to follow so that you can achieve your goals.

You may practice improving your self-discipline. Go out of your way to make yourself uncomfortable. Instead of avoiding what makes you uncomfortable, just face your fears. The more that you're able to practice discomfort, the better you will be with it. This will also allow you to control yourself more and stop avoiding the unfamiliar. Your mindset will change, and you may even enjoy trying new things and doing what once was uncomfortable.

Remember to focus on one thing at a time. Instead of overwhelming yourself with a huge list of new habits to try, only focus on 1-3 goals at once. This will allow you to fully commit to them and focus on what truly matters to you. If you come up with a dozen goals to try at once, it won't be as effective. You likely won't remember to work on all of them at once, have the time to focus on them, or be able to commit to so many changes at once.

What self-discipline can help with

Self-discipline can help with many aspects of your life. Often, we associate it with diets. You may think of self-discipline when you imagine resisting junk foods or the like. However, it can help you with all areas of your life. You will become more productive, form better relationships, be a happier person, become more positive, accomplish more goals, and overall be a better person. It will take effort, though. You must be consistent with your actions and practice patience when it comes to self-discipline. You won't achieve results overnight, but you will become stronger with more practice and greater knowledge. Knowing how self-discipline can benefit, you can help you stay motivated to get on the path to being more disciplined.

Self-discipline is a practice of consistently. When you master the art of discipline, you will be able to be more consistent with your actions. It will require you to power through challenges and remain strong despite facing obstacles. You may practice consistency with both positive and negative actions. You will learn how to consistently avoid bad habits as well as consistently practicing good habits. By doing so, you allow yourself to fill your life with more of what matters most.

Self-discipline can help you to be a kinder and more emotionally stable person. You may practice self-discipline with your emotions and reactions. Instead of letting your mood influence them, you may discipline yourself. Often, we use life as an excuse for feeling upset or thinking a certain way. However, when you're in a negative mood, everything seems different. Your perspective of the world will completely flip, having you think that everything is wrong with life. If you can train yourself to acknowledge your moods and pause before reacting to them, you can save yourself a lot of hassle. Instead of overreacting for no reason, you may understand that you aren't in a good place mentally. This will not be an optimal time for you to make decisions or complete important tasks. Know when to stop yourself, and you may prevent negativity. Pause before reacting to your emotions.

Pause before saying something that you'll later regret. This can help you tremendously.

Your relationships with others will also improve. When you practice self-discipline, you will follow through with plans. You won't make plans or say yes to plans that you know you won't follow through with. You won't over-commit yourself. You will also understand the importance of dependability, and you won't let small issues get in the way. Self-discipline also goes hand-in-hand with honesty, loyalty, and integrity. When you can control yourself, you will stay true to your values and act according to them. People will respect and appreciate you for it.

Self-discipline can also help you to achieve your goals. In order for you to accomplish your goals, you must stay committed to them. It's important for you to remain motivated despite any obstacles that you may face. There will be challenges, yet you must be able to stick through them.

Decisions and discipline

When you're disciplined, you will also be able to make better decisions. Instead of giving in to temptation, you will choose the path to success. It will be easier to make choices that align with your goals, and you'll be able to stick with them. You won't let others get in the way of your success or influence you otherwise. It will be up to you. Small issues won't bother you, and you'll still be able to make the right choices. It may be easier for you to plan out your goals and commit to a decision as well. Self-discipline can help you to solve your problems.

When you build better habits, you are already making better decisions. Self-discipline will allow you to create good and healthy habits that you'll stick to. This can eliminate the potential for making bad decisions, as you will have already made the choice beforehand. For instance, you may plan out your diet and what you want to eat. One who masters self-discipline will stick to that diet and resist temptation. This will make the choice for you of what to eat, and you won't have to feel guilty about going against this choice in the future.

You will also accomplish more goals that you want to accomplish. One who is disciplined will have their goals written out and prioritized. They will accomplish what they want to. You won't have to make as much of a choice on what you want to do, as you will have already planned that out. You will also make better decisions in regards to your productivity. Instead of choosing to procrastinate or give in to distractions, you will make the right choice. A disciplined individual will realize that it's better to get all of your work done before you play. When you procrastinate, you still have the task hanging over you. Yet, getting everything done first will allow you to fully enjoy your fun without feeling the stress of what you should be doing instead.

In general, the decision-making process will be better. When you learn to control your reactions, you will become less impulsive. Although it is good to be spontaneous every so often, the wisest decisions require some thought beforehand. You may weigh your options and reach the proper conclusion with time. However, this requires you to practice patience.

Discipline can help you to overcome laziness. Instead of making the choice to avoid work or not do the right thing because you aren't in the mood for it, you will recognize the importance of pushing through and accomplishing what you must. The easier option is not usually the option that leads to success. In fact, success takes hard work. You have to face challenges. You will make mistakes. Rejection will occur. Others may not fully support you and believe in you. However, those that succeed have great discipline. They recognize that success will take hard work, and they're willing to put in that work and suffer now to achieve results later.

Self-discipline can make a huge impact on you. It will help you to learn how to practice it, as you can help yourself to achieve your goals. You may also learn how to practice self-control over your thoughts, which will influence your behavior, feelings, and actions. Self-discipline can help you improve many aspects of your life, and you may form better habits while avoiding unhealthy temptations. You'll be much happier with yourself and realize your full potential. Additionally, your decision-making skills will improve, and you'll be able to make choices that have the best possible effect on your life.

Chapter 22
Goal Setting

S etting goals goes hand-in-hand with time management. You cannot claim that you are good at managing time when you lack goals. It is important to stop and question yourself about how you set your goals. Are you the type of person who sets big goals and takes massive steps toward achieving these goals? Or rather, are you one of those individuals who opt to set SMART goals and develop practical measures to meet them? Without a doubt, there are plenty of theories out there about setting goals. Therefore, it can be easy to get blown by the wind if you don't know what is right for you.

One of the main reasons that people set goals is to increase their productivity. This means that more work will be successfully completed in less time. So, having goals implies that you will be managing your time well. This discussion aims to take you through goal setting in time management. Through the information delivered in this, you will be better placed to create realistic goals that are measurable and time-bound.

Essential principles in setting goals

Most people set goals for anything that they plan to do. Often, we find ourselves planning for the day even without our knowledge. If you have developed a habit of setting goals, it will not be difficult for you to list some of the things that you wish to achieve in the next two months or one year. However, this is where most of us go wrong. Goal setting is not just about deciding what you want. There is more to this than what we actually understand. According to professors Gary Latham and Edwin Locke, there is a science behind the entire concept of setting goals (Casano, 2019). This is what influenced them to write A Theory of Goal Setting and Task Performance, which features the following principles of goal setting. These principles are succinctly deliberated in the following paragraphs.

Clarity

This is the first principle, which defines whether your goal is effective or not. Just as the name suggests, your goal ought to be clearly defined. A clear goal should be one that you can picture yourself reaching. You should find it easy to envision yourself after achieving the goal that you have set.

Setting unclear goals is not advisable because it will cause you to fumble around with what you want in your life. This happens due to the fact that you are never certain about what you want. The worst thing is that there is nothing that you will achieve which will impress you. There was nothing that you had set out to obtain. Accordingly, expect to get lost and settle for less.

Take an ordinary example of a weight-loss goal that one states because they simply want to shed some pounds. Yet, this goal is vague. You cannot envisage yourself on the other side of losing weight because you don't know how much you will be losing.

Challenge

Clarity is not the only ingredient that you require for your goal to be deemed effective. It is crucial to make sure that the goal you set is challenging. Why should your goal be challenging? You will gain nothing good by setting easy-to-achieve goals. In fact, you will only be lying to yourself. Conversely, challenging goals will bring a sense of accomplishment. As such, you will have a valid reason to celebrate.

Using the example of the weight-loss goal mentioned above, you will not feel excited if you lost three pounds in a span of three months. What this means is that you did not put in extra effort to lose weight. Your goals should drive you. They should be something worth sweating for. This is the best way for you to feel the joy of winning.

Commitment

The third principle, as proposed by Latham and Locke's theory, is commitment. It is vital that you show concern about what you are doing. When setting your goals, you shouldn't just set them for the sake of doing it. Rather, you ought to display some emotional commitment to what you are doing. As pointed out in the preceding principle, your goals should be challenging. This means that you will need some level of dedication to overcome these challenges. Without this, you will easily surrender on your mission.

Feedback

Goals also need reliable and consistent feedback. After setting your monthly goals, it is essential that you get feedback as to whether you are on track on not. In addition, feedback will give you some insight to understand what works and what doesn't. This allows you to polish your goals along the way to make sure that you focus on what you think will serve you best.

With reference to the example of losing weight, the last thing that you need is to find out two months later that your weight-loss plan didn't work. Ideally, the best strategy would be to gauge your performance weekly and find out the best exercises that will contribute to rapid weight loss. Therefore, feedback is highly important in goal setting.

Task complexity

Another principle that you should bear in mind when setting goals relates to task complexity. Sure, you will be setting a challenging goal to achieve. However, there is a trick that you can utilize to make sure that the goal is less challenging and attainable. This involves breaking down the bigger goal into smaller manageable goals. The advantage gained here is that you will feel that the task is less complex than it was before. You should avoid discouraging yourself in the process of trying to achieve your goals. For that reason, breaking down complex tasks comes highly recommended.

Setting SMART goals

As a means of ensuring that your goals meet the principles detailed in the preceding paragraphs, you ought to make sure that your goals are SMART goals. The term "SMART" is an acronym used to describe the aspects of a specified goal. A SMART goal is:

Specific

A good goal is specific. It should be clear-cut about what you want to achieve from your mission. What are you going to do? Setting specific goals will motivate you to find ideal ways of achieving them. To determine whether your goal is specific or not, you should be in a position to point out clearly what you expect to achieve.

Measurable

Can your goal be measured? Depending on how you are working toward your goal, it should be possible to track your progress. Through regular assessments, you will determine whether or not you are moving in the right direction. Take note of the fact that tracking your progress also provides feedback to make you aware of the tactics that work and those that don't. You can, therefore, adjust accordingly based on the results you get.

Achievable

It goes without saying that your goals should be achievable. In other words, they should be within your reach. Whether in business or in real life, the goals you set should be practical. In business, for example, you cannot set goals that demand a lot from your enterprise when you lack the required resources. Hence, your goals ought to be reasonable enough.

Relevant

This aspect relates to the notion of ensuring that your goals matter to you. They should reflect what you really want to achieve in life. It should drive you to the end of the tunnel where you realize your ambitions. In line with your personal goals, they should embody the type of person that you are. You cannot set personal goals that do not reflect who you are. As such, it is vital to make sure that your goals are not only realistic but also relevant.

Time-bound

So, you have set your goals and you are ready to put in effort toward achieving them. Well, before anything else, you should ask yourself whether you have a defined timeframe for achieving these goals. When are you going to complete your mission? Will you be done in a week, a month, or a year? Timely goals will guarantee that you prioritize your goals accordingly. This means that you will attend to more urgent matters first and schedule others for a more appropriate time.

Benefits of setting goals

From a general perspective, one would argue that goals help in giving people a direction in their lives. Of course, setting the right goals will guarantee that you make sound decisions that will ultimately bear a positive influence in your life. Take an ordinary example of a weekend that you failed to plan for. It is quite likely that you will spend time lazing around. Since you don't know what to do, you will feel bored. You will be ready to engage in any activity as long as it can keep you busy.

A reason to wake up every morning

Perhaps you have been feeling that your days are longer and that there is nothing serious to fill up your day's schedule. If you have been feeling this way, then most certainly you should set goals. Having a purpose to push toward will give you a reason to rise up early in the morning. People who have developed a habit of setting goals will attest to the fact that there are times when they can wake up without using their alarms. This is because the mind has been programmed to work and strive to meet set goals.

Get rid of distractions

Going through life without goals will also lead to many distractions. Usually, you will feel confused about what you should do. The moment anything comes along, you will not hesitate to jump into the wagon. Normally, this is not a trait that you would associate with successful people. They always have a goal to keep them focused throughout the year. Interestingly, sometimes they are too focused to spare some time to have fun. Eventually, their efforts pay off and they are the envy of society.

An opportunity to improve

Having goals also ensures that you improve in what you do. Setting clear and concise goals provides one with an opportunity to grow. You will wake up every morning striving to be the best version of yourself. Athletes are a good example of how goals can help you improve in what you are doing.

Athletes have goals that drive them to train every day. Their aim is to win competitions and all kinds of prizes that are ahead of them. This is what pushes them to train so that they can be the best at what they do.

Live your dreams

Set clear goals and you will live to see your dreams come true. With the constant motivation that will drive you toward your goal, there is nothing that will stop you from living the life that you have always yearned for. As such, goals not only motivate you, but they also provide you with a clear path toward success. Often, you will surround yourself with positive thoughts relating to your anticipated success. By the law of attraction, there is a guarantee that bliss will come your way.

Chapter 23
Forgetting Your Past

Getting rid of your junk

Another factor that contributes to our worry is our constant clutter in our closets and other places. When we have a lot of clutter in different places, we may become really stressed and overwhelmed by the amount of stuff that we have. But what if we could make it simpler? Why not get rid of the stuff that is holding us back from living a meaningful life? That is what this discussion is for—to show you how to get rid of your junk and live a minimalist lifestyle.

What if the new more is less? That is what the minimalists are saying. With more people graduating from four-year universities with student loan debts of more than $30,000 and people unable to get a decent job that pays the bills after graduating, it is no wonder that many millennials are in deep sludge. They cannot buy a car, let alone a house. Therefore, financially, it is becoming more difficult to be a millennial. Millennials are not likely to be able to retire later in their lives because of all the debt that they have acquired in their twenties. It makes for a difficult situation in every sense. The solution to all of this: buy less, consume less, and live with fewer possessions. That is what many millennials are having to do, and it is helping them to alleviate the worry of having so much junk that is causing many problems.

The key point to realize is that stuff does not make us happy. Accumulating more wealth, junk, and other material possessions is never going to make us happy. It is just going to make us more anxious about taking care of the things that could easily break, get damaged, or worse. We find ourselves worrying more when we have a mansion to take care of and other things. But as soon as we get rid of our junk, we find ourselves free to do greater things with our time. Miraculously, we are able to take a load off and stop worrying about the things that could go wrong or tear up. We also spend a lot more money this way, and we find ourselves unable to pay the bills each month, which is more disheartening and stressful.

What is the solution? Purge, purge, purge, I tell you! It is to get rid of everything that is getting in the way. That includes items that we absolutely do not need or desire. Don't let little things get in the way of your life. You should try to do everything to rid yourself of the things that are robbing you of joy at the end of the day because it is not worth it. Cast off everything that is causing you harm and anything that is unnecessary. You don't need it. Try to clean the house at least once a month. Take inventory of your needs and surpluses and then get rid of the things that are not part of your essential items. It will help you get to where you want to be.

Forgiving the past

Sometimes it can be hard to forgive people and situations that have hurt us deeply in the past. However, what we have to learn to do is to get over the past and discover ways to forgive the hurts that have caused us great trouble. We must think of ways to overcome our various situations and forgive the past.

It is easier said than done, I know. However, it is something that you have to do to get rid of the emotional and psychological baggage that you have in your life. Perhaps you have experienced a breakup with a person. It was a terrible experience for you; you are trying to figure out how to move on, but it is continually nagging at you. That's where you must learn to let go and forgive the past of the many things that you may have gone through and move on to the things that motivate you.

Forgiving past mistakes, misjudgments, and heartbreaks will give you the ability to overcome your fears and find peace within your soul. I'm sure that sometimes you feel troubled by the things happening in this world. There are things that can cause you anxiety and stress because they make you remember some childhood trauma or other difficult experiences in the past. When this happens, you begin to relive the painful things of the past.

You need to learn to forgive your past. It is not going to happen automatically. Often, forgiveness is a process that involves a great deal of time before you can carry it out. The only way to get over it is to forget about what happened. Granted, it may take you years to overcome the damage that someone has done in your life, and you may spend a lifetime trying to forgive them. However, the sooner you do that, the better off you will be.

There are many cases of people who have walked through life with the emotional baggage of childhood trauma. One such example was Robin Williams, who had a lonely childhood. His parents put him in an attic of the house, where he was forced to play with his toys all by himself. He rarely saw his parents, except during private dinner gatherings. In that case, Robin felt that he was constantly seeking the validation and love of other people. Many people loved Robin, and they showed it, but he struggled to love himself because he had not felt that as a child. Consequently, he went through his life, struggling with the concept of love because his parents had not shown him love. That deep sadness followed him all the way to his grave after his suicide in 2014.

What Robin Williams shows us is an example of someone who had childhood worries and challenges follow him throughout his life. He was never able to forgive and forget the past, even though it would have helped him to live a more fulfilling life. We can learn from this example that childhood anxieties and trauma can follow us well into adulthood and that if we are not careful, they may follow us all the way to our death. It can be difficult to articulate our concerns to people because they are buried deep within us. Inside our psychology, there are hurting children who are struggling to overcome the difficulties of the past, but the sooner we can overcome the past, the sooner we will be happy and able to live a life that is full of love, joy, peace, and good fortune.

Another example of a person who released the past hurt was Will Hunting from Good Will Hunting (1997), a movie with Ben Affleck, Matt Damon, and Robin Williams. Matt Damon's character, Will, is the main character who has been hurting from his past because he was abandoned by his parents and lived a life as an orphan with no family. He tried to mask his insecurities by drinking, smoking cigarettes, and using physical violence against others. However, he met Dr. Maguire, a psychologist who was played by Robin Williams. The psychologist was able to connect with Will on a deep emotional level and provide him the support he needed to overcome his past trauma. In one emotionally gripping moment, Robin Williams was able to get all the hurt out of Matt Damon's character as he burst into tears and hugged him. To calm him down, Robin's character, Maguire, kept saying, "It is not your fault." It was helpful to see this moment because it showed that the past could be effectively forgiven and wiped clean if a person wanted to do that. Maguire was able to get the pain out of Will and bring him to the point of forgiving the past. Although he might never forget what his parents had done to him to abuse him and eventually leave him, Will would be able to move on and do what he was meant to do, which was to "go and see about a girl." The touching story showed us how the past could be erased so that a person could go forward and discover his destiny. With moments of healing and wholeness, Will would be able to leave behind the darkness of his past and pursue his dream of being in love with someone.

What can we do to forgive our own past? The important thing to do is to realize that we need healing—spiritual, mental, and physical healing. Our minds and hearts are not in the right place. We have hurt from the past, and we feel that it is a dark chasm that we cannot escape from. However, we have to bring ourselves to repenting of our own misjudgments and the things that have caused us pain and anxiety and then also forgive those around us who have hurt us in some way. It is not easy, but it is a path that is well worth it because then we can find a way to feel better and heal. It is a lifelong process in some cases, but as we get rid of our excess emotional baggage, then we can find a freer and more prosperous future in our minds. It is crucial that we release stress, anxiety, and other things that are holding us back. If we don't do that, then we may be holding to something for the rest of our lives that could ultimately lead to our own downfall and destruction, as in the case of Robin Williams. Let's look at the ways that we can do this. How can we emotionally release the past from our hearts and minds?

Practical applications

1. Write down all the things that are causing us anxiety and worry and leave them for later. We should allow ourselves to release all the pain into the paper. After that, you burn the paper, shred it, or do anything to it to show that it is gone forever.

2. Say you're sorry to people you have hurt. What you have to do with this application is to say sorry to people whom you may have caused pain and anxiety. You may not realize how much this has put a rift in your relationship, and you will have to take the initiative to do it because it is highly likely the other person will not take the first step. You have to be proactive about this point.

3. Keep yourself super busy with things that you won't have time to worry or dwell on the past. You should find some ways to keep yourself busy so that you won't think about the things of the past. Do many kinds of projects that will help you experience joy and meaning in your life? Do things that give you passion.

4. Spend time with the people you love and don't spend time with negative people. Another point that you should think about is spending time with people who give you joy and avoiding Negative Nancy and other people who will just bring you down. This will help you to live a happier life.

Chapter 24
Deliberate Thinking

To do something deliberately is to do it with intention. Deliberate thinking, then, is quite simply the act of thinking thoughts with deliberate intent. Very often, individuals can feel as if they have no control over plaguing thoughts. It is as if these thoughts come into your line of focus and demand your time and energy like bullies or authorities that are out of one's power to control. This is not necessarily an exaggeration. If we do not practice keeping our thoughts in check, they will start to bully us and it can feel futile to try to cast those thoughts aside. They are so loud and so aggressive that we feel it is necessary to focus on the thought now and until it is resolved.

In reality, this is a choice.

The average individual is capable of navigating and managing thoughts of their own accord, but it is the lack of practice doing so that makes it feel useless. If you have never driven a car before, it does not mean you are incapable of driving; it means you have not been taught to drive. If your intention is to truly get a grip on overthinking, then you can do this with the practice of deliberate thinking. When you notice thoughts beginning to demand more of your time and attention than feels good to give it now that is the perfect time to practice deliberate thinking, rather than allowing your thoughts to run wild and unchecked. This is an opportunity to reclaim more power and influence over the outcomes and results you see in your daily life.

When you practice deliberate thinking, it means taking responsibility for what happens in your life; for what will happen in your future. You cannot ask for your power back only to relinquish it when something undesirable happens to you. You cannot take responsibility for the goodness that is coming to you, and leave the responsibility of the discomfort. You are responsible for it all, or you are under the control of external elements of which you surely have no control.

If you accept this responsibility, it means you no longer blame other people and other circumstances for your position. You have, in one way or another, brought the position to yourself. It may feel uncomfortable to accept that you are primarily the cause of your own discomfort. However, if you are brave enough to accept this, it comes with incomparable freedom. If you are responsible for all that has come, then you are responsible for all that will come. If you learn to effectively use tools like the power of positive thinking and the power of deliberate thinking, and then you are free to sculpt whatever future you desire.

Deliberate thinking, like positive thinking, is more about a change in attitude than anything else is. It is about the deliberate intent to train yourself for better thinking, and better-feeling thoughts. When something happens that is not in alignment with that goal, it is your job as a positive, deliberate thinker, to change your perspective on the subject, or to acknowledge its presence and dismiss it from your attention promptly. This doesn't mean ignoring the issue altogether, it means dismissing it until it feels good to work with it, think about it, and figure it out.

There may be a subject that feels big, scary, and uncomfortable. It has been buzzing around you for a while now. It calls on your attention and demands your focus even when you do not intend to be thinking about it. The thought creeps in as you are working or as you are attempting to enjoy the company of a friend. It stomps and shouts at you and demands your attention, growing louder and more unruly by the minute. It is ok to dismiss that thought for now, even if the subject is something you certainly must confront. However, chances are you do not have to give your attention to it at this very moment. Practice dismissing those unruly thoughts and send them back to the waiting room. Eventually, you will regain a reasonable degree of confidence and power over your habits of thought, and it will, at some point, actually feel good to deal with and resolve the tormenting issue. Rather than fight with oneself, the deliberate thinker practices control and dominance over thought; dismissing the situation from focus, for the time being.

How to use deliberate thinking with positive thinking?

The combination of positive thinking and deliberate thinking is unbeatable and this is a major factor for the insight and focus on this book. These are your two most powerful weapons and there is nothing you cannot confront without them. These tools remind you that you have the power and you are in control. Not necessarily control of all worldly circumstances, but rather, how you react to them.

If deliberate thinking is to think with intent, this could, in theory, mean the intention of dwelling in uncomfortable, bad-feeling thoughts. Deliberate means intentional; not necessarily good. To practice intentionally, but without the benefit of positive thought, could land you in a similar or worse nightmare of overthinking.

Positive thinking without deliberate thinking is a pattern with no goal or destination; no sense of accomplishment. It can be easy to float through the day enjoying every butterfly and rainbow, but without intention behind your patterns of thought and behavior, there is little to be gained. Overthinkers generally want to regain control over their thoughts in order to accomplish something; a series of things. Happy thoughts without direction may feel good, but your train will be headed to an unknown destination. If that is your intention, so be it, but many of us have other intentions in mind and this will be most easily accomplished by a combination of deliberate and positive thinking.

Pros and Cons of Positive and Deliberate Thinking

It is possible for someone to fall into positive thinking but end up misunderstanding it and misusing it. These individuals can dig themselves even deeper into discomfort. Therefore, it is highly recommended that you familiarize yourself with some of the most common advantages and disadvantages of employing this method of positive thought modification. Let us assess the following list so you know what to watch out for and what to look forward to.

Disadvantages of Positive and Deliberate Thinking

1. Only positive thoughts - Eradicating all "negative" thought can be detrimental to the individual. Some of the thought processes referred to as negative actually helpful and beneficial to us. Considering a worst-case scenario can help us to plan and prepare for an outcome so that the impact is not felt so harshly. Emotions like fear and worry can, in some cases, protect us from dangerous circumstances. It is important to accept this as part of your repertoire and rather than see this as a negative, consider it a positive thought-behavior. However, do not let this thinking spiral out of control. There is a difference between mitigating damages by considering worst-case scenarios and stewing over worst-case scenarios for an excessive amount of time, or in a way, that exhausts you.

2. Ignore real life - It is possible to become so enamored with the idea of positive thinking that the individual may begin to ignore primary concerns. While it should be your priority to think about that, which feels good, it does not mean you should neglect important aspects of day-to-day life. Neglecting that which needs your attention does not actually feel good anyway. It may be a delay in dealing with those uncomfortable feelings, but you still know in your mind and in your heart, those issues are there and they need your attention. If you find yourself having to confront an uncomfortable circumstance, as a positive thinker, you do not mindlessly ignore it. Instead, you acknowledge its existence and make a deliberate decision to confront the issue now, or at a better time in the near future.

3. Positive Thinking as your only tool - While positive and deliberate thinking can be a powerful tool for thinkers, it is important to recognize that is not the only tool you have. Becoming overly reliant on this one method of thinking and behavior actually creates another automatic response for your mind and body to follow whether or not it is actually the best course of thought and action. You end up in a spot much as you started in, where your actions and thoughts are rote, mechanical, and not deliberate.

4. Judgment from others - Just because you're at a point in your life where making positive and deliberate changes to your thought- and behavior-patterns feels good, doesn't mean everyone around you is ready for it. Be as gentle with others as you are with yourself and do not expect others to fall in line and think positively along with you. Often times, this journey is one you make on your own. It is unfair to expect someone else to adapt so quickly.

5. Removing yourself from the fuss - This can be a difficult step to cross over because we are, largely, social creatures. We want to express and share. However, a brief looks around you will demonstrate that a great many conversations taking place are neither positive nor deliberate. Spending 45 minutes arguing politics online with another person is likely not part of your deliberate goal. By giving your attention to this debate, you are likely slowing down your train by conjuring feelings of frustration, helplessness, and even anger. This can send your train jolting the wrong direction down a negative path.

6. Self-punishment - It can be a natural reaction for many Overthinkers to punish themselves mentally, emotionally, even physically, when they find themselves slipping up and letting the negative train build momentum again. Do not punish yourself. You have not done anything wrong. Allowing the mind to naturally swing back to uncomfortable thoughts is absolutely part of the process. To be mad at yourself for slipping back is equivalent to the carpenter who hammers one nail into the wood and becomes mad that not all nails were hammered into the wood at that moment.

Advantages of positive and deliberate thinking

The advantages of positive and deliberate thinking are more obvious and easier to see than perhaps the disadvantages are. By now, you should have some idea that positive and deliberate thinking yields highly beneficial results, especially when employed by Overthinkers. Here are some of the most beneficial rewards:

- A sense of clarity and clear thought

- The power to acknowledge and dismiss thoughts without guilt or delay

- The decrease in stress, which plays an enormous part in how the body physically feels and reacts

- Lower rates of depression

- Greater resistance to immune-system illnesses

- Greater self-worth

- Higher levels of confidence

- Self-accomplishment and self-actualization

- A better general mood and attitude

- A sense of well-being and everything in its place

- A certainty that you can handle life's circumstances in a healthy way

- Your healthy practice becomes a model for others to follow

- Gained control over thought-patterns

- Removal of automatic responses that are no longer serving you

- Removal of harmful behaviors that are no longer in alignment with your deliberate goal to feel good.

Chapter 25
Exercises That Help Positive Thinking

Positive thinking is a good habit and like any good habit it takes time to inculcate. Here are a few simple and very effective exercises and methods that will help you to think positive – no matter what.

Getting rid of worrying

What is worrying? Worrying is misplaced imagination. The problem with worrying is that it has the power to stress you to no end—for no actual reason because in majority of cases nothing happens. When you worry, you think about the possibilities of things going wrong.

You need to get rid of worrying. To do so, instead of worrying prepare for the worst possible scenario. Think beforehand, "What could go wrong here?" and prepare for any of those eventualities. Worry comes when you are not prepared well enough because it makes you feel helpless to the outcome.

Counter the helpless feeling by preparing for all possible mishaps that could be controlled. The rest you leave to the eventualities of life, what will be will be. Accept that you cannot control everything no matter what you do. So, give your best possible shot and leave the rest to fate.

Side by side, ensure that you have enough to occupy your mind when you think you are prone for a worry attack. If you have something to do, it is least likely that you will worry too much. Do something pleasant and happy—preferably for someone else.

No complaints for 24 hours

Have a "24-hours of no complaints" period as often as you can in your schedule. You could have it once a month or once a week. When this period is declared, the rule would be that you cannot complain about anything you find annoying, no matter what. Instead, try looking beyond it and do something constructive.

A nice story can give you a fair idea of how useful this method can be. A lady was shopping at a supermarket and observed that the cashier was very grumpy. She was snappy bordering on rude. The people she served responded with equal or more irritation.

When this lady's turn came, the cashier almost threw her change on the counter. However, the lady did not take offence; instead, she smiled at the cashier and asked her full of empathy, "You had a rough day dear, didn't you?" Then, paying her a tip she said, "Here dear have a wonderful cup of coffee on me. It will make you feel better."

Surprisingly, the cashier smiled, accepted the tip and said, "Thank you so much. My daughter is in the hospital and I could not get off today. I am very upset. Thank you for understanding."

Very often giving the benefit of doubt is all it takes to make the day better for you and others. Unfortunately, we tend to jump to the worst conclusions when we should rather be a little empathic. Next time, when you feel like snapping a biting retort to someone rude, take a deep breath, count to 10 and reply with kindness. It will definitely make your day because you refused to allow the incident to make you angry; and it may change that person's day for the better, too.

3-6 Hours of pure kindness

Another way to make you feel good and encourage positive thinking is to give yourself a 3-6 hours' time out when you should be kind to everyone around you. Be warned that this could be stressful initially, because you cannot get angry with anyone or say an unkind word, or do anything unkind to anyone – no matter what.

The greatest gift you can give yourself and others is compassion. When you impose these hours of pure kindness, you will learn to see the good in every person. It is impossible to get angry with anyone if and when you see the good in them.

Like the example in the "cashier lady" story, you need to understand that when someone behaves badly it is because that person is unhappy for some reason. This person needs your compassion the most. If you practice kindness in spite of the response, you will realize that this helps you more than the recipient.

Kindness – when offered unconditionally - has the power to calm your mind and fill you with a tranquility that is beyond compare.

Thank you, I appreciate it very much

Learn to appreciate others. Say "thank you" as often as you can; say it with genuineness and feeling. Everybody loves to be appreciated for what they do. It is wonderfully rewarding and motivating to receive a well said "thank you." Whenever somebody does you a good turn, no matter how small be quick to say, "thank you."

Learning to appreciate others will make it easier to appreciate the good things in your life. Every person has a long list of blessings, happy hours, good times – but we tend to focus on the negative–what we do not have, what we lost, what we would have had and lose the chance to enjoy what we DO have.

Whether you say, "thank you" to God, your friend, your spouse, your children, a stranger or anyone who did something for you, the benefit of it comes to you first. When you say "thank you" you realize that you received something nice and you have a reason to be happy.

Learnt to be grateful for what you have and say it aloud as often as you can. Say "thank you" as often as you can. It will make you happy.

Sorry, I hurt you – please forgive me

Just as it is important to say, "thank you," it is important to say "sorry" as often as it is required and with genuine feelings. Whenever you realize you have hurt anyone, be quick to express your remorse. Say "sorry" as soon as you can. This will clear the air and allow healing on both sides.

An apology put forth appropriately will always create positive energy. Try this experiment. Next time when you are in an angry altercation with anyone, take a deep breath and say, "I am sorry if what I did (or said) hurt you." See what happens. In most cases, when you say you're sorry the anger dissipates like smoke.

With the anger gone, good vibes come right back in and you will be surprised how good it feels for you as well.

It's okay, I forgive you

It is important that you can forgive those who hurt you as well. Often, we carry a grudge forever, without realizing that the anger and hurt erodes the soul and mind. Revenge is a poison that you carry inside you. When you hold anything against a person who has hurt you, you are tying yourself to that person and reliving the hurt again and again.

Forgiving means letting the bitterness go, which in turn sets you free. All religions advocate forgiveness—with a good reason. When you forgive, you become emotionally free of pain. Try it; you will feel a weight lifted off your shoulders, literally. It is a wonderful feeling to let go of the hurt. Forgiveness is a gift you offer yourself more than the others.

Chapter 26
How to Make Important Decisions Today?

When it comes to making these important decisions without delay, there are a few strategies that may help you out. Many of us are so swamped with work and other stressors in our life that we often fail to realize how easy it often is to simplify more complex situations and processes, in order to make an important decision.

Decisions always have an impact on something, but the impact is not always at the same level. Sometimes, a decision may affect how you feel, such as when you decide not to pack lunch for the day. Often, such a small decision would not have a major impact on your life–you can go to the cafeteria and buy something to eat when you feel hungry or during your lunch hour.

Other times, however, decisions have a much larger impact–such as when you have to make a choice that could mean a client would sign a contract with your firm or rather go to another firm. This can be a major loss, especially when the client would be worth millions to your company, should you make the wrong choice and the client goes with their second choice.

The more of an impact a decision will have, the more you would have to consider the different options and ensure that the one you choose will have a most positive impact on your life or your career, compared to the other options that are available to choose from.

Know your goals

Prior to making a decision that will have an impact on your life or your career, such as those that may result in a hire from a client, it is vital that you completely understand the goals that you are trying to reach with the particular decision that hangs on your shoulders. Understand exactly what needs to be done with that decision.

For example, is your goal to buy a new house? Understand the smaller goals involved as well. When you are trying to buy a house, you want to ensure there is adequate room for your family, so your goal will be to buy a house that has enough rooms, as well as living space, to accommodate everyone. You also have the goal of choosing a house that is close to schools and to your workplace and that of your wife.

At work, you might need to make a decision on a specific client as there is a conflict between two that you can sign. While the primary goal would be to make money through signing one of these clients, another goal may be to sign the one that could provide your business with a longer-term relationship and projects that will last for several years, even if it means a slightly lower profit on the first project compared to the other client.

Be prepared and well-informed

You should be well-informed and very much prepared in order to make a decision that will be best for you, your family, or your business, depending on which party the decision will have an effect on. Thus, always ensure that you obtain as much information as possible related to a project, or whatever it is that is involved before you decide on which option you choose.

The same goes for a business-related decision. Have interviews with the clients that will be affected by your decision. Ask the right questions. Know what they expect. Know what needs to be done. Understand what is involved.

All this information will help you filter out the bad options and choose the option that is best suited for the current scenario.

Make a biased decision

It is okay to listen to that gut feeling you get sometimes and to hear out the opinions of other people in your life, whether colleagues, family members, or friends, but it is also important that the decision you made is biased. Even though many would advise being unbiased, I personally find that making decisions in favor of something or someone, such as the parties involved in the situation, really is the best way to go about a decision-making process, and ultimately to avoid constantly finding yourself making delay after delay.

Consider the parties involved and understand what would be considered in their favor when making the final decision. Perhaps your family prefers a dog, so opt for a house with a big yard as compared to a smaller yard or an apartment in a more convenient location – that would be a biased decision based on the preferences of your family.

Weigh out all the pros and cons

Each of the options that you can choose from when you make an important decision has pros and cons involved. It might not always be easy to identify all of the pros and all of the potential drawbacks related to a particular option, but setting up a list of what you know would happen, how you, your family, or perhaps your business could benefit, and what the downsides will be, can be a big help and will ensure making that decision becomes much easier in the end.

Make a list with all the options that are available. Then, set up a sub-list beneath each one. Write down some of the pros and then write down a couple of cons. Be realistic when you write down these factors. Consider all the research that has been done, the information you have gathered, and take the other points I have covered here into account as well.

When you look back at the list you made, you will start to get a better picture of which decision or option is the better choice to make, when comparing the pros and cons of each option in front of you.

Understand possible consequences and complications

Actions have consequences. Sometimes, even making the right decision in life can pose a threat to someone or to some party, and possibly lead to a series of complications. This is why making a list of pros and cons that can be associated with each option you are facing is often not enough. Additionally, you need to consider the chain of reactions that may occur once you make the decision – you need to do this for each of the options that you have listed.

If you choose a house with a bigger yard instead of an apartment in town, then you might have to drive a long way to drop off the kids at school and to get to the office. The reaction here would be the longer distance, which means a longer driving time in the morning and in the afternoon. In turn, you will have to get up earlier and perhaps move faster in the morning. This will also push up your monthly expenses for gas. Your car may need more regular services if you are going to be driving longer distances.

The same type of thought should go into decisions that will affect your career and the company you work at, whether you own the company or simply serve as an employee. If you are going to sign one client over another client, due to a conflict of interest or another related matter, then you need to consider possible consequences that may arise when you choose one particular client. If you need to select a venue, consider possible complications that may arise with each of the options.

Time for action

After you have done thorough planning, you know the pros and cons of every option in front of you, and you should have an idea of the decision you need to make. Things should be much simpler now and give you the opportunity to make the decision without further delay.

When it is time for action, make the decision. Don't delay again. You have all the information and data that you now need to make the right decision and choose the option that will be most suited to the current situation. Take action, make the decision, and follow the appropriate procedures in order to follow through on that particular decision that you have decided to make.

Following up on your action

This is a step that people usually overlook and, while it is not really a necessity, I highly suggest that you take a moment to reflect on those decisions that you have made. Consider how they have worked out. I personally take 20 minutes once a week in order to follow up on the decisions that I have made during the week. I do this on the weekend when things are calmer. I sit down and take a look at all my notes related to any important decisions that I made. I consider the options I had, and how the one that I ended up choosing affected the particulars and parties involved.

This way, you will be able to learn from your own mistakes and motivate yourself through those decisions that worked out perfectly. Congratulate yourself on successful choices. Don't scold yourself on those that didn't work out great – rather look at why they didn't work out and see what you could have done differently. This way, you can avoid making such mistakes again in the future.

When is it better to delay a decision?

I know I just gave you the old speech of never delaying a decision and to stop procrastinating, but I do want to touch a quick topic – sometimes, in rare cases, it might be better to delay the process of choosing between different options. It is, however, essential that you understand that this only accounts for special cases and the fact that I am suggesting a possible delay should not give you the opportunity to make excuses when your case does not meet the criteria I am going to discuss here.

First of all, if the decision that you have to make is small and will have no significant impact on your life or in the workplace, then don't delay. No matter how small, the fact that you still need to make that decision will linger in your mind and add to the clutter that may already be present.

For small decisions, consider your options, weigh the pros and cons of each option, and then decide.

When the decision you have to make will have a bigger impact, however, then there are cases where you might want to consider a small delay. At the same time, I want to stress the fact that delaying should not lead to further delaying! One single delay and then, when the time comes, you need to make a choice.

The only time when important decisions should really be delayed is in cases where you feel sick or very tired. For example, if you have caught the flu or you have stayed up all night working on a project. Such scenarios call for rest and healing. ONLY delay the decision up to the time when you have gotten some sleep or when the flu has passed, then immediately start to work on a plan-of-action to ensure you can choose the most appropriate option.

Conclusion

I t's so incredibly important to not only be comfortable with yourself as it pertains to healing yourself and the people around you while you go through that journey but to be able to actively make your life happier as you go through it. Often, you develop a lot of anxiety as a result of negative emotions or simply a lack of emotion. The apathy we feel is a direct derivative of anxiety, and we overthink because our brain doesn't have any emotions to focus on, so it creates its own out of anxiety, stress, and apathy.

The most relevant part of healing is having those positive emotions brought back so that you give yourself positive experiences without the need to stress yourself out unnecessarily. For example, going outside and disconnecting from your devices for a little while can go a long way in stimulating positive emotions. We feel good when we go outside and smell the fresh air, and we feel good when we feel the most connected to the ground beneath us. Because being outside stimulates this kind of very basic pleasure in us, you should seek it out when you can. This doesn't have to be a part of your regimen, which you keep up with daily, but you should go outside fairly often so that you can really experience the real world around you for what it is in a basic, carnal way. Going outside doesn't have to be a solitary experience, either. It can be relaxing and cathartic to just take a walk outside with friends or other loved ones. It helps you not only to calm down, but it can be a good way for you to talk plainly with the people you care about and who care about you. Letting them into your life in a more honest and up-front way is a good venue for you to be happier in the long run. Being in nature tends to have this effect on people—we feel calmer and more emotionally stable and relaxed when we're outside, so it makes sense that we might be more willing to reach out to people and talk with them honestly about their lives, how they feel, as well as our own experiences with them. Having these experiences mesh together over a length of time can be incredibly healing for everyone involved.

When you feel overwhelmed with the pressures of life, and you feel as though you might collapse under the weight of your own stresses, it's a good time to step back and have an in-depth look at why you are where you are and why you're doing what you're doing. Assess yourself and your position at the moment and determine how important that position is to you. Your mental and emotional health should always come before the wants of others and what they might demand from you. If there's someone in your life who's asking something of you and it would just be too much, you have the ability and the freedom to decline in an exercise of putting yourself first. Often, a lot of your stress arises from not knowing how to prioritize yourself above other people. When we learn this irreplaceable skill, we become aware of our place with our friends and loved ones and we understand better how we can make ourselves and our lives happier. If you're in a place or position where you don't feel happy, get out of that situation. You aren't being terrible or selfish for wanting the best for yourself and wanting to be happy for the sake of being happy. Even if you don't want people to view you as selfish, there are more important things in your life than pleasing others instead of pleasing yourself. Be hedonistic on an intimate, spiritual level. There are ways that you can please yourself on the level of the emotions and the brain which you might not have been able to do or work up the courage to commit to before you started trying to undo all the trauma done to you over time. Indulge in something you enjoy now and then, splurge on something you've had your eye on for a while, turn down plans if you don't feel like going out, and have days to yourself where you can just sit back, relax, and enjoy your own company in a way that you might not be able to if there was anyone else around, no matter how close to you they were. When we prioritize ourselves and learn to simply cut our losses emotionally, we free ourselves to so many healing experiences we would never have had if we didn't know how to make those changes and make decisions for the sake of our mental health instead of for the sake of the happiness of other people. Even so much as taking a day off from your obligations if you can, and having just an afternoon where you can indulge and treat yourself can be an incredibly healing experience in and of itself. Indulging yourself and accepting yourself as someone who needs to be cared for and loved, even if it has to be by you, can bring you so much joy and emotional release that you might never have had access to otherwise.

Ultimately, there might be people in your life who are preventing you from being this best version of yourself. These people are toxic people, and they might be involved in any part of your life. They might be your friends, your family, your coworkers, or anyone else in your support system, or out of it, who you talk to regularly and who are having a direct negative impact on your life. Toxic people can look at any range of ways, and they come in many disguises. You might have been a toxic person at one point—most people have toxic traits or traits in their personality, which could be improved to make them more pleasant to be around and healthy for themselves and for others. Regardless of whether or not you have toxic traits now or did before, that doesn't mean you can't be affected by them in other people today. The more you learn about people in your life, the more easily you might begin to see them for what they truly are. If you know a toxic person in your life, you'll likely know by the way they act before the way they look. Toxic people tend to manipulate others in order to get what they want, and they don't tend to feel a lot of remorse when they successfully manipulate other people into doing what they need them to do. Toxic people get other, submissive people to do their dirty work for them while they sit back and manipulate everyone else behind the scenes. Toxic people might have very depressive actions, they might be anxious, they might be narcissistic, they could have any number of symptoms of other mental illnesses or signs that they aren't all there or they have plans and abilities to manipulate you to get what they want and think they deserve. You have probably been manipulated by a toxic person at some point in the last month or two. You also probably have at least one person in your life who would be considered toxic. Consider if someone you know or someone even in your support system has ever used the powers of eloquence and their own words against you to blackmail you or guilt you into being in emotional debt to them. Do they hold grudges against you for things that happened ages ago and might not have even been your fault? Do they have any way of guilting you or gaslighting you by playing the victim until you give in to their rhetoric and do what they want? If this is the case, you're dealing with a toxic manipulator and you can free up your life and your soul if you drop them as quickly as you can. Once you eliminate them from your life, you can feel yourself healing from all the bad energy that was with you with that person. Don't think of it as a major loss if you lose them for good—manipulators tend to be dramatic and make large shows out of abandoning people and making them feel pretty difficult. When we do knock them down, they might try to re-enter or take advantage of other people or things in our lives, so we don't force them out. This can be incredibly disturbing, so always have a way you can protect yourself and other people from people like this who are potentially dangerous or obsessive. The point of cutting off dangerous or otherwise very toxic people is not to put you in danger or even to stand up for what is right. You should want to cut off people who make you sad and angry—people who make your life less enjoyable to live every day and people you have lost your precious time for having to take care of them and cater to them. You drop toxic people for no one else's sake but your own, no matter what.

That is the nature of toxic people and removing them from your life. When you initially take them out, it feels as though something is gone, wrong, or missing. However, as time goes on and the hole begins to close, we often realize the hole should never have existed in the first place. Something new and better and healthy might have even begun to sprout in its place. If this is the case, be sure to foster whatever is growing anew. It might be something healthy that will enrich your experience and help you to be happier overall. It might be something toxic that is growing in that place of its toxic parent, in which case you can nip toxic behavior in the bud before it gets too bad.

When we overthink, it feels as though it controls our lives. Every move we make and every thought we have feels as though it's already been governed by this force in our head, which tells us that no matter what, we'll fail. No matter what we'll feel worthless, we'll never succeed no matter what, and so on and so forth. This impact can be damaging, not only to our professional career but also to our intimate, personal lives. The way being constantly told we don't meet some kind of invisible standard and never will as a kid messes with you in a way that is incomparable to many other experiences you can have while growing up. However, while you grow up, reflect on who got you there. You are always growing up, no matter how old you are, so always assess yourself and reflect on how you did today and how you did tomorrow. When you're constantly self-assessing in a way that is constructive, you can get so much done and quickly become the best version of yourself. Being aware of yourself, your emotions, and your mind is the best way that you can stay on track and make sure you become the best person you can be.

MENTAL TOUGHNESS:

THE COMPLETE GUIDE ABOUT HOW TO STOP
OVERTHINKING AND PROCRASTINATING.
LEARN HOW TO BE MORE PERSEVERANT AND
RESILIENT WHILE IMPROVING YOUR SELF-
CONTROL AND YOUR ABILITY TO FOCUS

Mark Mind

Introduction

The mental strength is a going worry among people, associations, and nations. It is a significant subject of extraordinary reference and with the consistent increment in total populace and rivalry, the presence of firm rivalry which cuts over each division of the world economy and business has clarified that each individual who expects to endure must have to learn the rudiments of being a survivor.

It is interesting to know that long age standing discovery of the term "survival of the fittest" has come to prove the existence of a common factor that leads to surviving and that is the "fittest." Now the question you should be asking yourself right now is "am I mentally tough enough to fit into the hard situations in the society?"

Mental toughness, therefore, is not just a topic, it is something that affects every individual on the planet today, on the off chance that you are intense intellectually the odds of your endurance in the advanced also quick creating world is sure. As the population continues to increase and with limited jobs, how do you intend to survive in this information age?

This is the ideal opportunity for you to search internally and know how you can truly turn out to be intellectually intense. This book is bringing the best down to business ways that will give you what you have been missing and what you have not been doing well. I will open up your eyes to the facts and true reality of the nature of the world and you will see what is actually happening.

Then you will have the option to figure out where you really have a place by and by, how you can free yourself from where you are, and graduate or jump to your chosen place throughout everyday life.

You can actually take your destiny into your own hands and chose where to be and when to be and achieve greater heights. The mental toughness associates with certain factors and characteristics that will bring out the very best in you when you decide to make a change.

The issues identifying with progress can be found in individuals with mental durability. Thus, effective individuals are normally intellectually intense, there is something that drives them to turn out to be exceptionally fruitful, and one of those variables are identified with being intellectually extreme.

Are you having problems in your life? Have you been looking for a way out of your current situation and you are finding it extremely difficult to realize your dreams? Then, this book is actually prepared based on vast experience and research.

It will make you rediscover yourself and become a champion by right and merit.

Nothing comes simple in life aside from you are brought into the world lucky and wealthy, and even as at that, you may lose the wealth that you have acquired in the event that you don't have the mental strength or arranged to accept accountability for your life, for some have had the chance of acquiring incredible riches and they are unable to expand with it or manage it well.

Being mentally tough is for both young and adults.

So take the opportunity provided here and equip yourself for that challenge that comes your way.

Be a different person, stand out from the crowd, be a leader in your area of life and become the champion that you have always dreamed to become, the time is now. Follow the simple steps to become mentally tough to be a survivor and a victorious person.

Chapter 1
What is Mental Toughness?

The development of mental toughness will demand that your thoughts, emotions, and actions are reigned in and kept under tight control during the worst of situations and conditions. Exercise your skills to the point that jumping these hurdles can be as simple as breezing over physical hurdles for skilled athletes.

The basic way that the brain is designed and operates gives you leverage to develop a strong mental toughness for any situation. You can make a mental choice to develop the skills that will propel you toward success or remain quietly living in the background and feeling bitter that nothing about your life changes.

Being in touch with your emotional side is critical to developing mental toughness. Knowing when emotions are trying to formulate and take over is the perfect time to introduce distraction techniques. You can easily learn how to pull yourself out of an emotional funk that keeps you bound up and unable to move forward. The mental weakness is rewarded through being pliable to raw emotion. It does not that mean you have to completely switch emotions off. You can be a compassionate, feeling person that is not ruled by emotions.

The mental toughness determines a person's ability to show a consistent performance under pressure and stress. This personality trait is closely associated with perseverance, character, grit, and resilience. You have to be aware of your emotions and thoughts. Mindfulness is all about working with your emotions and thoughts to consciously decide your actions. In other words, it is all about responding instead of reacting.

Mental quality isn't tied in with acting extreme. You don't have to disregard your feelings to state that you're intellectually intense. The picture that strikes a chord when somebody says an intellectually tough individual is a chilly, oppressive, dispassionate, and forceful person who never looks for help. This isn't right. The mental quality is tied in with acknowledging how your feelings influence your practices and contemplations. It isn't tied in with disregarding passionate or physical agony. It is tied in with knowing the wellspring of agony and when to tune in and when to restrict.

You shouldn't act naturally dependent to show that you are intellectually intense. The mental sturdiness is tied in with acknowledging and recognizing that you don't have all the abilities and answers. You are happy to develop and look for help from others. The mental strength isn't just about positive reasoning. You need to think coherently and reasonably. Inordinate confidence can be as awful as cynicism.

The mental strength isn't just about accomplishing joy. You don't have to compel yourself to feel glad. The mental strength is tied in with accomplishing your maximum capacity. You can even now be intellectually extreme in the event that you have uneasiness, gloom, or different issues. Albeit creating mental durability needs more work, the outcome will be justified, despite all the trouble.

The mental sturdiness instructing can be used to oversee pressure. It very well may be valuable for youngsters too. A versatile individual can confront life's difficulties and manage the weights they will confront. The mental sturdiness preparing can likewise be remembered for other requesting interests. Experts who need to contend in forceful situations can profit from this.

Why Develop Mental Strength

The mental strength is essential for everyone because it explains the behavior of the person you're dealing with. It also improves your productivity and efficiency. The mental quality makes you increasingly cautious about the work you're doing. Great mental quality really directly affects an individual's instructive accomplishments.

There's a link between personal aspirations and mental strength. The individuals who are intellectually solid will in general be more decided than intellectually feeble individuals. They want to be better, and they know they're capable of getting what they want as long as they put in the required effort.

Show positive behaviors

Intellectually resilient individuals will in general show positive personal conduct standards. They have an inspirational standpoint and positive characteristics. These individuals don't leave issues. Rather, they face these issues and manage them head-on in a positive manner.

Find and keep a job

There's additionally a connection between an individual's capacity to get and keep a line of work and mental quality. In foundations that give advanced education, understudies with great mental quality will in general total their investigations and get passing marks than intellectually frail individuals. The last is bound to stop end-route.

Achieve a better sense of wellbeing

Intellectually tough individuals will in general have a superior feeling of prosperity than intellectually frail people. They are progressively equipped for taking care of misfortunes and terrible days. Intellectually resilient individuals are additionally more averse to be missing in school or work. They're more averse to engage in tormenting. Individuals with high mental quality can recoup from misfortunes quicker because they know to think about things from different viewpoints.

Chapter 2
Characteristics of Mentally Tough People

We as a whole would have run over explicit focuses in our lives where our psychological sturdiness was scrutinized. It might have come in the form of a toxic friendship, a dead-end job or a destructive relationship. Regardless of what the challenge is, you need to be strong, change your perspective towards life, and be proactive if you want to be successful. It sounds pretty simple, doesn't it? Who wouldn't want good friends, a happy relationship and a satisfactory job? It might seem easy, but it takes a lot of hard work. It isn't easy to be mentally tough when you feel like you are stuck. The ability to break free of the bonds holding you back and creating your path takes courage that only those who are mentally tough possess. It is interesting to see the manner by which intellectually extreme individuals put themselves beside every other person. Where others see an incomprehensible obstacle to cross, they see a test that should be survived.

In the year 1914, Thomas Edison's factory burned down, and several precious prototypes were destroyed, and the damage amounted to $23 million. Edison's reply to this unfortunate incident was "Thank heavens every one of our missteps were caught fire. Presently we can begin new once more." Edison's response sums up what mental toughness is about. It is about having a positive outlook towards life, seeing opportunities, and taking the necessary action even when things start looking bleak. There are a couple of characteristics that all those who are mentally tough share and they are as follows.

1: They Are Emotionally Intelligent

One of the building blocks of mental toughness is emotional intelligence. If you cannot understand and tolerate negative emotions and turn them into something productive, then you cannot be mentally tough. Moments that put your mental toughness to test are testing your emotional quotient as well. Your IQ or intelligence quotient is fixed, whereas your EQ, or your emotional quotient (emotional intelligence), isn't and it can be improved if you are willing to work on it. Emotional intelligence is a highly desirable trait, and all those who are successful have a high EQ. When you can analyze a situation objectively and not emotionally, you will be able to make a better decision. If you can be easily swayed by positive and negative emotions, you are opening yourself up for manipulation.

2: They Are Very Confident

Henry Ford once said, "Whether you think you can, or think you cannot—you're right." Your mentality can influence your ability to achieve success. Mentally tough people will firmly believe in Ford's notion. If you don't feel confident about yourself and your skills, you cannot expect someone else to feel confident about you. Real confidence is essential and not false bravado. People often tend to mask their insecurities by merely projecting confidence, instead of being confident. A confident person will always stand apart when compared to all those who are indecisive, doubtful, and skittish. Their confidence often inspires others as well.

3: They Are Good at Neutralizing Toxic People

It is not only exhausting but also quite frustrating to deal with difficult people. People who are mentally tough are capable of taking control of their interactions with toxic elements around them. A mentally tough person can keep his or her emotions in check while confronting a toxic person. Their approach would often be rational. If you want to be mentally strong, then you should be able to identify negative emotions like anger and shouldn't let these feelings get the better of you. Negativity simply adds fuel to the fire, and it doesn't take long for the situation to spin out of your control rapidly. Take a moment and try to see the problematic person's point of view as well and try finding some common ground or a solution to the problem. Even when things are going south, a mentally tough person will be able to prevent the toxic person from bringing them down.

4: They Can Embrace Change

Mentally tough people are quite dynamic and are capable of embracing change. They not only embrace change but can adapt themselves to any situation as well. They are well aware of the fact that the fear of change can stall their progress and prevent them from achieving success. A mentally tough person would look for any likely change and devise a plan of action that will help him or her in making the most of the possible change. If you don't embrace change, then you will never see any good in it. Keep an open mind and check for ways in which you can capitalize on such change. You will be setting yourself up for failure if you keep doing things in the same way while ignoring any changes. Ignoring it or avoiding it will not make it go away. So, stop doing the same thing over and over again and expect a different outcome. Well, that indeed is the definition of insanity.

5: They Can Say No

If you want to reduce your chances of experiencing stress and depression, then learn to say "no." Saying "no" is, in fact, good for your mental health. All those who are mentally tough possess the self-esteem and the foresight that helps them say no. If you have trouble saying "no" to others, then you should start working on it immediately. Saying "no" not only helps you in avowing unnecessary burden, but it will also help you in prioritizing your work and cutting off toxic people from your life. While saying no, a mentally strong person would steer clear of phrases like "I don't think" or "I am not certain." Whenever you are saying no, say it with confidence. Learning to say no will help a person to concentrate better on the tasks they have on hand instead of taking on more work that they might be able to honor. The ones who are mentally tough have good self-control, and they can say "no" not just to others, but to themselves as well. Stop taking action impulsively and instead follow the rules of delayed gratification.

"No" is quite a powerful word and it can help you in protecting your valuable time. When you have to say "no," just say it. Don't make use of phrases like "I am not sure," "I don't think I will be able to" and so on. If you won't be able to take on any additional commitments or if you feel that you have got a lot of work to do, then don't take on any new obligations. Just say no. If you get stuck with something that you won't be able to do, then this will only create additional stress, pressure, and just burn you out eventually. Learn how to say no, and this will help in improving your productivity.

6: They Know That Fear Causes Regret

If you never take a chance, you will never know what could have happened. Unless you try, you wouldn't know. Instead of lamenting over the opportunities you didn't take, it is better to control your fears and make the leap. Don't be afraid of taking risks. However, this doesn't mean that you will take on any risk blindly. What is the worst thing that can ever happen to you? Death isn't the answer. The worst thing is regret. Regret about the things that you could have and should have done. Regret can eat you up from within. Mentally tough people know that fear causes disappointment, and this is where self-awareness steps in. Mindfulness will help you in adjusting among abiding and recalling. Harping for a really long time on your mix-ups will make you on edge and cognizant, though overlooking them builds your odds of rehashing them everywhere. You need to learn to transform your failures and look for an opportunity to improve.

7: They Can Embrace Failure

Failures are very common, and everyone has their fair share of failures in their lives. Mentally tough people are capable of embracing their failures. No one can experience success without knowing what failure is. When you can acknowledge that you are on the wrong path, are aware of the mistakes you are making, and can embrace your failures, only then will you be able to achieve success.

8: They Can Let Go of All the Wrongs

Mentally tough people are aware that what you concentrate on will determine your emotional state. When you stay fixated on a problem that you are facing, you tend to create and drag on the negative emotions, which in turn stalls your progress. When you start focusing on yourself and the circumstances you are in, you will feel a sense of personal efficacy, which helps in generating positive emotions and improve your productivity. Mentally tough people are capable of distancing themselves from their mistakes without forgetting them. Keep your mistakes at a safe distance, learn and adapt from them, but stop dwelling on them for prolonged periods of time.

9: No One Can Limit Their Joy

If you derive your sense of pleasure and satisfaction from comparing yourself to others, your happiness no longer lies in your own hands. You are essentially giving up the control of your happiness to someone else. Those who are mentally tough would feel good about something regardless of what others think or say. No one can take away your joy or happiness from you. It isn't possible to completely ignore what others think of you. However, you don't have to compare yourself with others. It is better if you take people's opinions with a pinch of salt. People who are mentally strong know that irrespective of what others think of them at any given point of time, one thing is for sure, they are never really as good or bad as others seem to believe. You should stop comparing yourself to others; physically, socially, or even financially. It is a trap that you should be aware of. You will always have people around you who have got more money than you have, have a better social life or are more successful in their respective careers. Instead of focusing on what others have, you should focus on yourself.

10: They Won't Limit the Happiness of Others

A mentally tough person won't be critical of others because he or she knows that everyone has something different to offer. They don't have to bring others down for them to feel good about themselves. By comparing yourself to others, you are only limiting yourself. Jealousy, envy, and resentment can drain you out of your energy and suck the life out of you. Mentally tough people will never waste their energy worrying about what others think of them, and they certainly won't spend their energy sizing others up. Instead of allowing all sorts of negative emotions to manifest, you should concentrate on channelizing your energy towards something that's more positive and something beneficial. Celebrate others' successes and rejoice in their victories, it won't diminish your accomplishments. Learn to radiate positivity.

Chapter 3
Assessing Your Mental Strength

Are you mentally tough? Do you have what it takes to be mentally tough? Do you wish to be mentally tough? If so, why? There are numerous misconceptions about what mental toughness means and why everyone should purpose to master its art. The mental toughness is about having the ability to manage your emotion in the face of adversities and the ability to uphold productive behavior always despite the circumstance surrounding your environment. Just like developing physical strength, building mental strength requires a lot of hard work, time, and energy input. Additionally, just like you track your physical workout progress, it is also advisable to track your mental toughness progress and determine the areas where you have improved and where you need to put in more effort. However, assessing mental toughness may not be as simple and straightforward as assessing physical workout results. This is because you can determine a person's physical strength and workout progress just by looking at them which is not the case when it comes to mental toughness assessment. In some cases, a qualified psychologist may be required to conduct a thorough mental toughness assessment on an individual especially among elite athletes who rely on their mental toughness to win. However, for people who are trying to develop mental toughness for their own benefit, it is possible to assess progress at home by answering a few crucial questions as noted herein. The effects of mental toughness are felt by an individual and are more internal than external. Therefore, an honest self-reflection exercise is paramount to developing and maintaining mental toughness. It helps in understanding your strengths and determining the areas that require more input in order to enhance your mental strength. Start by answering the following questions.

Are You Good at Regulating Your Thoughts?

The personal conversations you have when alone are core ate boosting your overall well-being. Though is common to be harsh to yourself at times, talking to yourself about some of the issues that affect you or the challenges you may be facing like you would to a best friend is actually very healthy and core at developing mental toughness. However, it is important to reason realistically because having negative thoughts always can be damaging and prevent you from being productive or achieving your goals. On the other hand, too many positive thoughts can also be harmful because they do not prepare for negative eventualities. Your brain is only prepared for success and not a failure. So, when a failure occurs, it will be hard for you to accept and move on.

How Do You Keep Your Behavior Productive?

Developing mental toughness is all about understanding when you should change your behavior and when you should change your environment as well. There are times when you can work on improving self-discipline so that you are able to deal with temptation better, and there are times when the only thing you can do is change your environment so that you can bring out the best in you. Other times, productive behavior entails doing the things that you would not wish to do. It may also be about performing behavioral experiments that help you in proving your negative predictions false. Mastering mental toughness helps a person to respond to different hardships effectively as well as overcome obstacles with ease. This way, you are able to make better choices about yourself and when the decisions you make are not very popular. Answer the following questions to determine whether your behavior is productive.

Why Assessing Your Mental Toughness Is Important?

Behavior can be easily observed but it is hard to know what a person is thinking in their head. This can be easily misdiagnosed, and it occurs more often than we think. This enables consumers to create a level of self-conception that is hard, perhaps impossible, to accomplish by other means. It enables them to work with customers. In addition, this measure is a normative measure that allows for an evaluation of where a change happened before and after a program. Similarly, the evaluation of mental toughness and aggregated outcomes with organizations and entire populations is feasible to gather views on a main aspect of culture. That is essential as well. There is a clear link between cultural and behavioral impact. While the study demonstrates that our mental toughness has a genetic factor, our mental toughness is also a reflection of our experiences. We have learned to be mentally hard or emotionally delicate based on the events that have unfolded in our lives. Consider the present "snowflake generation" discussion. It's a warning. There is no implicit necessity for our mental hardness to evolve. Instead, self-awareness and reflection are essential to our lifelong journey. Some mentally delicate people will gladly stay as they are and profit from studying and adopting methods that the mentally difficult ones will embrace.

Chapter 4
How to Develop Mental Toughness

You need to be mentally tough to squash and stomp out any doubts that may creep into your mind. Mental toughness is a valuable asset when it comes to overcoming your distractions and becoming a more self-disciplined person. Mentally tough people are not quitters. They have the drive to do what it takes to succeed; to get back up ten times after falling for nine.

A strong character is also essential for self-discipline. Often, a lack of self-discipline is a sign of weak character. Building a character will enable you to withstand any challenge you may face. If you are successful, self-discipline will never be a struggle in your life.

How to Build Mental Toughness:
Develop a strong support system

Create a positive, strong, and encouraging support system to gain strength from whenever required. During challenging times, we must be able to share our feelings with a close, trustworthy, and motivating group of people. Exchange thoughts and feelings, enlist the support of people you trust, learn about people's journey, gain constructive feedback, enlist support, and discuss possible alternatives. The people you surround yourself with contribute largely to your thoughts and mental framework. Speaking to trusted people can help you gain new insights, views, and solutions about challenging situations, which in turn boosts your mental toughness.

Take cold showers

You might think this is unnecessary suffering, but it is not because taking cold showers has a lot of benefits such as boosting your immune system, increasing levels of testosterone, reducing inflammation, and so on. When the cold water touches your skin for the first time, try not to yell or wince. Just bear it and keep your mind and body as relaxed as possible by taking deep breaths. Try to stay in the cold water for at least 30 seconds and just make it longer as you get used to the coldness.

Minimize social media usage

It takes a lot of mental toughness to unplug from social media. You can either stop using it completely or try to use it only when necessary, like for communication or sharing important stuff. But minimize social media usage as much as you can and just spend your free time doing more productive things. Believe it or not, Steve Jobs didn't let his kids use iPads because he knows how toxic it can get once people start to go online and use social media.

Get out of bed right away

When you hear your alarm go off in the morning, do not press the snooze button, and do not stay in your bed even for just one minute longer. Get out of bed right away and do something to keep your blood flowing. Splash your face with cold water, make coffee or tea, prepare breakfast, and just do anything to wake yourself up. This is all just mind over matter. And you will feel a lot better when you realize how much you were able to finish in a day because you woke up early.

Sleep on the floor

You can also try sleeping on the floor once in a while. You don't necessarily need to give up your comfortable bed for good. Just do this from time to time to help you build your mental toughness. For a really tough challenge, sleep without a blanket. Use a thin sheet if you are not ready for the difficulty level.

Do small exercises

This will not be your regular full-blown workout. That is another thing that you should be doing even if you are not trying to lose weight because it will keep your body strong and healthy. These mini workouts are workouts that you can incorporate in your everyday life.

Move slowly

You might think that this tip is counterintuitive because slowness is often not associated with success and achieving goals. But this does not literally mean working at a slower pace. It just means that you do not make impulsive actions and snap decisions.

Get dirty

Some people are so afraid to get themselves dirty because getting dirty is way out of their comfort zone. Although being clean is something that we should all strive for, there is nothing wrong with getting yourself dirty from time to time.

Read

Reading can make you tougher mentally because it helps you improve your mental focus for a long period of time. Read a book for a couple of hours every day; that can teach you a thing or two about delayed gratification, unlike television and online videos that are passive entertainment and do not really contribute anything to improving your mental toughness. Reading is also an activity that allows you to use your mind active and learning new words and information is always a welcome bonus.

Take a break

When something doesn't help you achieve the desired results, go on a break or change your strategy rather than giving up. Tackle the task with a rejuvenated, fresher, and brand-new perspective after recharging your batteries. True success and glory come to people who do not quit.

Build a mindset

When faced with tough situations, brainstorm. Think of solutions, ideas, alternatives, and possibilities for resolving the situation instead of giving up. There are various ways to work out a solution strategy by keeping your mind more open, flexible, and fearless. You may require a change in the approach or a slight strategy change. Recognize various ways to deal with a challenging or overwhelming situation.

Develop a sense of humor

This is a simple, easy, and enjoyable hack for people to develop mental toughness, yet a good number of people fail to see its virtues. When you experience challenges, humor can help you sail through the situation with ease. Look at the lighter side of things. This helps us overcome stress, disappointment, and anxiety connected to it. You gain a totally different perspective about challenges by viewing them using the lens of humor.

Build a positive or constructive view of your skills and abilities

An individual's sense of self-esteem, self-confidence, and self-image is largely affected by perseverance. Keep reminding yourself about your strengths, achievements, skills, abilities, and wonderful moments. Make a list of tough situations you have tackled, and how you battled them. Draw inspiration from winning and positive moments of the past.

Observe your self-talk

What is your mental talk sound like? If it isn't positive, abundant, and successful, latch on to a different frequency. Our self-talk has the power to determine our chances of success. This self-talk can help us sail through challenging circumstances or dive into failure. Realign your self-talk for success by making it more positive, balanced, and constructive.

How Mental Strength Improves Self-Discipline

The mental strength is one of the most important elements of self-discipline. Knowing how it contributes to self-discipline will help you to see why you need to be constantly working to enhance it.

When you are mentally strong, it allows you to conquer self-doubt so that it is not able to interfere with your level of discipline or cause you to procrastinate out of fear.

Motivation comes from your mental strength. When you are not mentally strong, you will find that it is much easier to lose your motivation before you even have a chance to take full advantage of it.

You can easily tune out comments and advice that are simply not going to help you. This is critical for self-discipline since it is all about efficiency and removing unnecessary baggage.

When you are mentally strong, you are able to face your fears. Fears are one of the biggest reasons that people are not able to develop a strong sense of self-discipline.

You can more easily rebound from failure with mental strength. When you quickly come back from failure, it's more difficult to disrupt your ability to be disciplined.

Lastly, you can easily learn from your mistakes. Remember that learning and accountability are paramount when working to enhance your discipline level.

Chapter 5 What Does Habit Have To Do With My Mental Toughness

Habit 1: Goal Setting and Achieving Goals

People with goals succeed because they know where they are going." Earl Nightingale.

Setting clear goals gives you a sense of direction in life. Without goals, it is easy to drift through life without a main agenda. When you don't have goals, you become open to anything. Suddenly, nothing will seem important to you. If you hit a detour or the going gets tough, you will simply give up, change your mind and go after something else.

Setting goals helps you realize what is important to you and what isn't. Once you become clear about what you want in your life, committing becomes easier. One of the reasons you may jump from one activity to another and fail to push through when times get tough is because, at the back of your mind, you know that whatever you are doing may not be very important after all.

Goal setting changes all that by giving meaning to whatever you set out to do, and by doing that, it helps sharpen your focus and enables you to go after your goals no matter what stands in your way. That is why it helps to improve your mental toughness.

The Right Goals

Before setting goals, it's important to know what the right goals are. For one, you must be able to differentiate between goals and fantasies or daydreams. Daydreaming and/or fantasizing aren't just shallow and unsystematic but can also be counterproductive in terms of succeeding in life. On the other hand, the right kinds of goals can help you register continuous improvements in the quality of your life. These improvements include upward career mobility in both traditional and unconventional careers.

Another thing to consider when figuring out whether the goals you're setting are the right ones are your life purpose and passion. Goals that aren't in line with any or both of these two things aren't worth pursuing. This is because accomplishing them won't provide any real sense of satisfaction and worthwhile accomplishments. Pursuing goals that aren't in line with your life purpose and passions will just render your efforts futile. And given your very limited time, energy, and resources, you should choose the right kinds of goals.

You must also be able to distinguish between goals and desires. Why? Your ability to do so will determine how successful and satisfied you can be in life. How do you determine which of your "goals" are actually goals and which are merely desires?

Goals should be things that you have a great deal of or complete control over. Desires are the things you want to accomplish, acquire or experience that are greatly or completely dependent on the cooperation of other people, events, or circumstances. For example, let's say you want to become an actor in Hollywood. Your goals might consist of you auditioning across the world, attending acting workshops, starting off in television, and then working your way into films. Your desires would be to work with Robert Downing Jr., Kevin Hart, Julia Roberts, or any other great actor in the industry. You'd feel a great degree of satisfaction from working with these people, but it is not necessary to achieve your true goal. Furthermore, reaching top-level status, building a raving fan base, and a pinch of luck would probably be the necessary potion to fulfill that desire. These desires are out of your control compared to the actions set in the goal creation. Why's it important that you properly classify the things you want to accomplish, acquire or experience as goals or desires?

How to Set Clear Goals that You Actually Achieve

So how do you go about setting clear goals that motivate you and enable you to achieve your goals? Just follow the steps covered below.

Step 1: Start by visualizing what you want to achieve

The first step that you need to take is that of forming a mental picture of what you want to achieve in life. You cannot achieve anything unless you first see it in your mind. Any great achievement by someone else started as a mere thought. And that is why you need to start there.

Many times than not, this is always the hardest part. For many people, knowing what they want in life can be a tough question to answer. So, it helps to give yourself as much time as you need so that you can come up with an accurate assessment.

A good starting point would be asking yourself a question like, "What do I want to offer the world, the community or my family." You could also try, "How do I want to grow?"

It doesn't matter if you come up with broad and vague answers at this point. Long-term as well as short-term goals are just as good. You can redefine them.

Step 2: Redefine your goals: Ensure they are specific

Being very specific about your goals makes you push yourself to achieve them as opposed to those that are general and vague.

As an example, let us look at a goal like, "I want to be rich." Wait a minute, exactly how rich do you want to become? This goal is very general and non-specific. The very nature of this goal gives you no motivation to set out and achieve it. Look at a modified version that says, "I want to make one million dollars." This one is more objictified and specific. You are more likely to act on this one than the first. Moreover, you need to know why you want your specified amount. Wanting one million dollars is cool, but for what? It sounds nice to be a millionaire, but it may far exceed the necessary wealth required to live life the way you truly desire. Figure out the specifics of your desires and how much they cost to find the total sum of your true goal. Write these rewards down and keep them in very close visual proximity to your goals.

Take the same approach to every goal that is on your list. Revise the list and come up with an entirely new list that contains goals that are specific.

Step 3: Ensure that the goals are measurable

What does it mean to set measurable goals? This simply means that you should be able to tell when you have achieved your goals. If we go back to our example of setting out to becoming rich, you will see that the goal itself is not measurable. At what point, will you be able to tell that you have attained your goal. It helps to know the destination of your journey.

The more refined version of making a million dollars is measurable. All you have to do to be certain that you have attained this goal is a look at your bank balance. So, go over to your list and try to ask yourself, "At what point will I be certain that this goal has been achieved?" Write the answer below the goal.

It also helps to set small checkpoints, otherwise known as milestones, along the way so that you can check your progress, especially when it comes to long-term goals. Therefore, in the case of the one million dollars, you can have milestones/short-term goals of making 100,000, 250,000, 500,000, 750,000 and then 1,000,000.

Habit 2: Managing Time Well

"Time = life; therefore, waste your time and waste your life, or master your time and master your life." Alan Lakein.

So how does embracing good time management enable you to become mentally tough?

Well, to help you understand how time management works to make you mentally tough; it helps to look at one technique of time management, creating a to-do list. One advantage of a to-do list is that it helps you keep track of all tasks that you need to do on a given day. It also allocates enough time for each activity on the list.

Apart from doing the above, a to-do list also holds you accountable. When you have a to-do list, you have an obligation to complete the tasks on the list by the end of the day. In a way, a to-do list keeps you in check. If you think about it, when you do not have a to-do list, it is easy to give in to small excuses so that you end up not completing tasks. If a distraction pops out of the blue, say, an invitation by a friend to a party, you will easily divert your attention from your goals and procrastinate. When you have a to-do list, you stay committed to the tasks that help you accomplish your goals in the long run. To some extent, a to-do list helps streamline the process of making you disciplined enough to chase your goals no matter what. And that's the essence of mental toughness.

Can you now see why time management is an important habit and how it helps you develop mental toughness?

Chapter 6
Controlling Fear or Failure with Mental Toughness

Fear comes in a lot of flavors. We fear disappointing others. We fear not meeting their expectations. We fear not meeting our own expectations. We fear failure. We fear success. We fear the unfamiliar and unknown.

Regardless of its form, fear sabotages our psychological resilience. It erodes our resolve, releases unhealthy emotions, and causes us to focus on potential negative outcomes. We freeze up, overwhelmed by the possibility of disaster.

Fear distorts reality. It implies that catastrophe and ruination are certain to follow our performance. If we allow fear to gain a foothold in our minds, we end up feeling defeated before we've even taken action. The truth is, the odds of catastrophe resulting from whatever we're doing are so infinitesimal that they're unworthy of consideration.

Fear takes every potentially negative outcome and amplifies its impact. For example, if we're about to give a presentation, our fear may tell us that we'll be ridiculed by our audience and forever branded an incompetent failure. In reality, we're likely to leave a favorable impression on our audience even if a few things fail to go as planned.

Fear is an emotion that opposes the development of mental toughness. Once the latter develops, fear is rendered powerless.

You've likely heard the phrase "that which doesn't kill us makes us stronger." It typically refers to tragedy and misfortune, but it's equally applicable to failure. If we interpret failure as feedback, it toughens us.

Each incident further desensitizes us from the crippling emotions that might otherwise surface.

Throughout this process, we become steadily more courageous when we're faced with uncertainty. The idea of making a wrong decision or committing a mistake, and consequently experiencing a negative outcome, holds less and less fear for us. A negative outcome becomes nothing more than feedback, which presents us with an opportunity to learn and improve.

The more prepared we are to interpret failure as feedback rather than a pronouncement of inadequacy, the more courageous we'll become. Eventually, we'll adopt a fearless mindset. We'll notice practical lessons in every negative outcome, an attitude that'll embolden us and reinforce our resilience when we confront setbacks and misfortune.

Our willingness and readiness to learn from our failures aligns perfectly with this frame of mind. It's an admission that we're imperfect, as well as an acknowledgment that we're capable of learning anything we need in order to persevere and eventually succeed.

This attitude affects every area of our lives. It influences our decisions and actions at school, in the workplace, at home, and with friends and loved ones. It shapes our responses to unexpected obstacles and emotional distress. When we learn the right lessons from failure, we develop greater awareness of ourselves and our capacity to handle pressure and overcome challenges.

5 Lessons to Learn Whenever You "Fail"

So, what are the correct lessons that we should learn from failure? How can we ensure that we're taking maximum advantage of the feedback we're presented with? Following are five takeaways that'll reward you as long as you're willing to perceive failure as a stepping stone to improvement and eventual success.

1. Practice positive self-talk

Part of the BUD/S training program involves staying underwater with breathing gear. This is known as "pool comp." While the trainee is underwater, his instructor will break his breathing equipment. The trainee must remain calm and fix the problem. Positive self-talk is essential to keeping panic at bay and completing this test successfully.

Application: Whenever you feel overwhelmed, whether at your job or at home, remind yourself that your skills, abilities, and knowledge will help you to prevail. Tell yourself to remain calm and relaxed. Tell yourself that your current circumstances are temporary and will dissipate when you give them attention.

2. Continue training after you master something

Navy SEALs must master a wide variety of disciplines. The problem is, most of their time isn't spent in the field where they can put these skills to use. SEALs experience a lot of downtimes. If they neglect to constantly practice their skills, they'll get rusty. So they train over and over, guaranteeing they'll be ready to perform when they're on deployment.

Application: Keep practicing skills that are essential to your long-term success, even if you feel you've mastered them. Try to use them each day to ensure they stay sharp. For example, writing is obviously a major part of being an author. But it's tempting to take significant time off between books. Many authors, myself included, resist this temptation and write every day to keep our writing "muscles" in tiptop shape.

3. Focus on small wins

Like most of us, Navy SEALs set goals for themselves. But their goals do little to help them endure the mental punishment associated with their jobs. To stay mentally strong and achieve their goals, they practice "segmentation." They break down their larger goals into micro goals. For example, rather than focusing on completing a 20-mile run, they focus on reaching the tree they see in their path in the distance. Once they reach the tree, they focus on scaling a hill that's within sight. And so, on until they complete their run.

Application: Break down intimidating projects into small steps. Ideally, these steps can be completed within a single day. For example, suppose you've been tasked with giving a presentation at your workplace. Segment the project. Write down each step, including selecting a topic, writing the content, preparing slides, and brainstorming questions for your audience. You can further segment writing the content into creating your introduction, the body of your presentation, and your conclusion.

4. Visualize your desired outcome

This is something that Navy SEALs and world-class athletes (e.g. Olympians) have in common. They mentally rehearse their activities and visualize their success. This technique is effective because, according to psychologists, the brain doesn't differentiate between actual experiences and imagined experiences. Because of this cognitive quirk, visualization prepares our minds for success and squelches our fears in the process.

Application: If you're worried about something you need to do, visualize doing it successfully. For example, suppose you're concerned about a big presentation you're expected to give at your workplace. Close your eyes and see yourself giving the presentation. Take yourself through each step, each part of your speech, and each slide. Visualize completing your presentation and responding confidently to the audience's questions. See yourself in the ideal state you hope to experience.

5. Anticipate everything that might go wrong

A large part of a Navy SEAL's mental conditioning is to control the innate fear that surfaces in the face of adversity. For most of us, adverse circumstances are unpleasant and frustrating. For SEALs, such circumstances can be deadly.

To combat this fear, SEALs rehearse relentlessly, trying to anticipate every problem that might prevent them from completing their missions.

Before Navy SEAL Team Six descended upon Osama bin Laden's compound in May 2011, they created a life-sized model of his compound. They then spent three weeks training for the operation. During this intense training, they brainstormed and simulated unexpected complications and rehearsed their responses to them.

Application: If you're working on a project and worried that something might go wrong, ponder the difficulties you might experience. Let's again suppose you're planning to give a presentation. The audiovisual equipment you're using to display slides might malfunction. What will you do if that happens? You might forget a piece of your speech. How will you recover? Someone in your audience might ask a question for which you lack an answer. How will you respond to this individual? Try to anticipate every possible complication, and then rehearse your responses. You'll feel more comfortable and confident that you'll be able to handle any problem that surfaces.

Chapter 7
How to Change Your Mental State and Increase Mental Toughness for Personal Success

S uccessful people are always celebrated, success is like a light that cannot be hidden, whenever there is a success recorded somewhere, either in a competition, games, business, education, technological advancement, science, medicine, arts, etc. there is always some form of awareness created either in any of the sector involved.

Like I have enumerated, successful people have mental toughness. To achieve success, you need to holistically put into practice what needs to be done and you will definitely achieve it. It is a combination of so many factors that leads to success. Majority of it depends on you. You can decide to achieve success and you can decide to choose where you want to belong.

To achieve success, you need to begin immediately, and how do you get started? You will need to begin by doing the following:

Leave Your Comfort Zone

Success is not usually achieved by continuing in your normal state or doing what you have been doing that is not making you to advance, no! Success cannot be achieved if you are not ready to do what successful people do to become successful. Hence, you need to adjust and adapt to a lot of changes. You need to work harder and begin to train like it was your last chance to become successful. Successful people usually go the extra mile, it means you have to cut what you eat; it means you have to reduce the amount of times you spend at the club or relaxing.

Maximize a better usage of your time by drawing up a program that will guide you in whatever you are doing, make sure you allocate every time you have in a day, week, months and year to some form of activity that will make you to become successful.

Take stock, fall back and assess your activities and analyze areas that need improvements and where you need to step up.

Take action immediately, avoid procrastination and get things done promptly without being urged to do so. Make sure a day doesn't go without you achieving something that will bring you success. Be persistent about it.

When you have achieved success, make sure you manage it very well, because success can be achieved and can also be lost if not properly managed.

The champion is in you; bring it out by being mentally tough!

Confidence

Confidence is when you have "self-belief." You have the ability to make yourself mentally tough by having that confidence and you have the ability to make yourself irrelevant by not having confidence in yourself, so the ball is in your court.

Before you can say that you are confident, you have to be truthful about it. You can only be informed by your conscience, when you think and discern about being confident. Hence being confident is more of a personal thing, if others have confidence in you, it means you have developed yourself and you have proven to them that you are confident and they also know that you are confident. But when you are being personal with confidence, it means you have the conviction that you are confident about yourself. Therefore, for you to be confident you must possess the following characteristics;

High Self Esteem

It doesn't matter what it takes, there is one thing that matters most when it comes to confidence and that is "low self-esteem." Low self-esteem is dangerous because it kills the spirit of a person who has it. It is also very important to know also that when you have low self-esteem, people easily notice it and that can be used against you. Low self-esteem tends to expose the weakness of a person who has it. For instance, if you are competing for a prize and your opponents realize that you have low self-esteem, you are in for serious trouble because, a clever opponent will start by using mind games against you, your opponents will try as much as they can to talk you down and make you crumble in the competition. Make sure you always maintain a high level of self-esteem. Don't quit, don't think or form the opinion that you are not the best when it comes to competing with others, start realizing that you can make it and beat your chest and say to yourself "I'm confident, I'm going to succeed!"

Self-Belief in Fostering Confidence

There is nothing as solid as believing in yourself, and there is no way you can talk about self-confidence without you believing in yourself. To be mentally tough you have to believe totally in yourself, you have to believe in your own abilities. If you do not believe in yourself, it means if someone else believes in you, you will let them down. You don't let people down by not believing in yourself, you give people inspiration and they will see you as a role model if you believe in yourself and become successful.

To believe in yourself, you need self-conviction, talk to yourself every day, that you are good, talk to yourself every day that you are the best, you owe no one apology for claiming to be the best, whenever you want to perform a task, say to yourself "I am the best" and you will drive your mindset towards that direction. As much as self-confidence is important, many people lack it and that's why we have so many people who are average, even with the potential of advancing, they just don't want to move to the next level. It's all because of a lack of confidence because they don't actually believe that they have a potential that can improve their lives.

Points to note:

- Avoid low self-esteem

- Build up your confidence level

- Think greatness

- Don't think small

- Meditate on your life and think about advancement

- Contemplate on yourself and see through your inner self

- See yourself as someone that is about to explode

- Say to yourself, the world is waiting for my arrival every day

Chapter 8
Using Mental Toughness or Self-Confidence, Self-Discipline, Willpower and Self-Esteem

Willpower is the distinguishing ability that enables you to exercise power over or to influence you will positively. Willpower allows you to resist harmful impulses and stick to an informed decision.

Willpower and self-discipline are often used interchangeably, but they are not the same. Although both qualities are essential because they work together towards helping you to accomplish your goals, they have distinct differences. Willpower is the exertion when you are determined to accomplish a task. It is the level of control that individuals use to restrain their impulses.

Willpower can be short-lived and only used when the moment calls for it. Sometimes, it could be as simple as following a set of temporary rules to achieve a short-term result, like dieting or quitting smoking. In short, it is the ability to push and control yourself and your actions when needed.

Self-discipline, on the other hand, is about your mindset. It is focused on getting in touch with yourself, what you want, what you believe in and shaping your life around that belief. Self-discipline is a trait that is built for life. There is no short-term solution or rules to be followed. It is a quality that is built for a lifetime. Willpower can help you do just that.

Willpower is a powerful tool that can help you dominate your life and enhance self-discipline. However, caution is advised. You need to know that your willpower differs depending on the time of day and circumstances. When you are tired and stressed out, your willpower is usually at its lowest.

When you fortify your willpower, you will be able to stand strong and accomplish your objectives even when circumstances are not that favorable. The good news is that despite what many people think, willpower can be strengthened without exerting too much effort.

Let us look at how you can do this:

Build Your Pressure Capacity

It starts with the little things like resisting that voice that tells you to resist doing something until the next day. As the popular saying goes, "tomorrow never comes." There are always other tomorrows, and thus, if you keep postponing what you need to do, you may end up never doing it. Stop postponing. Stop procrastinating. Little by little, you will be able to fortify your willpower. Additionally, because you've enhanced your capacity for pressure, you will be able to exercise your willpower even when you need to make difficult decisions.

Calm Negative Emotions

When you fortify your willpower, you take charge of your emotions, actions, and reactions. Notice that although the emotions are still there, what changes are how you react despite having them. You need to be on the lookout for things such as anger, boredom, and tiredness among others. This is because when you experience powerful emotions, your judgment is usually clouded. This is why you need to still and calm such emotions.

Manage Inner Conflict

Experiencing inner conflict is common since we are constantly making decisions, or we have to take action. One voice pulls you this way and the other that way. You may want to do something, but somehow, you convince yourself that doing it is not worth the effort.

Meditate

Meditation is good for the brain. When you meditate, the gray matter in your brain builds up. The gray matter is responsible for regulating emotions. Also, it is where decision making takes place. This is why meditation is great for your willpower. It enables you to make decisions without the interference of emotions. The act of meditating itself requires discipline. Meditation fosters willpower and leads to personal improvement.

Exercise

Everybody knows that exercise is beneficial. However, few people religiously follow an exercise regime. The main reason for this is that people view exercise as a tedious job. They find excuses not to start it, and thus, they never reach the point where exercising becomes routine. However, it is vital that you embrace exercise. Exercise is linked to enhanced mental performance and improved willpower.

Get Enough Sleep

The human body needs sleep in order to rejuvenate itself. This is why sleep deprivation is dangerous. It wreaks havoc on the prefrontal cortex. This area helps control cravings and your response to stress. When you have adequate rest, you give your brain the energy it needs to do its work well.

Focus on "Later"

Willpower calls for taking charge of your actions and emotions. Unfortunately, sometimes, this is not easy, especially if you have a bad habit you want to get rid of. Intense cravings are hard to ignore especially since you know you won't even have that thing you were used to.

Be Accountable

Accountability is a word that means a lot. It causes people to pause and think about the consequences of what they are about to do. When you are accountable to others, you strive to behave in a manner that will not cause them distress or displeasure. You would also not want to let such people down.

Have Self-Belief

When you are talking about self-belief, always remember that the keyword is self. Self-belief is that strong conviction you have that gives you confidence that you can accomplish what you set your mind to. In life, you will find it difficult to unleash your potential if you don't believe in yourself. A self-belief is an interesting tool. It can be sharpened or dampened by others but ultimately, you need to make up your mind about it.

Mark Your Starting Point

The first thing you need to acknowledge is where you are when it comes to believing in yourself. This is the point where you need to honestly search your deepest thoughts and feelings. Note down your feelings on different aspects of your life. Are you living your ideal life? If not, what is holding you back from achieving what you want? Think of the limiting beliefs you possess and trace where they came from. Did they come from someone else or were they conceived due to past experiences? Once you know how you view yourself, you will be in an excellent position to adjust your view and improve yourself.

Quiet the Negative Inner Voice

Your inner thoughts, whether positive or negative, are always present with you. They can be loud, or they can be quiet depending on how much attention you give them. You need to know that having negative thoughts is not a crime.

Turn Weaknesses to Strengths

One of the things that can limit your belief in yourself is your perceived weakness. Many people don't want others to be aware of their weaknesses. In fact, many would rather suffer silently than let others know of their struggles. However, self-belief is not a false belief in your abilities. It is not about presenting a perfect front. You need to acknowledge where you fall short and figure out how you can turn those weaknesses into strengths. Self-belief gives you the freedom to pursue your goals even in the face of opposition and limitations.

Develop Useful Traits

A weakness that you can correct is one that requires knowledge or skills. As long as you are capable of it, you can learn a new skill. You don't have to be clueless when it comes to a skill that may be useful to you. You need to learn all you can about something you are dealing with. This will boost your confidence and belief that you can indeed tackle any situation that arises in the course of you doing your job.

Re-imagine Yourself

Focus on the new you that you've created and seen yourself transforming into that person. This way, you will be able to remove yourself from a position of helplessness to that of power and self-belief. When you re-imagine yourself, you will have the needed motivation to work towards achieving your goals. Ensure that you visualize what being a new you will achieve and how it will make you feel. The more desirous the benefits, the more you will work to achieve your goal.

We all have great willpower; you just need to show yourself that. Well, with these exercises you can easily begin the journey to making that kind of proof available to yourself. With greater willpower comes the ability to improve your overall self-discipline.

Chapter 9
Achieve Success Using Mental Toughness

Though most people do not realize it, a person's perception of the world greatly depends on their inner state of mind. For instance, we all know how alienating and disturbing things become when we are in a bad or frustrated mood. On the other hand, there is another state where everything we wish for seems to flow just right and everything you do feels effortless. These two states define your mental state. Therefore, it would be great to understand how to have full control over your mental state in order to control your moods, feelings, and actions that eventually lead to success. Having the power to change your mental state proactively means that you can control how you feel and how you perceive things around you. You get to be in control of how you function and most importantly how to feel about different circumstances. Every emotion is triggered by something and if you have the power to choose your reactions carefully, your mental and emotional state would not be determined by what happens in your life whether good or bad.

People grow up with a certain expectation of how their adult life will be and no one envisions a life full of challenges and failure. But unfortunately, life rarely turns out as envisioned or as planned. In most cases, the milestones that people long to achieve are derived from other people's perceptions of what a good and satisfying life should be. In reality, you only have one life and therefore, you should live it as you imagine by doing the things that make you happy and give you satisfaction as opposed to living by other people's rules. To achieve this, start by forgetting all the opportunities you missed and all the failures you might have encountered in the past. Regret does not change your life the bad choices you made before; instead, it wastes your valuable energy and time that you would have used to build yourself. Give yourself a break from everything and refuse to heed to outside expectations of what life should be. Focus on working out what truly makes you happy and propels you to achieve your life goals. If you get to this point, you will have mastered how to control your mental state. The following step would be learning how to improve mental skills for success as explained below.

Mini Habits for Great Goals Every Day

Take Control

You have to know how to be in control of yourself if you are to be mentally hard. The mental toughness and overall achievement rely mainly on your ability to control the mind. The mental skills and state control are some of the most significant things that a person should learn. This is because many other things flow quite smoothly when you can control your thoughts. Life itself ensures that it is not simple to be in control of your thoughts. This is because of the many uncertainties that make up life. Yet something you can regulate will always be there. And you can find most of the factors. For instance, there could be predictions of an economic downturn. Many individuals automatically become afraid, stressed, and possibly take actions such as the sale of some of their assets. But did you know there's a different alternative? Other alternatives are always available. You can simply decrease your expenditure and retain your property until things get better. You can contact a family and all of you agree on cost reduction policies. Thus, while many are stressed and glued to their TV screens to updates on when the economy is eventually crashing, you plan for those difficult moments ahead. This plan will keep you in control because you thought about the scenario before it actualized.

Quit Thinking About Things You Cannot Change

When you are in control of your thoughts and mental state, you will understand that your van only changes matters that affect you. Other things that affect your life may be changed but it is never a guarantee.

This is because most situations occur as problems that require solutions in the form of changing how the situation occurred. However, there are a few situations that cannot be changed no matter how hard you try. When you overthink such situations, they become a source of stress and demotivation and end up hindering your success. To avoid this, it is important that you change your perception towards particular situations that you cannot change. To save your precious time and energy, it is advisable to always change your view about situations you cannot change. Evaluate them from a different perspective and you will definitely get an idea of how to tackle them effectively.

View Failure as a Learning Opportunity

Failure is inevitable if you are going to accomplish anything tangible in life. You must fail before you succeed. As soon as you know this reality, life will be better for you. It is therefore very important with this understanding that you learn how to look at mistakes in a different and positive perspective. It is essential that you realize that if you fail, it is not a sign that you are headed for total failure. It's a sign that you're trying to achieve an objective instead. View failure as an opportunity to learn, become mentally tough and emotionally resilient. Avoid the view of many that failure is bad and should not occur. This is a lie based on how people misunderstand failure. Such lines of thought tend to somehow pursue perfectionism. Even in tiny quantities and practically undetectable the spirit of perfectionism will always get you frustrated. This is because you will never be in a position to view failure as a life lesson. But if you fail to realize that it isn't the end, it's easy for you to rebound and play on the field again. Failure is thus a friendly stepping stone, not an enemy. Just view it at the right angle.

Chapter 10
Improving Your Emotional Intelligence
Using Mental Toughness

Train your brain is necessary to stay calm under pressure. It helps you to increase your mental toughness. In case of any disaster, it helps you to look beyond what happened. It gives you prudence to observe the elements of disaster with a new lens, examine your thoughts, get the shortcomings, recompose the actionable parts in a new frame and get the work done seamlessly. However, life does not always follow an easy-going road, and everyone has to face failure. So, do not worry about your failure or do not feel sad due to failure. Your mental strength is actually your true friend who always stays with you like your shadow. It stays with you in success and as well as failure. So, it is always with and all you need to strengthen it more.

Practice Meditation

It has been proved time and again that meditation can improve the level of mental toughness you have. Even soldiers who are about to go on a mission or are being trained for combat are advised to practice meditation and for good reason. They do not become too emotional in their career or in other words, their mental toughness is improved.

In the world of mental toughness, there are usually three types of people. The first one is the marshmallow. As the name suggests, these people are very soft, both inside out and so any little amount of pressure on them can cause havoc. The second group of people is the jellybeans. They have a soft inner core but a hard shell. They are obviously tougher than marshmallows but at times, even they can buckle up after a prolonged period of stress. The last group of people is the rocks, who can literally handle everything that is put in front of them. They are not only hard from the outside but also from the inside.

When a person learns to adopt a lifestyle that includes a regular time set aside for meditation, then he/she eventually starts developing a growth mindset. In this mindset, people do not see their failures or obstacles as negative things but rather learn from their mistakes and events of life. You will learn to harness the power of meditation and then use that energy to stay positive throughout your day. Your idea of mental toughness will be elevated to a whole new level with this new routine of meditation.

At an average, a person has over 70,000 thoughts in a day. What meditation does is that it helps you seek that quiet place inside your head that is present but is hidden under the pressure of all those thoughts weighing you down. But people often confuse meditation with mindfulness. Mindfulness is a different thing and you can say that it is a type of meditation. But with the help of meditation, you will be able to analyze so many thoughts that got buried in your subconscious and you will be able to do so without being judgmental at all.

The first way in which meditation promotes mental toughness is that it helps you enter a state of calmness. When you are calm, you have the time and concentration required to judge which thoughts are worthy of your attention and thus you can invest your time in them. You will also learn a rational way to respond to anxiety in your daily life. Moreover, with meditation, you can distinguish between noise and static. Your recalling power will increase, and you will also learn how you can control your mind so that you do not get affected by any distractions. In short, meditation can improve your capacity to handle stress and thus enhance your level of mental toughness.

Don't Beat Yourself Up For Things You Cannot Control

There will always be things in your life that are beyond your control and this is the ultimate truth. If you cannot make peace with this fact, then you will have a tough time on this planet. When people cannot get over the fact that they can't control everything, they end up becoming control freaks.

Thus, if you want to train your brain to have mental toughness, then you need to stop picking fights on every small matter that comes your way. Frankly, you need to understand that everything is not worth it to waste your energy fighting over it. There will always be some troubling times that you have to face in your life. But don't fret or don't give in to depression just because you cannot control the situation. The simple fact is that the situation cannot be controlled. And when something goes wrong, don't beat yourself up for something that didn't happen because of you.

Yes, you can influence people, but you can never or rather you should never force your will upon others. For example, you can do everything you can to make the party good, but you cannot do anything to make the people have fun. It is their own decision and choice. Sometimes, the feeling of being a control freak intensifies even more when you have the tendency to jump to catastrophic outcomes which might not even happen. So, judge your thoughts and think whether you are indulging in such a practice or not. If you are, then think about what is the worst that can practically happen. Usually, it won't be as bad as you are thinking it to be.

You also need to have a stress management plan. As already mentioned, you can practice meditation, or you can also do something you love. Practice anything that is stress-relieving to you. You can even go out and have a good time with your friends if that is what you want. Create your own positive affirmations that you can tell yourself in a situation of stress. For example, if you are thinking 'Important members of the board are going to be present at the meeting' then you need to tell yourself 'I can handle it'.

Give a Name to Your Emotions

Dealing with your emotions is important in all aspects of your life and not only when it comes to mental toughness. When you name your emotions, the process is called labeling and it is also the first step for everyone towards effectively dealing with their emotions. It might sound easy to you now, but it is way tougher in reality. You have to pinpoint what it is that you are feeling and sometimes you might label your emotions as something that it is not.

There are so many reasons as to why labeling your emotions is a difficult task. For starters, right from your childhood, you have been taught that it is necessary to suppress your strong emotions. Moreover, sometimes there are unspoken organizational and societal rules that stop you from expressing your actual feelings. Or sometimes a child is never actually taught in what way they should speak up and express what they are feeling. All of these things cumulatively act as a barrier to correct labeling of emotions.

The most common emotions that are visible in a workplace setting are stress and anger or at least that is what they are labeled as. But in most cases, these two labels mask way deeper emotions than they actually seem to be. The tendency to avert from showing or talking about one's emotions is a growing concern in today's world especially when mental health issues are increasing each day. When you avoid speaking about your emotions, you automatically create a distance between you and your emotions. This affects your ability to identify how you are feeling at a particular moment.

As already mentioned above, sometimes adults do end up labeling their emotions but they do it in the wrong way. For example, if someone is feeling sad, then instead of saying 'I'm feeling low' they might say 'My eyes got watery, nothing more'. Do you see the difference between the two ways of expression? You must spend some time every day with yourself and you must acknowledge the fact that you are feeling what you are feeling. You should also think about how these emotions affect or are going to affect your decision-making abilities. Whether it is about something that happened in your workplace or your personal life, if you have some emotion on your mind, it is more likely to get spilled all over your life and create havoc.

When it comes to your emotions, you need to concentrate on developing a more nuanced vocabulary. I am not saying this just because I want you to be precise. No, that is not what I mean. What I mean is that when you use the right vocabulary, you will also gain the power of describing your emotions correctly. Correct diagnosis of your emotions is essential if you want to respond correctly to them. Also, don't stick to basic descriptions like angry or sad as sometimes your emotions are way more intense than that. There is a variety of flavors and levels of every emotion. Being angry might also mean that you are grumpy or annoyed. You need to label your emotions the way they are.

Maintain a Balance in Your Emotions with the Help of Logic

Whether it is a family dilemma or a financial crisis where you need to make important decisions, being mentally strong is very important. But for that, you need to implement logic to balance your emotions. So, if you see that your emotions are running high, take a stand immediately and increase your level of rational thinking. If you are confused as to how you can achieve this in your life then here is a tip that works for most people—whenever you are making a choice, consider the pros and cons and write them down somewhere. When you finish your list of pros and cons and read it again, you will realize many things and may even be able to separate your emotions from your decisions.

Decisions are something you cannot spend your day without. Even if you are not doing anything and simply chilling at home, there will be several decisions cropping up in your mind, for example, 'what should I eat for lunch?' Do you see it? Your daily life is filled with so many such small and big decisions that sometimes we even tend to look past them. If you are planning to quantify your decisions in a day, then don't try to walk on that path because it is nearly impossible. Your decisions are not always huge. They can even be hidden in mundane things like whether you want to get a coffee or make yourself some tea.

It is often said that 80% of the choices made by humans are influenced by their emotions. So, do you favor logic or emotion when you are making some decisions in your life? Unsavory situations in life can arise at any moment and they are all due to momentary lapses in your judgment. Yes, you might feel constant friction in your mind when you are trying to create a balance between emotions and logic and your emotional self might even try to break free and dominate, but you have to deal with it all if you want to achieve mental toughness.

Chapter 11
Leadership Skills and Mental Toughness

After perusing you may have a strong understanding of basic crest execution and administration principles—and how mental execution can affect results and victory. You may pick up information on how to create your mental sturdiness preparing more profitable by utilizing Top Execution Progression™.

Peak performance and leadership are not pure sciences. Success and the attainment of a specific goal involve self-awareness, customization, action, and flexibility. Provides you with a basic education on the science and art of peak performance, superior leadership, and success.

The Art of Leadership

Although leadership can be studied scientifically—leadership is not a pure science. The quality of leadership is more of an art that must be studied, nurtured, and diligently practiced in order to develop and maximize it.

Leadership is often misunderstood, misapplied, and ill-defined.

True leadership is not defined or determined by any of the following:

- Seniority in an organizational hierarchy

- Title or position

- Personality

- Management style

When referring to leadership—far too many people talk about only the senior ranking members of an organization. Leadership doesn't just automatically happen when you hit a certain pay grade or job title. The truth is that leadership can be found at all levels of any organization. It does, however, make sense that we would expect to see more leadership at the most senior levels of an organization, but it is not guaranteed.

The art of leadership can be demonstrated in sports, work, business, and your personal life. The quality of leadership can be found in people from all types of backgrounds and education.

Don't be fooled into believing that only certain personalities can be effective leaders. Contrary to popular (but false) beliefs—you do not have to be a super high-energy extrovert or naturally charismatic to become a highly effective leader.

Lastly, leadership is not synonymous with management. Being a manager of many people or things does not make you a great leader. Management is a critical and important skill for any organization but being a good manager does not automatically make you a good leader.

So, what is leadership?

The art of leadership is defined as follows: the practice of successfully compelling a group of people to perform at their individual peak while maximizing their collective efforts to achieve a desired result.

Of course, leadership requires a leader, a follower, and a goal. But, the true art of effective leadership is much more about "influencing" people than it is about exerting authority or power.

One thing that all great leaders have is mental toughness! Great leaders must lead by example, which means that they must become highly skilled mental warriors who can use their mind power to maximize their personal peak performance under any circumstances, which in turn allows them to effectively influence and lead others.

The Art of Success

Success is the accomplishment of an aim or purpose. Success is associated with winning, happiness, and a favorable outcome. To succeed—a person (or team) must achieve something desired, planned, or attempted.

In practical application, the precise definition of success is ultimately a personal definition and can vary greatly from one person to another based on their core values.

For some people—advancing to the playoffs for their designated sport, or losing the first five pounds on a weight loss program or getting an entry-level job in their chosen field—all constitute success and significant achievement.

For others—success in these same areas might require a higher level of achievement, such as winning the championship trophy in the playoffs; losing twenty-five pounds and reaching target weight; or getting promoted to Director, VP, or CEO in their industry.

Most people have been conditioned to use the "pyramid theory" when assessing their personal level of success. The pyramid theory is one way to measure your success, and it compares your achievements to others striving for the same general goal. In theory, the higher you are able to go on the pyramid of achievement—the less direct competition you have—and consequently, the more successful you are (when compared to everyone on the entire pyramid).

For example—obtaining advanced knowledge through higher education, developing superior skills, or fully leveraging natural talents are all proven ways to elevate and differentiate yourself on the pyramid of peak performance and success. To win a national championship or world championship in sports places you at the top of the pyramid and clearly demonstrates success through peak performance.

Unfortunately, most people don't have the mental training or skills to reach their full innate potential. Consequently, far too many people end up settling on a lower level of the pyramid.

You are not going to settle! You will learn how to excel at the science of peak performance and the arts of leadership and success.

Art is the expression or application of human creative skill and imagination. Success is an art—and it comprises your personal values, goals, circumstances, knowledge, perceptions, and actions. The art of success is concerned with how we as human beings can uniquely (and effectively) define, imagine, and achieve highly favorable results based on our desires.

From the perspective of beginning mental toughness students—the repetitious nature of mental training and skills development is sometimes perceived as tedious. However, for the experienced mental warrior and champion—the consistent action of training and performing is a captivating journey that provides intrinsic joy, motivation, and opportunity for creativity. Successful extrinsic results, accomplishments, and rewards are merely a reaction to the diligent application of art and science to training and peak performance.

Elevating to the highest levels in any sport or career (achieving peak performance), requires that you progress from a solid scientific foundation to the apex of artistry—from learning principles and skill development—to experiencing personal transformation and skill mastery.

Preparation, training, and performance repetition is the best way to influence outcomes in a positive manner. However, and contrary to popular belief—hard work does not guarantee success. To achieve peak performance and master the art of success in your sport or industry—it is imperative that you also work smart by leveraging the best training tools and strategies.

Learning how to exploit relevant scientific and technological advances is an art unto itself and should be an area of focus for the aspiring peak performer and future champion. Keep your focus on consistent progress and improvements—and you will set yourself up for breakthrough results and big wins.

Study champions in any field, and you will find that they are always working to enhance their skills and improve their game. They genuinely approach self-improvement as an art!

The art of success is simply a cumulative connection of smart choices and effective actions over time.

Peak Performance IQ

Peak performance is partly physical (external actions; external reactions; external results), partly emotional (internal reactions; internal results), and partly mental (internal thoughts; self-talk; visualization).

Physical performance involves your body movements and the outside world.

Emotional performance involves your feelings and physical reactions inside your body.

Mental performance involves your brain and the two-way communications inside your head.

Your mental performance has a significant role and impact on your emotional and physical performance. You cannot experience consistent emotional and physical control without consistent mind control. Consequently, you must become an internal leader and champion before you can become an external leader and champion.

Mental warriors have strong mental muscles. They use specific training to develop superior mental fitness and mental skills that facilitate superior emotional control and physical performance.

Mental fitness is the ability to remain strong, directed, and positive through your thoughts, feelings, and actions in the face of physical, mental, and emotional stressors. The mental fitness has a direct effect on your performance, results, and success.

Lack of mental fitness will always lead to inferior mental performance, sporadic emotional control, subpar physical performance, mediocre results, and limited success. Conversely, dominant mind power is the foundation for superior mental performance, consistent emotional control, peak physical performance, excellent results, and continuous success.

Talent and luck can definitely play a role in winning. However—you can't change your genetics—and the best way to invite more luck into your life is to be thoroughly prepared for success. This "pre-luck preparation" starts with developing mental fitness (mental toughness)—the undisputed core trait of all consistent winners and champions in every area of life.

The ability to control your mind despite conflicting subconscious thoughts, conscious thoughts, raw emotions, physical sensations and cues, social cues, and environmental cues—is one of our most precious and powerful gifts as human beings.

You do have total control over your thoughts and actions. Your ultimate power is always in the present moment. My goal is to help you utilize this awesome truth and power to make dramatic improvements in your performance, results, and happiness!

If you want to win more consistently in sports, business, and life—you must increase your peak performance IQ (knowledge and understanding). I created the Peak Performance Progression™ concept to increase your peak performance IQ and help make your mental toughness training more productive. All mental warriors and champions have mastered the application of this continuous improvement tool for peak performance management.

The Peak Performance Progression is made up of five key elements and their connection to each other. Following, are the five components of Peak Performance Progression:

1. Mental Toughness

2. Mental Performance

3. Emotional Performance

4. Physical Performance

5. Results

The components of the Peak Performance Progression are positioned to flow in a specific order based on scientific research and outcomes from studying high performers in a variety of fields.

The practical science of peak performance requires optimal engagement and productivity in every component of the Peak Performance Progression.

Mental Toughness Tip

The mental sturdiness will donate you the uncommon capacity to do the things that most individuals cannot or will not do. With mental durability, you'll significantly increment your chances of joining the beat 5% in your field since you may be able to reliably make way better choices and take way better activities.

Too often, I encounter beginning students and clients who falsely believe that mental toughness is predominantly an inborn or predetermined trait. As with any sport, profession, or personal activity—to deliver consistently superior results, you must focus on developing and maintaining superior skills.

Superior skills = superior results!

The same holds true for your mental skills. In order to exhibit superior mental toughness—in the form of willpower, focus, mental stamina, and self-discipline—you must engage in consistent and effective mental training to unlock, transform, and maximize your mental skills.

Victory through top execution does not happen by wishing or trusting! The extraordinary news is that your mental skills—and subsequently your mental toughness—will move forward with legitimate preparing and hands-on encounter.

Remember, the purpose of this is to "separate you from the pack" and transform you into a mental warrior and superior leader by showing you how to maximize the mental attributes and skills that will help you win more often and achieve your goals more quickly.

Chapter 12
Be Spiritually Grounded Using
Mental Toughness

Giving Up Control

Stress management is a very complex phenomenon. Something must be controlled to govern it—for example, testing your shower for the amount of hot water. You activate the water and adjust the hot and cold water mixture to regulate the temperature. If it's wrong, you walk into the shower and start lathering. Sadly, at your discretion, you do not have "warm" or "cold" pressure faucets. You cannot merely turn positive thoughts and emotions while at the same time, turning off disturbing and painful feelings.

Managing means understanding that all the factors involved in any situation cannot be controlled and governed. You know that when you handle something, you cannot manage or operate around all of the variables involved. You live together with a lack of control and continue to advance towards your target.

Let's use the leadership of a girls' softball league team as an example. It involves drawing, teams, family, grounds, facilities, weather, arbitraries, schedules, travel time, and opposing parties. How many variables are you able to control? You might be able to control some machinery, time, and schedule with a little luck. The other factors are beyond your power. You can see that the overwhelming majority of your work factors are beyond your ability. So, what are you doing? Throw your hands on, and ask yourself, "Can't I get rid of that lack of control?" or, "I know I can't control most of the variables involved, but I'm willing to accept it and take values-congruous action and manage the team." If you think about how to influence it, the mind takes data from the past, brings it into the present, and leaps forward into the future. The brain is beneficial to plan things you can monitor, like your actions and specific aspects of your physical environment, for "past, present and future."

Studies show that it is getting worse to try to control, stop, or remove disturbing thoughts, own script, visual images, and unpleasant emotions. By concentrating your full attention and trying to control disturbing thoughts or uncomfortable feelings, it intensifies your strength of mind.

You can even demonstrate this by thinking of a genuinely fun picture, not stressful like a bright red, white, and a blue beach ball. Think of how you feel when the ball is thrown up and caught as it drifts quickly back to you. Close your eyes and think about that luminous beach ball you throw up and down thoroughly. Think of it for a few seconds. Stop thinking about it now. I want you to work hard to stop worrying about the beach ball, which is bright red, white, and blue. Come on, try to stop thinking about the beach ball very, really hard. Continue to read this and stop thinking about the beach ball. What happens when you try to control the beach ball? Are they gone or intensified? In most situations, it did not make them go away when trying to control your thoughts.

Body Awareness

When talking of meditation, a lot of beginners to the practice start fantasizing about having an out of body experience. Reality is far more anticlimactic. Meditation is a deeply "in the body" experience and, if anything, you get far closer to it. If you want an out of body experience, you only need to open your eyes and look at how you usually live.

We constantly travel between the past and the future, loaded with worry and pain. We fret about our future and worry about our past. We regret decisions made and fantasize about correcting them. We envision futures where all our problems vanish, and we're in bliss. All the while, the present lies there ignored and unattended. What is this if not an out of body experience?

Being present is being deeply connected to your body at the moment and truly experiencing everything that is going on with it. It is to explore it and see where knots exist and where certain aches and pains exist. Where do pleasant sensations exist and so on? The thing is that not all of the stuff your mind communicates to you, come to you as words or emotions.

They manifest as physical sensations, and once you bring awareness to them, you'll unearth what your mind is telling you.

For now, you can take a moment to travel inwards and spend time within your body to see how certain body parts feel. Something must be in pain or sore somewhere. Don't judge this, but marvel at how easy it is to disconnect from your body and pay no heed to it.

Dealing with Pain

Pain is quite literally a painful topic to deal with, and we have powerful inbuilt mechanisms to deal with it. There are two types of pain that you need to be aware of. The first is acute pain, which cannot be cured through mindfulness. This is the pain that results from a physical injury or a problem that has occurred in your life. The pain of this kind needs a medical solution and not a spiritual one.

The second kind of pain is chronic pain. The origin of chronic pain may be physical, but there is a huge emotional and cognitive component to it which mindfulness can address. While the elimination of pain is a stretch, reducing the burden you carry as a result of it is certainly possible. Research shows that meditation and other mindfulness practices can help address chronic pain (Penman, 2019).

While meditation by itself is very effective, applying an entire framework of mindfulness to the issue is a better approach. So, how do you do this? Well, the first step is to begin by investigating the pain.

Recycled Thoughts

We're notorious for recycling ideas, so it flaws the current moment.

We aren't necessarily present but swept up within our heads.

Orgyen Chowang supports, "the very first move is to comprehend your mind is naturally immaculate, and your emotional events are only passing through. You have to profoundly accomplish that.

Remember back into an occasion when you had participated in a leisure activity such as for example a game, a pastime, or spending some time together with friends. Remember how time passed, and you are consumed in the present moment, perhaps not contemplating the near future.

Being at the stream way to function as from the zone. It involves being chilled in your activity, which means that your thinking exists as opposed to stuck in the future or past.

To keep away from overanalyzing notions, you have to first recognize it's an all pure process that you must work together with.

To simply accept we cannot stop mental poison, which means detaching ourselves out of being spent included. We aren't getting active from the emotional drama and allow thoughts to flow throughout your brain, unopposed.

I love Orgyen Chowang's information to apply meditation together with your eyes open. He summarizes three powerful methods to deliver our ideas back into the current moment employing the pristine mind meditation:

Inch. Do not adhere to days gone by.

Chapter 13
Applying Mental Toughness in Different Fields

Steering clear from the various challenges in life is an impossible feat for anyone. Rather than hiding or running away from them, you should mentally prepare yourself to handle them properly or to minimize their impact on you.

Below are the common challenges that you may experience in different aspects of your life. Learn how you can exercise your mental strength while dealing and overcoming tests of patience, courage, determination, and self-control.

A. Challenges to Your Financial Stability

Mentally strong individuals are on top of their finances because of two things—they are guided by their financial goals, and they recognize their limits.

Problems in this area arise either due to the person's own lack of control or due to external events that are normally outside one's control. Whatever the case may be, those who are mentally strong prepare themselves for financial challenges by developing and practicing good spending, investing, and cost-saving habits.

Here are the top 5 ways on how you can also mentally prepare yourself to maintain your financial stability even during trying times:

1. Align Your Financial Decisions with Your Personal Values

You cannot mentally prepare for financial challenges when your spending habits go against what you deem as important in your life.

Those who have high mental strength know that their purchases and investments are reflective of their personal beliefs. As such, they feel motivated to work hard to earn money that could be spent on the things and for the people that matter to them.

In comparison, those who just spend their money without thinking about their core values tend to overspend on things that they would regret later on. Furthermore, due to the irrational spending, they have lesser resources to use when an actual need arises.

2. Establish a Personal Budget

When creating a budget, you would have to assess your current financial status, and acknowledge the amount of money that you should only spend. Though it can be quite a stressful task to do, it is essential for your goal to be mentally prepared for the probable financial challenges that you may face.

With a budget, you will be able to make financial decisions without fearing that you would go over your means. Furthermore, it will also protect you from giving in to the impulse to buy something as a result of your emotions.

3. Differentiate Your Self-Worth with Your Actual Net Worth

Mentally strong people know that their value cannot be measured by the amount of money they earn, or the size of their house. They also do not brag about it to others because it would only incite negative emotions and strain relationships.

As such, by separating their self-worth from their financial status, they are able to focus more on mentally preparing themselves for the unexpected changes that may affect them financially. Their concern lies more in being ready for any eventuality rather than making themselves feel better by acquiring as much money and property as they can.

4. Avoid Engaging in Unhealthy Rivalries and Competition with Others

Comparing your financial capabilities with other people will not only waste your time and energy. It will also undo the hard work you have put into mentally preparing yourself for financial difficulties.

When you envy what others have, you are more likely to break the rules and limits that you have imposed upon yourself in order to remain prepared for anything that can go wrong in your finances. Before you know it, you are buying luxury items or the newest gadgets even though you don't actually need them—or worse, even if such purchases go beyond your current means.

5. Take Calculated Risks

Those who have mentally prepared themselves are less likely to be blinded by supposed get-rich-quick schemes, or high-payout gambles. However, they also do not shy away from potentially sound investments that could make their money grow.

Such individuals are able to remain rational and objective because they do not let themselves be carried away by the excitement of the moment. If needed, they take a step back to better assess the opportunity in front of them. Only when they are confident enough to risk their hard-earned money are they going to push through with an investment or a big purchase.

B. Challenges in Your Career

When it comes to one's career, majority of the challenges that you would likely face can be divided into two categories: starting a new career and working on your current career.

Each category requires a different kind of preparation, so what follows are some practical tips that could help you navigate your way and excel in your chosen career.

New Career

Preparing yourself mentally for a new job is equal parts exciting and scary. After all, you want to make a good impression on your boss and co-workers, who are essentially strangers to you at this point.

For a great first day at your new job, take note of the tips given below:

Gather Information About the Background and Culture of the Company

Since your first day would likely be more about memorizing the names of your co-workers and figuring out where to go after, it is best to familiarize yourself ahead of time with the kind of working environment and culture that you may expect while working for that company. Mentally preparing yourself through research will keep you from being completely disoriented in front of your new colleagues. Furthermore, you will be able to ask more insightful questions about your position and their expectations from you since you know, more or less, the general bits of information about the company.

You may begin your research on the official website of the company. Ideally, you should have checked this prior to applying for a job there, but in case you have not, explore its pages and entries. If it has its own blog, read through the posts to get to know the company a little bit more.

Extend your search to the job posting sites because they normally feature company reviews from the employees themselves. For a broader scope though, social media sites would likely have posts about the culture and reputation of the company. Again, you should have checked these out while you are searching for a job.

In terms of company culture, you may focus your research on how they interact within work hours, as well as the kind of relationships that you may build with your new co-workers. Are the employees formal with one another, or do they follow a familial approach? Can you call them by their first names, or are honorifics a requirement while doing business with each other? Finding out the answers to these interesting questions would help you figure out the right tone and attitude that you should take while working there.

C. Challenges within Your Family

According to a study about intense levels of stress, families are more vulnerable to suffering from the combined pressure of financial and work problems. Though raising and being with your family can be happy and fulfilling, it can also be quite demanding of your attention, time, and energy.

To help you mentally prepare for the challenges that you may face within your family or as a family, below are several tips on how you could do it together:

Set Aside Time to Talk About the Worries and Problems of Each Other

Having regular conversations with the whole family offers a lot of benefits for everyone involved. Front and foremost, it brings each member up to date on what is going on in their respective lives. Having this level of awareness and understanding would give everyone a chance and more time to handle any problems or issues that need to be addressed.

Furthermore, moments like these can be used as a channel to teach the younger members about the proper ways of dealing with the challenges that they face on their own. By teaching them how to use tools and techniques at their disposal, they will be more equipped to manage stress, anxiety, and fear. Remember to educate them as well about the unhealthy ways to cope with or escape from problems.

Make the most of these conversations by sharing your personal experiences too in order to create stronger bonds between each family member.

Chapter 14
Improving Your Odds with Mental Toughness

The ability to endure through whatever may be going on in the moment is clearly related to qualities we have already looked at—a positive mindset and patience—that is, to the ability to expect a positive outcome, despite what may be going on in the moment. At its root, all endurance is mental, and it is a necessary quality for mental toughness. In fact, it is one of the qualities that most people think of when they consider someone as mentally tough.

The value of endurance is a little different from patience. Patience is about letting things bake, without hurrying it or getting frustrated while you wait. Endurance, on the other hand, is about actively doing something, repeatedly expending effort, despite negative or insufficient outcomes, until you achieve the outcome.

To be successful, you need to be able to fall and get back up again and again. It doesn't matter how many times you fall—it only matters when you decide to stop getting back up. As long as you keep trying, you are not a failure—you are just a work-in-progress.

This is another one of those reciprocal relationships, a road that goes in both directions. If you never give up, you develop a stronger mind, and the stronger your mind gets, the less you will give up. One day you may even become like Edison or one of those diligent entrepreneurs who set their sights on accomplishing something and don't rest until they make it happen.

We tend to think of endurance as to how much we can run, walk, or work, as a kind of marathon, as the distance we can go without running out of energy. In athletics, that can be an accurate description, but when it comes to our mental strength and the inner force that drives us, endurance is about how indifferent we are to the time it takes to achieve success at a task, or how much we need to do or go through to achieve our goal.

If you can envision a goal and commit to doing whatever it takes until that goal is attained, you will build your endurance. You can remind yourself to "do whatever it takes" at the moment, as a kind of a mental "hack." When you measure what you are doing against a distant goal, you can feel like you're stuck or standing still. Instead, if you don't benchmark the outcome to an arbitrary measure of time, you can put the importance on getting the objective completed, step by step, instead.

If you break your goals down into smaller bite-sized tasks, you can keep giving the mind the rewards it needs. The feeling of "success" is experienced as a reward. As a result, you will be more motivated to keep going. The mind focuses more easily on smaller tasks at hand than on those distant, overarching accomplishments with rewards in some far-off future, those big goals that you have to relentlessly remind yourself to move toward.

Remember, you build mental endurance the same way you would build physical endurance—with practice. Endurance is practiced, not inherited. The smaller objectives you set, the more you aspire to and successfully achieve, the more you will form a habit of enduring. It's like fasting. You start by skipping a meal. Then you skip two. Eventually, you can progress to skipping meals for a full day. In a short time, incrementally, you build up your endurance, and you can find yourself fasting for seven days in a row.

Whenever you want to build your endurance, whether it is in swimming, running, fasting, or succeeding, you need to take it up a notch at a time, using baby steps. There is no other way. One step at a time, without fail, without pause. Doing that, you will begin to experience the confidence that comes from having demonstrable evidence of being able to do what you once doubted or thought impossible. That confidence helps the mind endure even longer.

One of the best ways to develop mental toughness is to start with developing and practicing endurance. Weaker minds tend to give up, not because they don't know how to do something, but rather because they get tired and give up. Endurance has a lot to do with working through fatigue or discouragement.

That fatigue is much like the fatigue a marathon runner experiences. Fatigue is real and can be the difference between life and death. The willpower to go on in harsh conditions only goes so far. Sometimes, you need to keep going through the wall of fatigue. Other times, endurance is knowing when to take rest or a break in order to continue moving forward. Consider the soldier, of ancient legend, who ran from Marathon to Athens to tell the people that the battle had been won. He ran through the night, for 23 miles, without stopping once. He got to the town square, yelled "Nike," collapsed, and died of exhaustion.

There is something to be said for willpower. It can get you past the mistaken sensations of the body and the bouts of laziness we all have in these situations. But you should never push your mind and body so far that it breaks. There are times to heed the warning signs and take care of your mind and body. That's one of the reasons to build up endurance gradually.

When you build physical endurance gradually, you give your body the time it needs to adjust. You need to do the same when you are building mental endurance. When you build it up slowly, your endurance will be more reliable and longer-lasting.

One way to develop mental endurance is to set yourself mental challenges that require you to keep going in the face of frustration or other obstacles. You could, for instance, start doing crossword puzzles, forcing yourself to complete the entire thing. Each time aims to reduce the time to complete the crossword by five percent. If it took you 60 minutes last time, aim for 57 minutes. Once you start, don't stop to do anything else, keep at it until it's done. If you pass the time allotted, don't stop, just keep going until you finish.

You can start playing a game that's a physical sport. Get your heart pumping while you are in a competitive state and go into the game with an intention to win-one point at a time? Play a full game through at least once a week.

Elite military persons, like Navy Seals or others, all go through rigorous training to develop endurance, to push past what they perceive to be their own limits and to persist and ignore all the things that would pull them away from completing their task, no matter how onerous.

For more ordinary individuals, setting challenges like training for a marathon, or taking on some sort of 30-day challenge in a favorite subject, such as joining thousands of writers in their annual NaNoWriMo (National Novel Writing Month) challenge to write 50,000 words (a short book) during November, will build up endurance. You can build up your own endurance with activities like those, and, more importantly, train yourself to recognize that some of the limits you have been accepting as real have been self-imposed.

Chapter 15
The Secret to Staying Motivated

Goals give us direction. They help us determine our destination so that we know where we are headed and what it will take us to reach there. We know what we want to accomplish in life and can gradually take steps in the right direction. Goals are the targets that keep us on course even when the going gets tough. Without goals, you are aiming in the dark, hoping that it hits the bull's eye. Goals give you a sense of purpose and direction. They give you a roadmap on which you can embark to lead a successful, abundant, and glorious life. Here are some goal setting secrets that give more purpose, focus, and directions to your actions:

Keep Your Eyes Fixated on the Larger Picture

If you are employed in an organization, and simply concerned about getting to work each morning, finishing your work and returning home, you are not positioning yourself for success.

Do you know the company's corporate strategy? Do you know the company's vision or revenue generation model? How about its long-term profit generation and expansion strategy? Avoid being married to short-term goals or keep a myopic vision. Always stay fixated on the larger picture where goal setting is concerned.

While setting work goals, keep a keen eye on the larger picture or vision. What do you wish to accomplish from the venture? Why are you doing this? Combining strategy, long-term goals, and planning are vital to achieving success. What do we need to do to keep our employees satisfied, productive, and happy? What exactly can you do to keep your customers happy?

What is your top goal in life? A majority of people seek to be financially free for living a happy, rewarding, and fulfilling life. Financial freedom in its real sense is about possessing all the time and all the money to enjoy it. While some people have all the time in the world but no money to enjoy their free time, others have all the money but no time to enjoy their money. True financial freedom is about both; the time to enjoy your money and the money to enjoy your free time. Is it your financial goal to achieve financial freedom—or do you want to achieve something else?

Some youngsters want to retire at 35 and travel around the world. This pushes them to toil hard, give it everything, and save enough money to fulfill their dreams.

Keep an eye on the larger picture. This will give you more focus, clarity, and energy when it comes to working on the goals. It will push you to be more self-disciplined, action-oriented, and dedicated to your work.

The larger vision includes both: what has happened and what the future looks like. Use your innovation and go deep into building the larger picture.

Here are some techniques to build your big picture:

Free Writing, Brainstorming, Thinking, Sketching, and Drawing

If someone awarded me a dollar each time my thought wandered, I'd be a billionaire by now. However, some of the most resourceful and inventive insights occur to us when we think freely. Dip into your creativity to work out your goals and the larger picture. Ideas are never right or wrong, good or bad, and correct or incorrect. Don't evaluate your ideas or obsess about them being too unrealistic or impractical. Carry a notebook or phone wherever you go to list down all interesting things you observe and witness around you. It will expand your vision and feed your mind with more ideas.

Write down ideas as they dawn upon you or as you observe them. It can be while driving, jogging, watching television, spotting a street sign, showering, watering your plants in the backyard, and so on. Ideas can dawn upon you anywhere. You can have your own 'Eureka' moment just about anywhere. Be prepared to record them or risk losing them. Build an atmosphere and ambiance for optimizing your creativity. Set up a personal creativity corner in your house or patio. Play soft music and allow your free-thinking process to begin. Do not worry about good or bad your ideas appear—just allow them to flow unrestricted. What do you really want to accomplish in life?

What are the various possibilities of achieving your ultimate goal in life? For example, you desire to make money by traveling around the globe. What are some ways to make this happen? What is the bigger picture behind your goal? Do you wish to live a more adventurous, action-packed and exciting life? Do you wish to keep away from a more mechanical 9-5 job? Do you wish to build something interesting that inspires youngsters to give up their regular life in exchange for traveling around the world? You may like to sketch your ideas rather than writing them. Sketch or doodle ideas—sketch a larger goal or your bigger picture and encircle it by tinier sub-goals needed to fulfill the bigger goal or larger picture. The objective is to clarify your wants by staying fixated on the larger picture before accomplishing it to make it easier to work in the desired direction.

Breaking Your Larger Goal into Tinier Sub-Goals

Though your vision should be on the larger picture or purpose of a task or goal, avoid taking your vision away from the next step. The most vital step in any goal fulfillment process is the next step. Think that you are given a task of scaling the planet's tallest mountain. If you look straight at the summit, you will feel overwhelmed and intimidated. You will never believe a mountain as high as this can ever be scaled. It appears to be a super challenging task if you view the tallest summit from the base. The summit obviously appears unachievable and practically impossible to climb.

Your confidence in reaching the camp a few feet over the base will be more than the confidence of reaching the summit because the camp near the base appears way closer than the summit. Can you climb to the camp just above the base? Of course, yes! You will reach it easily, quickly, and without any hassle. Once you access this camp, look at the next camp located a few feet over the present camp.

Do you believe you can reach the next summit? Again, of course, you can reach it quickly and easily. It is merely 500 feet above the existing one and isn't a big deal. Keep looking at the subsequent step every time until you access the peak. This should also be your attitude towards success, money, goals, and life mastery. Keep your vision firmly fixated on the next goal or camp instead of worrying about the final goal or mountain summit. Keeping your eyes on the next step makes it seem more doable and realistic instead of feeling daunted by the prospect of reaching a goal that seems too far away right now. When you start a business or an Instagram account, you'll tend to think about having a million followers immediately. It will seem highly impractical and scary in the beginning. It may deter you away from your goals.

However, if you think in terms of more realistic milestones, the targets may seem more doable. You can build on one sub-goal at a time until your ultimate goal seems more realistic and attainable. In business, you don't think about huge profits immediately. Initially, the business may run on a loss, then the focus will be on breaking even, and finally, it will be about making and growing profits. Imagine how overwhelmed you will feel if you think about making large profits on the first day itself. Keep your goals big and be fixated on the larger picture. However, while taking concrete steps to fulfill the goal, keep your eyes on the next step.

When you think about a big goal, you are likely to feel overwhelmed by the prospect of achieving it. This isn't to advocate that you should not set large, seemingly unrealistic and ambitious goals. You must know where you want to go but keep an eye on the subsequent step to make it appear more realistic, balanced and achievable. Once we go past a camp, our confidence to access the summit soars. With every step you access or every tiny goal you achieve, your confidence in achieving the bigger goal grows. If you have read Brian Tracy's Focal Point, it refers to a strategy that if implemented can bring a considerable change in the way you perceive and approach your goals. Tracy mentions if you feel overwhelmed or intimidated by your goals, concentrate on finishing the first 10 percent of the task needed to meet the goal. When you complete 10 percent of the tasks needed to achieve a goal, you gather the momentum to go on. Once you gather momentum by starting with one-tenth of the task, there are higher chances of you completing it. Let us say assume you desire to create an information-filled social media page with a hundred high-quality posts. Now, obviously, you cannot create all hundred posts in a day or week. However, if you make a list of all topics for the posts a write a rough idea for every social media post, you have finished 10 percent of the task. This one step will reduce the gap between you and your objectives and drive you into a hustle-mode.

Measuring and Evaluating Goals Frequently

Measure, assess, and evaluate your goals at periodic intervals to check where you are with reference to the overall goal. Where are presently standing where the larger goal is concerned? Sometimes, evaluating and measuring goals can be tough, in which case you just need to keep recording outcomes and measuring them against the larger goal. Let us say your bigger goal is anger management. You wish to prevent and bursts of anger and fits of rage that are leading to plenty of problems in your personal, professional, and evaluating social life. Firstly, your objective is to prevent flying into fits for rage for a year. How will you measure this? Keep a record of all situations where you felt a compelling urge to fly into a rage but controlled the urge. This can be a monthly or weekly process. Count all the times that you succumbed to your impulses and reacted. How many times did you manage to resist from flying into a fit of rage? How many times did you vent your anger? What did you do or speak in anger? Was your emotional or impulsive reaction justified, or did you respond on an impulse? Did you misplace your anger elsewhere? Could you have controlled your anger had you tried slightly harder?

Ask yourself these questions before going to bed. Keep measuring, analyze, assessing, and evaluating your goals frequently to stay on track with the bigger goal. Certain goals can be measured more precisely than others. It is simpler to record your progress in some cases where exact figures are involved. If you have enlisted for a degree and successfully write each paper to earn the degree, you know where you are once the papers as assessed. You know precisely how much you have scored on each paper. Evaluating progress, in this case, is much simpler.

Chapter 16
Improve Focus and Concentration with Mental Toughness

O f course, what is self-discipline without any focus? You must be willing and able to focus if you want to ensure that you can, in fact, figure out how to be self-disciplined. After all, how can you really and wholly dedicate yourself to making the right decision if you cannot focus on what is right in the first place? When you cannot focus, you cannot really make a meaningful, practical decision because you are not giving anything the actual levels of focus and attention that they would deserve.

The state of focus is one that is fleeting for many people—they struggle to find that state in which they are so incredibly engrossed, they fail to ever make the proper decision in the first place. Focus is that feeling when time ceases to matter. It is that time in which you are so completely in tune with the world around you and what matters that you do not feel like you are wasting major amounts of time. Your entire mind is homed in on one thing to ensure that you can, in fact, make that decision without wasting time.

What if you could turn that intense focus on at will? Think about the potential that you would have to succeed—you would be able to succeed simply due to having the drive to do so, and that is important. You would be able to completely and utterly engross yourself in that particular activity, and because of that, you would be sure that you could actually make what you wanted to happen actually come into fruition.

You would be so absorbed in what you are doing that it hardly seems like work in the first place. You are too busy focusing on what you are doing to notice that the time continues to creep by. You do not feel the fatigue that those around you seem to feel because you are naturally engrossed rather than constantly forcing your mind back to it.

The Benefits of Focus

When you learn to be self-disciplined and therefore focused, you begin to reap all sorts of benefits in your life. These benefits include:

- You get stuff done sooner: Just by virtue of not having to jump around so much with what you are doing; you often find that whatever task that you have on hand at any given moment becomes infinitely easier. You do not struggle to make sure that you meet your tasks because you simply do them without worrying. You do not find that you feel tempted to check your phone for messages every two minutes, nor do you feel like you need to flip-flop between several tasks at the same time. This means that you can focus entirely on one task at a time and make it happen quickly and simply.

- Your work improves: Along those same lines when you are focused and entirely dedicated to what you are doing, you will find that your work gets done better. You focus on one task entirely, and that means that you are able to really give it the attention it needs in order to double-check all of the necessary details. You will be able to focus without mumping around so you will be able to ensure that you have made the appropriate decisions and given it the appropriate amount of focus in the first place.

- Your stress levels decrease: When you are no longer concerned about how to get your work done because you are focusing entirely on it, you will very quickly find that you are able to better regulate yourself. You will be able to avoid being stressed because you know what you are doing when to focus on it, and how to make good use of your limited time in the first place. You will make sure that you are avoiding outside stressors simply due to not paying any attention to them, and you will also recognize that you can better ensure that everything is done according to command.

- You allow the subconscious to take over: Your subconscious mind is almost like a copilot for your body—you and your conscious mind are obviously the pilots, but your subconscious is along for the ride, taking care of all of the lesser tasks that have to occur. If it is muscle memory, your subconscious mind will do it. When you strongly focus on what you are learning to do, you teach your subconscious mind how to do what you are doing. Over time, your subconscious becomes capable of activating automatically and taking care of the brunt of the repetitive, mindless work.

The Struggles of Focus and How to Defeat Them

When you struggle to focus, however, you start to see problems. Focus is something that is, unfortunately, in short supply these days—you cannot often find the focus that you need without intensively learning to do so. Focus has been dwindling as the need for it has dwindled. Even cars have begun to take away some of the mental loads for drivers, allowing for uses of sensors, cameras, and other articles that will directly manage the road right around you for you. There are some cars that will even auto-manage so you are kept in the right lane, so you do not have to do it yourself.

With the focus being hit from all around you, you are going to find that you struggle. You are inundated with advertisements when you try to watch a 3-minute video online—the advertisements may even last longer than the video in some situations, and you are likely to see at least one in the middle as well. When you see these ads breaking up the video that you are watching, they damage your focus. They remove your focus from what you were looking at in hopes of telling you, at least subconsciously, to buy their products. They try to snipe you away from actually making sure that you make good choices with your money and that can be a problem for you.

This is exactly why it is so important to learn how to focus in general and why self-discipline puts so much focus on the art of being able to focus in the first place. Thankfully, even if you currently lack the mental capacity to really focus well, you can learn to do so. You can develop your ability to focus, training the brain to really harness its abilities to stay on one task before switching to a new one. When you learn how to do this, you will find that you can create the sharp focus that you need to avoid the distractions. You will be able to cut out all of the distracting stimuli from around you to ensure that at the end of the day, you will be able to achieve your goals with ease.

When you want to learn how to focus, the most important thing that you can do is ensure that you repeatedly correct yourself. Every time that your mind wanders, you must be willing and able to pay closer attention to what you were doing. You must return your wandering mind to where it belongs. At first, you may feel like you are desperately trying to gather up a bunch of ducklings on a mat, and every time you set two down, three more takeoff running. You may feel like you are fighting this impossible uphill battle. You may worry that you cannot possibly manage to develop this focus to the capacity that you need it, and that can be absolutely terrifying.

Chapter 17
Mental Toughness Techniques That Can Help You Achieve Your Goals and Be Strong in Every Situation

Difficult situations come up often, and there is really nothing you can do about it. You cannot stop all difficult situations from entering your life—if it were possible, people already would have. Stop and think about the last week at home. Was it perfectly peaceful? Did you find that you did not have a single conflict?

Chances are pretty high that, somewhere in your life in the last week, or even the last day, you found that you had some sort of conflict in your life. It is impossible to avoid it all of the time. However, you can learn how to handle them better than ever before. You can teach yourself to cope with the negativity in the world without letting it wear you down. You can learn how to protect yourself from handling your difficult situations in life with ease. Whether it is a fight with your spouse or an argument at work where you did not agree with what your partner wanted you to do, it can be difficult to deal with the aftermath if you are not self-disciplined. You could find that you would prefer to lash out at the other person—you would rather do something that makes the situation worse.

We are going to address how to handle yourself better. We are going to take a look at how difficult situations can become a sort of pit in which you are stuck and unable to pull yourself out of without knowing what you are doing, and then we are going to switch gears to handle those difficult situations, learning to make the most out of them rather than allowing yourself to wallow in them. It is when you begin to wallow that the difficult situations in your life can become quite out of hand. It is only when you can develop your own self-discipline that you can finally break free from the cycle of negative situations and struggles that you are probably accustomed to by this point. You can learn to do this to ensure that you are successful. When you learn to defeat the difficult situations in your life, you learn how to bring yourself closer to success. You bring yourself closer and closer to being able to get exactly what you want in life, and it takes an ample amount of self-discipline to do so.

Getting Trapped in Difficult Situations

Imagine that you have just taken a mental health day off from work. You have spent the day at home, making sure that you are able to really relax because your job has been stressful lately. You needed the time to decompress and help yourself begin to cope with the negativity that it has been bringing to your life lately.

Your spouse, in seeing that you decided to take the day off, suddenly leaves you with a laundry list of tasks for you to take care of. You are left to figure out whether you want to anger your spouse by not doing anything because you took the day as a refuge from mind-numbing work, or whether you want to sacrifice the entire purpose of the day that you took off. You eventually decide that you are going to keep the day off as intended and do not do any of the things on the list that was given to you.

Of course, when your spouse gets home, you end up in an argument. You are told that you were home all day and should have had plenty of time to take care of something. Of course, you did have time—you just chose not to do so. You wanted to take the day as intended and make sure that your own mental health did not suffer too greatly. So, you took the argument instead, knowing that at the very least, you got the time that you wanted and needed. You then yelled that you only took the day off so you could catch up on sleep and then told your partner that they could take a day off to take care of all of the chores if they were that big of a deal, but you wanted your time for yourself as it was intended. That was a personal day, so you took it to enjoy yourself. The argument ended up getting worse over time, and eventually, the two of you slept in different rooms, utterly furious with each other.

The problem here was that you got put into a trap in the first place. Oftentimes, the difficult situations that you end up in do not have a clear-cut answer. There is no one way to answer what is best to do and how to make sure that it happens. There is no possible way for you to be able to see the future to figure out which situation will be the best for you. Of course, you can usually make a relatively educated guess— such as in this case, you have chosen to recognize what would happen. You did know that you would get a fight for not doing what you were asked—but you did not care.

However, the entire situation was poorly handled in the first place. You could have saved yourself a lot of hassle if you had been more upfront at first about what you had intended to do. Instead of telling your partner what you intended to do, you allowed your partner to believe that they would come home to a list of things done that were not.

The problem with situations like these is that they exist in a cycle as well, just like procrastination. When you are trapped in this cycle, it will eventually spiral out of control. You will eventually find that you are unable to manage the situation regularly. Your problem will worsen. The problem, however, is that they will continuously worsen with every iteration of the cycle. Now, let's go over this cycle briefly:

• Problem worsens: You begin with the problem. This is where you have one in the first place to some degree. In the example above, this is where your spouse asked you to take care of the list of chores for the day. You thought to yourself that you could do it, but you really didn't want to since it would defeat the entire purpose of having a day off to begin with, so you shrug it off.

•   Tensions rise: Of course, ignoring the problem just makes the tension worse. Your partner comes home and discovers that nothing got done on the list. This raises the tensions in the argument.

•   Problem gets worse still: Then, you end up blowing up about the whole situation as a whole. You could have avoided it—but you didn't. The cat is out of the bag, and you made the argument worse.

•   Tensions get worse: As a direct result of your actions, you find that the tensions get worse still, and you wind up spending time sleeping on the couch instead of in your bed because you do not want to be around your spouse.

•   Repeat.

Making the Most out of Difficult Situations

Of course, if you had taken the time and self-discipline you needed to stop and really think about the situation, you probably could have saved a lot of hassle. Instead of a major argument, you could have found that things were calmed down. You would have been able to stop and realize that the best thing to do in this situation would have been, to be honest. You would have been willing and able to recognize that you were not acting in the best situation possible and that, long-term, your decision would hurt everyone. However, you chose to go with instant gratification for yourself. You choose to intentionally forego, ensuring that everyone in your household was, to some degree, happy. Instead, you focused on making yourself happy—so you ensured that your one day would be calm and you refused to acknowledge the problem at all.

When you use self-discipline in difficult situations, you can begin to see the best way to approach the situation. You can recognize that what you really need at that point in time is some decision that will limit the risk of making things worse. You may choose, for example, to make sure that you communicate in this case. Communication is difficult for the best of us—it runs a major risk of being misunderstood or of causing further issues for you if you simply happen to say the wrong thing and offend someone somewhere along the line. You must be willing to take that risk; however—when you are willing to take risks like that, you can ensure that you know that you are making the right decision. You are choosing to do the genuine right thing for the long-term rather than focusing on short-term benefits.

Of course, the best way to figure out how to deal with your own emotions in order to think clearly enough to do so is usually through figuring out some sort of grounding method that works for you. When you do so, you are going to find that you can calm yourself down enough to make the objectively right choice in many different contexts.

Let's take a moment to look over a popular grounding method that gets used to help people calm down from heightened emotions. In this method, you will be engaging with all of your senses, one by one, in order to intentionally calm yourself down enough to be able to cope with the emotions to clear your own head.

First, you want to identify five things that you can see around you. Take a big, deep breath through your nose and try to spot the five things. Make sure that you really note the details for yourself—you want to note that you see a fuzzy, black dog walking down the street and a big, fluffy cloud that looks strangely like a bunny wearing a silly tutu. You find five different things that you can see with your eyes, and then you move to the next step.

Next, you must identify four things that you can hear around you. Sometimes, it can help to close your eyes at this stage—you will be able to more clearly focus on your hearing without your eyes distracting you.

With the things that you hear out of the way, you want to then turn your attention to three things that you can touch. This could be grass under your feet, the feeling of your phone against your palm, and the feeling of the air from the fan blowing over you. It could be something that you are touching or something that you sense from elsewhere.

Then, you must find two things that you can smell. This may seem strange to you—after all, we rarely pay attention to the scent in the air when it is not particularly pungent or powerful.

Finally, you must find one last thing that you can taste. This could be the gum that you are chewing or the taste of your coffee lingering on your breath. Identify this last sensory stimulus and then take a big, deep breath once more.

Chapter 18
Watch the Pros Not the Joes

D id you know that you can increase your in-game skills just by watching your idols perform skills that are relevant in your chosen sport? It's called the engraving technique.

The Engraving Technique

In The Little Book of Talent, Daniel Coyle talked about something that he called the engraving technique. The technique shows that young athletes can improve their talents if they continually and consistently watch top performers in their field perform the skills that they wish to get better at doing. Daniel Coyle proved that when young athletes watch these top performers over and over again, they engrave the skills in their subconscious mind and develop an HD mental blueprint.

So, when it comes to learning a skill, reading an instructive book on it is good, listening to a trainer talk about it is also good, but the engraving technique is such a great option that several top athletes have used it to become the stars we know them as today.

Here is some proof of how the engraving technique works.

Timothy Gallwey, a great tennis teacher and author, demonstrated the engraving technique in a video that was aired on an old TV show 60 Minutes back in the day. He had a group of middle-aged people who were new to the game of tennis participate in this experiment. At the beginning of the experiment, he studied their abilities through a couple of tests. He then picked one student who showed the least amount of skill in the group. He made the student focus on him and watch his actions while he performed tennis skills. After twenty minutes of this exercise, the student who was the worst at the skill showed a lot of improvement. When that same student started physically practicing their improvement shot through the roof! Surprising, isn't it?

Another example is the Suzuki method for learning music that was developed by Shinichi Suzuki, a Japanese violinist. The method emphasizes the need to provide students with a musical environment that is kind of like the linguistic environment that we use for learning a language.

Suzuki believed that this could be replicated in a music learning environment, and that is exactly what he did. Every day, students learning through the Suzuki method listen to several professional recordings of songs that were graded from simple "Twinkle, Twinkle, Little Star" to more complex tunes. The songs were performed by masters of the violin so that the students got to hear high-level musicians play the songs that they were working on. As the students listened to these songs, just like the toddler listens to languages, the songs become engraved in their minds. Pretty cool huh?

Just like most other techniques, there is a correct and incorrect way to practice the engraving technique. Let me show you how you perform this technique effectively.

Make a playlist of things that you want to master. Like a Steph Curry 3-point shooting playlist or a Kyrie Irving finishing around the rim playlist. You should not just watch random videos; you should watch videos of the skill you want to master. While you are watching you should imagine what it feels like to do the skill.

Watching your favorite stars participate and dominate in actual high-level competitions will put you in a competitive state of mind.

If you want to excel in your chosen sports, watch the pros.

Five-Minute Engraving Technique Exercise

We all know people tell us we play like. We also know what we need to work on. Like when Richard Williams wrote, "Serena, you need to learn to put more topspin on the ball." Here's what you should do. Find videos on YouTube of a current professional athlete who is great at performing that one skill that you need to work on. Dedicate at least fifteen minutes of your time every day to engrave a skill that is relevant to your chosen sport.

Chapter 19
Time Management Strategies

The Value of Time

No matter who you are, what you do, how much or little money you have in the bank, whether you own five properties or live in a tiny rented studio apartment, you possess something of immense value. This thing, which along with your health is probably the most valuable of your assets, is also (like your health, again) something you take for granted. What is this thing? Time, of course.

From beggar to billionaire, every human being has twenty-four hours in a day. No amount of money can buy more hours in a day; it's up to you to squeeze the maximum potential out of these precious hours. How we use our time ultimately determines who we are tomorrow, and someone who uses their time productively will see success and the attainment of their goals in the future. Also, using time efficiently is just like investing money wisely; you may not see immediate returns tomorrow, next week, next month or even next year, but you absolutely will after a few years. The problem is, however, most people don't think about time in this way. They squander the hours given to them in a day, neglecting it just as they neglect their health.

How then do we go beyond this squandering of time that so many of us are guilty of? How do we learn to use this valuable resource as efficiently as possible? Your Energy Plays a Big Role in All of These

I've mentioned energy an amount of times, and I want to talk about our energy as it relates to our efficiency. Like it or not, we're biological beings, and much of what our bodies do and how they run is out of our control. While we can't control what time and for how long we have our most energetic periods during the day, though, we can learn when these periods generally occur, and make the most of our peak energy periods. In this way, we can use our time and energy incredibly efficiently and give our productivity an enormous boost.

As every one of us has no doubt experienced, our energy (and with it, our motivation, ability to work hard, focus intensely and concentrate on tasks) fluctuates during the day, generally tapering off in the evening and fading completely away at night until it's time to sleep. According to psychophysiology's Peretz Lavie, our energy fluctuates in daily patterns which he calls ultradian rhythms. Our energy levels rise and fall during these times. For most of us, our peak energy levels occur in the morning, and we often have a mid-afternoon slump. Energy can return in the late afternoon or early evening, and then usually trails off through the night.

Everyone is different, but regardless of the pattern of your own ultradian rhythms, you will generally see your energy rise and fall at the same time every day. While some people say that managing time is most important, others say that managing energy is more important. If you want to maximize the efficiency of your time and energy, however, you need to get them working in tandem, and manage them both; one cannot work efficiently without the other.

First, figure out what times of day you're generally most energetic and focused. These are the times of day you're going to assign your most important tasks to. Working at your most important tasks when your focus and energy levels are at their highest will ensure that you get quality work done rapidly.

Second, don't try to fight your ultradian rhythms! Work with them, not against them. If you know you generally have a slump in energy after lunch, don't try to power through it. Instead, take a walk outside to get some fresh air, or even take a fifteen-minute power nap. Trying to force yourself to be productive when your energy levels only result in further loss of energy and a prolonged inability to focus and concentrate.

Similarly, when your energy levels are high, don't waste this precious energy on things that aren't important! Make sure that you're focusing on things that matter during your energy peaks throughout the day. And remember that rest is extremely important too; if you try to do too much without taking a decent break, you'll burn up all of your energy early in the day and won't have enough left to do things. Make sure that when your natural energy rhythms start to dip, you give yourself time to rest before moving on to the next thing.

Scheduling Your Day-to-Day Activities

Never underestimate the power of a good schedule. As I explained about Parkinson's Law, when you assign yourself a deadline for any particular task, you're far more likely to get that task done quickly and efficiently. I'm going to take a detailed look at some ways we can get the most out of schedules and scheduling.

First, let's look at the Most Important Task method, abbreviated to the MIT method. Realistically, we can only focus intensely on and effectively work on a certain number of tasks during a day. While you might think that you're able to get ten major tasks done every day if you simply write them into your schedule, the truth is that you can probably only do half of these, if that. Therefore, to make the most of your time and energy you need to figure out what your one to three most important tasks are in a day and give these things priority in your schedule. Put these tasks in at times your energy levels are at their peaks, and when you do these tasks, give them your undivided attention. Save less important tasks for later in the day.

In line with this is the productivity power that comes from the block scheduling method. Instead of simply writing out a list of ten things you need to get done during the day, you go further: you schedule a time slot for every one of these tasks. For example, you schedule your most important work project for 8–9 am. Then you have a short break from 9–9:05, then you schedule another important work task from 9:05–9:45. Since your energy level is likely to begin dipping at this point, you schedule a fifteen-minute coffee break, followed by ten minutes of answering emails. The more meticulous attention you pay to dividing up your schedule into blocks like this, the more efficiently and productively you'll use your time. In fact, you may well find that the seventy hours you were putting into a workweek formerly become thirty hours of actual work. This method is used by many incredibly productive people like Bill Gates and Elon Musk, and can be applied to any tasks you need to do in a day.

Another tip to make the most of your schedules is to organize tasks into batches. This means grouping similar tasks together. An example would be if you need to go to the grocery store at the mall, you may as well also do the other shopping tasks for that week while you're there instead of making a number of separate trips to the mall. This doesn't mean multitasking or trying to juggle multiple tasks at once.

Finally, the first ten minutes of your day, when it comes to scheduling, can make a huge difference in terms of productivity. Few people start their day off by getting into the right mindset for that day, which is a pity considering how much it can boost your productivity. When you begin your day with the right ten minutes, you can make a difference that affects you throughout the day. A great way to start off your working day is to check your schedule for that day, and then reflect on the day ahead. Clear your mind and be present; don't let your thoughts bounce all over the place and don't get stressed about things that are outside of your control. Focus on your breathing and close your eyes, and make sure you're comfortable and ready to work. Simply doing this at the beginning of each day can make a tremendous difference to your focus.

Taking It One Step at a Time

Multitasking is often portrayed as something impressive, something to strive for, but the truth is that few people are capable of doing it effectively, and for most people, trying to multitask ends up harming their productivity rather than helping it. Generally, it's far better to focus on one thing at a time instead of trying to multitask.

Focus generally comes from the area of our brains called the prefrontal cortex. A number of studies have shown that our brains can't handle focusing on more than one activity at a time—at least when it comes to intense, productive focus. Whenever people try to do more than one task simultaneously, the quality of output of both tasks suffers.

However, "can't you save valuable time by doing two things at once?" I hear you ask. Again, the answer is no; research has shown that when people try to do this, the test subjects work more slowly and less efficiently than those who focus on one thing at a time. To put it quite simply, attempting to multitask is generally going to result in fractured focus, a decrease in efficiency of work, and poor quality of that work, not to mention the fact that you're actually going to take longer and waste more time by attempting to multitask. Therefore, despite how highly many people regard the idea of multitasking when it comes to productivity, the truth is that focusing on one task at a time is always going to be a far more efficient and productive use of one's time and energy.

Chapter 20
Declutter Your Mind, Body and Environment

Finding Yourself in the Larger World

Have you heard the expression, "Look at who you are with, that is who you are"? You could also say, "Look at where you are; that is who you are." However, you would describe yourself or however others would describe you, you were not created in a vacuum.

Besides physical traits like height or eye color, there are very few traits that you were always destined to have. If you consider yourself quiet, there is a reason for that. Maybe you grew up in a calmer, less boisterous family. Maybe you looked up to fictional characters who fit into the strong, silent type.

But whatever personality you think you have now, it can change. The prefrontal cortex, the brain region right behind your forehead, created your personality based on the information you took in from your environment. Some of it, you decided to incorporate into your personality.

If you spend more time observing the thoughts going through your prefrontal cortex and reflecting on how your environment created these thoughts, you can make yourself whoever you want to be. Control your environment, the way you spend your time, and the people you spend time with, and you will control yourself.

Keeping Track of Your Habits to Change Them

When you think of mindfulness, you probably think of sitting cross-legged somewhere in the mountains of Tibet, humming "OM." This is one part of mindfulness, but it is just one.

A person who spends all their time on the reflective aspect is not practicing mindfulness. Find a place where you can make notes, even if it's an app on your phone. Write today's date and the date will be one month from now. Set a recurring reminder on your phone during a time that you are not busy.

When you get this reminder, don't meditate, but take a few minutes to think about what you did that day. Don't overthink it. If you went shopping, vacuumed, and sorted through bills, listing all those things is all you need to do. It doesn't seem like much, but if you do this every day, you will become more aware of what your life consists of.

When the month ends, think of one thing you want to change about your life. Think of one small thing you can do every day to make it happen. Your brain has become what it is today because of the stimuli you have had in your environment. This is about the practical ways you can go about making these changes.

Mostly focused on changing the people in your life, this one is about your habits and how they made your brain, yourself.

I've said repeatedly that your brain changes depending on the inputs you give it. We've gone over multiple examples of how we know this to be the case.

If you introduce a new habit into your routine, the habit will change you over time. You just have to be patient. Slowly, you will notice a lot of things that you thought were set in stone about yourself are like putty— you can mold them however you please. There are so many different goals that you could have in mind with wanting to change your habits and change your brain. I couldn't possibly cover all of them, but we will use the nine intelligences as a framework for different goals you might have. Becoming a master of your own brain takes a healthy amount of self-awareness, too. If you can't be honest with yourself about where your talents currently are, you won't be able to improve. If you aren't able to repeat a pitch, lying to yourself about what you are currently able to do is not going to help you get better. On the contrary, you have to think about what you still don't know how to do.

Take musical-rhythmic intelligence as an example. You might not be able to repeat a pitch or keep a beat, and you shouldn't just assume that you can. You have to actually test these things out for yourself.

Ask a friend who is already musically inclined to test it out for you. Are you able to repeat back the same pitch as they give you?

Don't be discouraged if you can't do it. All that it means is you have some practicing to do. If you keep at it and don't give up, you'll be able to pick up this skill just as you picked up any skill.

Chapter 21
Some Apps for Productivity

Focus Booster

It works like a timer with more features, allowing you to manage your time in small bursts while avoiding potential distractions. The great thing about this app is that its records sessions and presents it in a detailed spreadsheet that allows you to analyze your time. Together with this, you can get suggestions on how to use your time better.

Rescue Time

Unfortunately, Rescue Time isn't free. On the plus side—it is an excellent app to have with more features to speak of. It is the perfect app for people who do most of their work online or through a computer, whether its PC, Linux, Mac, or Android. Rescue Time essentially tracks down your computer activity and presents you with a chart showing how much time was spent on websites.

Any-Do

A comprehensive app, "Any-Do" is ideal for people who often work with others in a group. It is because of the main perk of "Any-Do" is to share the list with other people who are working on the same project.

Other than that, "Any-Do" carries the most essential features of a typical time management app. It includes shopping lists, "To-Do" lists, notes, reminders, and events. You can also sync the app with other devices.

Toggl

Toggl works mainly as a time tracker. What you do is turn it on and off whenever you're doing a task and labels it for future use or reference.

You can even organize time tags, and for those who get billed by the hour, you can use it to track billable time. It's currently one of the apps being used by those who work remotely. Timesheets may be sent, exported, printed, and examined.

To Do Calendar Planners

Electronic calendars are so much more efficient, allowing you to create a task list and have yourself reminded before the crucial moment. It is precisely what the app can do, including synching of data, prioritizing tasks, and even attaching Google Maps to your tasks.

Remember the Milk

An app to remember, Remember the Milk lets you organize and manage your time through several devices. It works in computers and mobile phones and may connect with your Twitter, Google calendar, and Gmail. You can also separate task lists depending on priority or if they're for home, work, or even school.

Time Doctor

Another one for the team, this app helps track your time, provides reminders, reporting tools, and integrates with other computer networks. It has the additional benefit of monitoring sessions through screenshots, therefore allowing you to find out whether your workers are working. Unfortunately, the app isn't free.

Google Calendar

Something free from Google, this Calendar presents a task list with an estimated time of starting and getting them done. You can add or remove tasks as you go. You can put in new tasks, set appointments, and block time for certain activities. The great thing about Google Calendar is that it's very pervasive so that you can put it in your phone, your tablet, and your laptop. If you happen to lose your gadget, you can always obtain your account from Google so there nothing is nothing lost.

Todoist

Another time management app that works for both single users and group work, the Todoist lets you arrange tasks, set deadlines, and have yourself reminded of anything that needs to be completed. It helps you keep track of urgent projects and collaborate with other people in your team. It's available in several languages and can be synched through all your gadgets.

Focus@Will

This app uses the power of music and neuroscience in boosting productivity. The app essentially provides a continuous release of music that is proven to help with brain activity. It is meant to be used for those cerebral activities like paperwork or when you're trying to write a paper. For menial tasks like cleaning the house: however, it won't be as effective. It's NOT available for free, so you have to consider that.

ATracker

This personal time tracker lets you find out everything you do the whole day through a comprehensive reporting. You can customize the options for the tracker, add more tasks, and check the ones that have already been finished.

If This Then That (IFTT)

Another unique time management product, it makes use of a basic logical precept wherein one action triggers you into doing another. It has the same principle used in the "Rhythm Routine." The app, however, uses the term 'recipe' and offers a host of preset and customizable recipes. For example, IF you're in the office, THEN you put your phone into silent mode. IF it's Friday, THEN you take your laundry to the cleaners. It also comes with a "To-Do" list that works with GPS and Maps. Hence, if you go to a certain spot and your "To-Do" list has something that is to be done there, it would alert you to that task.

Chapter 22
Improving Family Relationships

Show Respect and Consideration

The old saying goes we get to pick our friends; however, we're stuck with our loved ones. That is accurate; however, there are numerous things which we can do to assist our relatives become our friends in the order we feel stuck. We may not enjoy our brother-in-law; however, he's a part of our loved ones, and unless we've got a great excuse not to, then we have to show him honor and attention. In doing this, we'll have taken a step toward a much better connection.

Prevent Getting Up Conversations that Challenge or Provoke

Most importantly, you understand household members to understand what challenges them provokes them. Avoid those themes and activities. If your Uncle Tim has an inferiority complex, do not bring up things which make him feel bad. Think before you talk! If your jobless brother is sensitive to being jobless, do not speak about your advertising, and when somebody else brings it up within his firm, change the topic.

Do not Accuse or Blame Openly

If you believe a relative has to be called to the carpet, detained or involved doing something that's damaging to the household, face them privately, not openly or in a family gathering. Give them the chance to supply an explanation and also to answer your queries or accusation before between the remainder of the household.

Prevent Strife in Family Get Together

If you may keep your peace, do this, even though it means having to swallow your pride. Family arguments at parties, including vacations, seldom accomplish anything more excellent than hurt feelings and destroyed family moments. If you're hosting your family room, be confident that you look closely at the seating arrangements. Do not chair two feuding relatives near one another. If Aunt Judy and Aunt Samantha are quarreling about who gets the best pies, make sure you mention something beautiful about every one of the pies. Go out of the way are the peacemaker.

Agree to Disagree

One factor which may be relied on in every household is they will not agree about everything. Within every family, there are religious thoughts, philosophies, belief systems, lifestyles, views, etc. The very best thing every family member may do is agree to disagree on a few matters. Bear in mind, and this only works if every relative practice it, instead of merely says. Agree to disagree then get on with all the joy of spending some time with all the family!

Contemplate Another Point of View

While agreeing to disagree, reveal other household members who you admire and appreciate them enough to listen to their point of view and then think about it. Do not tell them they're wrong and you're correct and shed it. Give to hear what they must say, and do not assert since they're sharing their perspective. Thank them for sharing.

Take a Grateful Attitude

Before you meet other relatives for family occasions or vacations, prepare your spirit using a joyous attitude. Each individual has some decent qualities for that you could be grateful. Concentrate on these excellent qualities as opposed to the qualities you don't take care of in the individual.

Restrict or Forego that the Alcohol

Free lips sink ships... and start family fights! In case you've got an affinity to exaggerate it in family parties and state more than you would like to or say the off-base things, it is likely best to limit or forego your liquor utilization within the parties truly. It is distant way better to lose out on a few drinks compared to hazard harming or irritating relatives, or indeed making a trick of yourself.

Living without Neighborhood Conflict

If you are lucky enough to possess acreage or even a large city lot, then there's a distance between their home and your neighbors. However, for nearly all individuals, their home is quite near their neighbors. Sadly, this may create a battle! Below are a few methods for how to prevent conflict and mess with neighbors.

Do not blame the Neighbor for Living in Their Home

A friend once explained, "My neighbors could be fine if they'd only stay in their home and be silent." To put it differently, she had been stating that she desired the best to reside in her house, but she'd instead the neighbors never bother her by appreciating the same right! If you agree with everything your neighbor would or not, and if you enjoy them or not, doesn't negate their best to be viewed and heard in their own house.

Pick Your Battles!

If you decide on what your neighbor does, by allowing the water out of their sprinkler get in your flower bed, for their dog barking once or two if its master goes home, you'll be fighting along with your neighbor each the Time. Your neighbors are individuals, and they reside in their area, which will occasionally be a hassle for you. If you always complain, then your neighbor will observe that you're likely to pick on what they do, and they'll soon quit trying to delight you. If the matters that matter to you have been talked about, then your neighbor will probably believe you are only complaining, again and again, will not attempt a remedy. It is far better to decide as to what you can't endure and get in touch with your neighbor or your government about just those matters and locate your very own sensible solutions for your small things.

Maintain up Neighborhood Standards

Part of becoming a fantastic neighbor is to get your role in preserving neighborhood criteria. Adhere to the homeowner association rules and town ordinances concerning yard/garden maintenance, look of the outside home, parking principles, and land-use principles.

Meet and Know Your Neighbors

Banners float across areas. Should you make a bid to meet and get to know your neighbors, then you might discover the rumors of them aren't authentic, and they might come across precisely the identical thing about you. It will go a long way toward preventing battle!

Participate in and Host Neighborhood Occasions

The feeling of community which has been widespread in times past appears to be lacking from contemporary areas. That does not mean it cannot be brought back again. Strategy or take part in local block parties, holiday open houses, lawn sales, secure community watch classes, potlucks and barbecues, and yard birthday parties and occasions to your kids.

Take Responsibility for Your Kids, Couples, and Pets

Keep your eye on your pets and maintain them adequately included so that they do not run amok in your area. Do not allow dogs bark too, use your neighbor's yard to get a squat toilet, or struggle neighbors' dogs or cats. Ensure that your kids and adolescents are considerate and respectful of neighbors, nor create difficulties or harm for those neighbors. Inform your teens not to give neighbors only cause to panic or stress. If they're out late at night, then inquire about being sure that they and their buddies are silent when they come and go—place curfews for listening to songs outside or speaking to the porch.

Chapter 23
Myths About the Mentally Strong

"You have power over your mind, not outside events. Realize this, and you will find strength."

(Marcus Aurelius)

So now that we've seen what mental toughness traditionally encompasses, it's time to take a look at some more myths about mentally strong people. The common thought is that these folks somehow possess superhuman courage. That is not the case. In extreme instances such as the military personnel or high levels athletes, this may be true. These individuals have certainly trained both mentally and physically to develop what seems like extraterrestrial capabilities.

But for the everyday person, they have simply changed their outlook on life. They have made a decision that they can handle whatever comes their way, and just get on with it. This could easily be titled "Attitude Determines Altitude" or "Persistence is the Key to Success," or my personal favorite "Just bloody do it!" In this sense, success is achieved by simply showing up. By putting in the work each day, not by continually overcoming insurmountable odds. Its small, consistent, incremental wins that we are looking for. Not scaling Everest each week!

I have talked in much greater detail about finding your purpose, so I'll save you the explanation again here. But needless to say, that it's a crucial thing to find. Then whatever you are trying to achieve won't feel like work. It will simply be doing what you were put on this planet to do I.e. to actualize and manifest these goals into your physical reality. Then things will become dramatically easier by default.

Human beings are creative creatures by very nature. We want to work towards achieving milestones and are happiest when on the path to doing so. This is how our cognitive mechanisms were designed to function. There are countless people I've counseled over the years who suddenly experience a sudden drop in confidence, or even full-on existential crises. It's almost always due to having achieved something big, such as the dream job or high-level sporting goal. These folks were laser-driven whilst on the road to accomplishing these feats but are now somewhat lost. They have reached the top of the mountain with nowhere else to go. All I get them to do is re-evaluate things and get a new goal. This reinvigorates them without exception.

The Australian shepherd dog is a prime example of this. It's a very hyperactive breed which requires high amounts of exercise and activity to keep it happy. In fact, it will start to go crazy if there are no animals to herd. Owners report that the dog will endlessly run rings around the house or dig holes in the yard in the absence of any meaningful work. Humans are very similar in this sense; we need focus and direction towards a worthy task in order to keep us happy and functioning well.

In addition to this, too many of us focus on the "how" something should be done, not "what" should be done. Everyone's heard the adage that if your "why" is big enough, then you'll find the "how to." Through fear of sounding like an esoteric law of attraction guru, I couldn't agree more. But for now, let's just say it's wise to focus on the process, which requires the following two principles.

Persistence Equals Results

"The wise man is concerned only with the purpose of his actions, not their outcomes; beginnings are within our power, but the outcome is ultimately up to fortune." (Seneca)

Again, results don't come from mere contemplation alone. It takes action, a lot of action. This is where most people trip themselves up when it comes to mental toughness. They get a momentary burst of motivation but give up on a new venture or activity at the first or second sign of trouble. But the magic comes from persisting past these setbacks. It lies on the other side of these hurdles.

Oil companies don't make money by continually drilling shallow holes. They do their research and calculations and drill a well deep enough until they hit the oil deposits. Those who benefited most from the midwest gold rush did so by drilling until they eventually hit the vein they were aiming for, not stopping "three feet from gold." It's as though our existence on this earth has been set up solely to test the will of human beings. To reward those with the persistence to push through problems.

In essence, you have to be a dolphin. Look around, make a plan, and be decisive about the direction you want to go in. Then dive and swim and swim for six months before eventually surfacing for air to re-evaluate things. Then after some adjustments, dive and swim again! I appreciate this is easier said than done in today's fast-moving world with untold amounts of distractions. But you will be amazed at how much you will be able to achieve by sticking to this simple productivity principle.

So just get on with plowing for your goals without distractions and you'll be just fine. We do need to make the distinction between being busy and being productive though. It's pointless to fill up your day with activity for activities sake. Remember that working hard as a means to an end is a myth. You've heard the saying that "If you want something done, then give it to a busy person." I would argue you should give it to the productive person. These people are conditioned to get results, not just fit a lot into their day. They have trained themselves to achieve a certain amount of output, so adding just one more activity is of little disruption.

Everyone has this innate drive and persistent hunger within them. It's not until we see the rest of society making excuses for why things aren't working out, and justifications for throwing in the towel, that we do the same. It takes a mental switch and much daily practice to become a mentally strong and driven person again. I get more done in a day than anyone I know. But I still frequently feel lazy and bogged down. It takes a conscious effort to recognize these instances and to reaffirm my purpose in order to snap back into the correct state for action. Once you do these enough times, your identity begins to change from a person who gets moderate amounts of activity done, to getting everything and anything done! You simply need to increase your activity thermostat and persist through momentary setbacks.

Excuses Are the Enemy

I always find it interesting how most people will show up on time for arrangements with others. They will turn up 20 minutes early for a doctor's appointment or business meeting, but half an hour late for a workout or study session they have scheduled for themselves. I'm certainly not suggesting you begin wasting other people's time, but simply start respecting your own to the same degree. And this entails not making any excuses.

Doing so will ensure you take maximum responsibility for yourself and your actions. Nobody is going to take care of your own success for you. Whether this is in business, academia or within the family setting. All of these areas require work which only you can do. Again, military personnel will have an advantage here, as they are all too aware of the importance of self-sufficiency and extreme ownership of responsibility. Excuses will just not cut it in their world.

But even within general everyday life, you learn that excuses aren't relevant anymore, results are the only thing which matters. Yes, there will be reasons why something happened or didn't go your way. You were overlooked for that promotion because your boss prefers your colleague who he/she socializes with. Or you got turned down for that date because you weren't smart or good looking enough.

If you allow these things to dictate why something did or did not happen to you, then you are powerless to fix them. That is really what we are getting at here. Become so invaluable that your boss has no choice but to promote you. Become so eligible that every single person in town is knocking down your door to take you out.

It's not denying reality or beating yourself up for no reason. It's a mindset which is simply the most beneficial for you to adopt. If everything is within your control, and your responsibility to fix, then the ultimate power lies with you. You become the driving force in your own life. You decide your circumstances. In essence, you now have complete control over your future, and can steer the ship in any direction you wish.

It's my opinion that every major psychological growth spurt in life is preceded by a definite and conscious choice to assume more responsibility. It might be taking that promotion which requires handling more staff, having a child or upsizing your home. Each of these instances takes an upgrade in the cognitive work you must perform to ensure you can handle the responsibility, and adequately deal with an expansion of your comfort zone. However, when you are fully committed to persistent action towards your true purpose, your creative faculties will take care of the rest. You will find a way around any problem as your desire is big enough to solve it. Excuses will simply not enter into the equation.

Progress in life will always cause additional and bigger problems to arise. It's the surest sign you are heading on the right path to growth. This is the crux of mental toughness i.e. learning how to deal with these difficulties with increasing competence and confidence. It doesn't take superpowers. The mentally strong are everyday individuals who have just learned how to get it done. If you want some additional pointers on how to cultivate this within yourself, then the following will show you how.

Chapter 24
The 80/20 Rule

The 80/20 rule, also known as the Pareto principle, was the brainchild of Vilfredo Pareto, an Italian economist. In 1896, he noted that 80% of the property and wealth in Italy was owned by 20% of the population. No one is surprised by this notion today, but it was a heady proclamation at the time.

Today, the 80/20 rule is typically in the context of business and workplace productivity. We're going to take a different approach. We're going to apply this simple, life-changing concept to every aspect of your daily experience. You'll find the 80/20 rule is a powerful tool that you can use to achieve maximum satisfaction from your career, home life, and relationships. It can have an enormous impact on your diet, physical fitness, finances, and education. It can propel your small business to remarkable success in a surprisingly short time frame.

In short, I'm going to show you how to use the 80/20 rule to optimize every area of your life.

What the 80/20 Rule Isn't

This isn't about implementing a system. We're not trying to squeeze your life into a stodgy formula. Rather, this is about cultivating a forward-thinking mindset, one that recognizes the tremendous value in focusing on items that matter and ignoring the rest.

Nor is this about minimalism. While the Pareto principle can help you move toward minimalism (if that's your goal), its practical applications extend much further.

A common misconception of the 80/20 rule is that it encourages doing things in a hasty, careless manner. But that's untrue. We're not trying to cut corners. Instead, we're dedicating our focus and energy on tasks that produce the greatest impact with regards to our goals.

In other words, why spend our limited time on things that have a negligible effect on whatever we're trying to accomplish? If we can get 80% of the way there with only 20% of the effort, why not do so?

This idea will become crystal clear as we progress through 80/20 Your Life!

The Name of The Game Is Leverage

At its simplest, the Pareto principle is about leverage. This leverage allows you to do small things that can literally transform your life.

Think of the many ways we use leverage today. We use bottle openers to remove metal bottle caps. We use hammer claws to remove nails. We use car jacks to lift our vehicles when we need to change tires. We use scissors, which is a combination of two levers, to cut through paper, cardboard, and rope.

Other levers have little to do with physical force but are just as useful. For example, a simple flick of a switch bathes an entire room in light. Depressing a trigger engages a drill, which can be used for a myriad of household projects.

I'm going to show you how to use the leverage promised by the 80/20 rule to dramatically improve every facet of your lifestyle.

80/20 Your Life! Is Open-Ended

Again, it's not my intent to give you a blueprint. I'm not interested in providing a plug-and-play formula. In my opinion, such an approach would do more harm than good. Any application of the Pareto principle should complement your circumstances.

Your circumstances are unique to you.

My goal in 80/20 Your Life! Is to inspire you to brainstorm—and experiment with—ways to apply the Pareto principle in your own daily experience. I'll give you a number of examples along the way, some of which come from my own life. You'll discover how I've used the 80/20 rule, and the leverage it offers, to make considerable changes in my lifestyle.

But these examples should serve only as a springboard for your own ideas. The 80/20 rule should reflect the context of your life and complement your personal goals.

Chapter 25
Know the Enemy to Know Victory

nowing what procrastination is by providing definitions is one thing, but knowing what procrastination is by examining what it looks like in your daily life is another beast altogether. The definition provided here is very simple: it is doing things that feel good at the moment, but that does not translate to long-term goals. For this definition to hold any water, it assumes that you have goals in the first place. Most people out there do. It can be anything from wanting to do better in life, to change your living situations, or even to become financially independent. These are all different types of goals, but they share one thing in common: they require hard work.

Procrastination then is a universal affliction felt by anyone who has a goal in mind. Even if the goal is the only subvocalization in the mind that nobody knows about, it is still a goal. Another word that fits here is desire. We desire fun and play (procrastination), but we also want some form of long-term change (requiring hard work). If you are stuck having fun and playing on your off-hours, then you are robbing yourself of realizing long term commitments. Procrastination then is both a thief of time and a thief of self-realization.

An examination of your daily habits begins with a breakdown of the big things. The most obvious will be time spent sleeping, at work, or at school. From here, you can move on to specifics. There are only 24 hours in a day, so it is crucial to figure out how these activities stack up. An example breakdown may look like the following. Most people will have very different breakdowns for any given day.

To simplify things, we assume full-time work in the example during a day in the week.

Time spent sleeping ~ 8 Hours (33%)

Time spent at work (including commuting) ~ 9 (37.5%)

Together, work and sleeping account for a whopping 70% of the daily time budget. This is some 17 hours in total that you have little opportunity to pursue long-term goals (assuming these goals are strictly unrelated to work). The other assumption is that work is engaging enough that long-term goals are impossible to work towards. This leaves another 7 hours to split up between leisure, responsibilities, and chores and so on. This is where things get tricky. These 7 hours can be split in a seemingly infinite amount of ways over various areas.

Many of these activities are further split across the week, rather than on a daily basis.

Time spent towards personal upkeep (hygiene, bodily functions, eating)

Time spent on home economy (chores, making dinner, buying groceries taking care of children)

Hobbies

Entertainment

Socializing

Exercise

Work outside of work (seminars, acquisition of new skills, practice, etc.)

Countless others

The rest of the activity is left to you. The most important part is finding the amount of time that is considered leisure or your "own" time. In general, these are activities that fall below #4 on the list above. Everyone is different in this regard. Parents will generally have more time spent on children than non-parents. There will be a marked difference between those who work full time, part-time and those who are unemployed. The more leisure one has, the greater the chances that they give in to procrastination.

The stereotypical image of an unemployed young person is someone sat at home doing nothing all day. Others who are unemployed treat their unemployment as a job, spending upwards to eight hours a day looking for work. Many of them also turn to the "gig economy" for extra cash by doing menial and specialized tasks for money on the internet.

Bad Habits as One's Personal Enemy

In terms of procrastinating, a bad habit is any habit that takes away from time going towards your goal. There could be several of these that you engage in throughout the day. These habits are also easy to identify. If and activity…

Occurs almost daily for no definite period of time but can often take up an hour or more;

Makes you feel good inside;

Distracts you from the stresses of life;

Is automatic in execution; autopilot-like;

Gives you nothing in return after countless hours wasted;

Simulates a sense of achievement without providing a proper return on investment.

This is not to say that any activity that makes you feel good is inherently bad. It's only when those activities outweigh your preferences for goal-oriented ones that there is a problem. Sex feels good and is a completely healthy aspect of human relationships. Porn addiction, out-of-control casual sex encounters, and masturbation addiction, on the other hand, are generally unhealthy. The porn addict is still missing out on a real relationship. The libertine may be looking for fulfillment in the partners he sleeps with, only to realize he can never find it.

Perhaps the biggest indication of a bad habit is time. Too much time spent doing anything relative to other activities is a sure sign of time being wasted. If it feels good while you are doing it, then doubly so. Chances are you have identified them in the past but did nothing to affect change.

Still not sure what your bad habits are? Everyone has them; unless you are ultra-disciplined, then there are some activities in your daily life that you indulge in too much. We call this overindulgence, which is just a fancy way of saying doing nothing at all. Chocolate is an indulgence because eating it is pleasurable, but it needs to be modulated appropriately. Playing video games is an indulgence but playing them too often can cause you problems. Unless you are a big eSports star, then you probably shouldn't be playing eight hours a day.

Identifying some of these habits will be easier than others. The type of person you are will also determine how difficult they are to detect. Someone working full-time is less likely to be addicted to something that requires a large time commitment, but they still may enjoy watching Netflix as soon as they get home. Far too many full-timers "clock-out" as soon as they get home and take relaxation to another level. In contrast, a student who doesn't work may find it easier to squeeze in time for their bad habits. These bad habits can be multiple and have a compounding effect on your time management. Even those without obvious addictions may suffer from the addiction of the "many." Having too many interests, obligations or artificial commitments.

Common to all bad habits is the set of criteria listed above. Going through this list and seeing which of your daily activities fit the bill are worth examining.

Occurs almost daily or daily for no definite period of time but can often take up an hour or more

Any activity you do every day isn't inherently bad. Most of us will drive to and from work every day and drive to run errands on the weekends.

Is driving then a bad habit? Potentially—yes. Others who place a premium on work location may elect to commute up to two hours both ways because the job has better pay. What they lose in those four hours to and from work is completely worth it to them. Once an activity becomes a daily habit and it takes up a significant amount of your free time, something different happens. Such a practice may be indefinite in nature, meaning that one day you do it for thirty minutes and the next day, you easily get carried away and do it for three hours.

This is common behavior for bingers. Social media addicts also do this. They firstly require a daily fix, and secondly, they may lose track of time if they enter a "sweet spot" during their activities. Gamers unlock new game content and don't know how to delay that gratification, so they keep playing rather than waiting for tomorrow. It is obvious to make the connection between procrastination and compulsive behavior. A gambling addict sits at a slot machine because they believe doing more of something will pay off eventually. Or that doing more is somehow preferable than going home empty-handed. This is, of course, the gamblers' fallacy. Setting up more bets will not increase the chances of a payout.

In contrast, few people get carried away doing chores, studying or exercising. In fact, these activities are designed such that they are time-dependent. Once all the dishes are clean, the dishwashing activity stops. After the essay is finished, we close the word processor and hope we don't have to see it again soon. After our muscles have been exhausted, we pack our things and go home. Nobody wants to spend more time at the gym than is necessary (bodybuilders aside).

Chapter 26
How to Accept Things the Way They Are

"Acknowledge—at that point act. Anything the display minute contains, acknowledge it as in case you had chosen it. Continuously work with it, not against it."

Eckhart Tolle.

We always have to choose in life.

We can choose to fight against the world and its troubles. We can choose to focus on life's negative aspects and desperate to change other people. We can choose to obsess ourselves with the things that we don't have and feel unhappy with the present as a result.

Or, we can choose to appreciate ourselves, everyone and everything around us. We can choose to be content with what we already have first, while constantly working our way to achieve better things. We can learn to accept and properly deal with everyone around first before we can find those people that match us most.

In fact, embracing life as it is while working towards a better future is often the best remedy for fear, stress and anxiety.

This doesn't mean that we should always agree with someone or stay passive in every situation. This is to say that, instead, we should let go of the matters we can't control first. After that, we can take control by thinking about a detailed plan and then taking determined actions to carry out that plan.

The point is, when we cannot change a situation, it's time to change our minds.

It's time to accept and let go of the past, with its failures, agonies and losses.

It's time to accept the uncontrollable.

It's time to accept the unchangeable.

Learn the hard lessons.

And move on with the next plan in life.

That's the real meaning of acceptance.

The Power of Acceptance

Since a few years ago I have learned the great power of acceptance.

For example, I usually hated the weather when it came to winter. I disliked the bitter cold temperature that caused me so much discomfort. As it eventually turned out, it was actually my point of view that brought me stress and worries in small situations like that.

Again, it's a choice I had to make.

The realization was that I couldn't do anything except adapting to the weather, finding exciting activities and enjoying it. Accepting the weather and learning to live with it was the only good choice I had. The other choice was to complain about the weather and suffer from the severe stress of that constant struggle.

I realized that I was much more peaceful and cheerful when I accepted what life had given me, instead of continually struggling to control everything.

Acceptance is being comfortable with what we're given. It is improving changeable aspects of our lives and embracing the unchangeable ones. It means letting go of the things we cannot control while staying active on the matters that we can deal with. Whether it's a terminal disease, a tragic accident, a sudden loss of someone we love, accepting things that we cannot control will help us stay in peace. Practicing acceptance will help us move on despite the unexpected ups and downs of life, in the moments that we're uncertain of what's going to fall upon us.

There are often times we're alone in life. Everyone else is busy with their life, with their own stress, hassles and anxiety. No one really cares about us, about our worries and depression. No one has spare time to care about our sadness or loneliness. As such, during those difficult times, it's ourselves and ourselves alone that we can rely upon. That's what we must accept to be a strong and independent person.

Learning to Accept

Learning to accept those aspects of life that we cannot change is a vital skill. Doing so will help us alleviate all burdens and be truly liberated.

Most of us want to possess many things in life. We want everything to be perfect. Truth is, that desire of perfection is often the ultimate source of our miseries. Life is so much paradoxical—the more you want to control it, the more you are controlled and burdened. The more you want to possess, the more stress and fear of losses you'll have to overcome.

On the contrary, the less you expect from life, the less troubling and painful you'll fight against it. And of course, the more fulfilling your life will become.

We hence need to accept and let go of unchangeable things.

Accept death. Everyone has to face death eventually, one way or another. So while we feel sad after the loss of someone we love, remind ourselves that death is an unchangeable part of life. It is indeed inevitable. Remind ourselves that maybe, we would ultimately join everyone we love in the afterlife. As such, do our best to make this life the most unforgettable one, so that we can share many wonderful stories with our beloved ones when we meet them in the future.

Accept negative emotions. Accept that life can be boring, brutal or difficult sometimes. Accept that we will fail times and times again. Every one of us exists for a different reason, so we don't need to gain glorious achievements to be valuable or worthy in life. As long as we treat others kindly, do our best, and have some inspiring dreams to strive for in life, we can march on to happiness with our heads held high.

Also, embrace your imperfections. Many people wish for a perfect family, a perfect body, or a perfect partner in life. But there is no perfect family. There is no perfect partner. And there is no perfect life. Everything has both positive and negative aspects associated with it. In reality, almost no one can find their perfect imaginations. The mere fantasy of perfection might even create cracks in our relationships when our expectations exceed what we can get from reality.

Instead, learn to accept our flaws as well as others'. Reconsider our improper expectations. Relationships are always two-way streets that need cooperation and effort from both sides. A great relationship is not something that we can find. It's something you and your partner must create together.

A New Life has Come

To get out of all troubles, first, we need to take a step back. We need to gradually accept every mistake, every hardship and every failure in life. Life is here for us to learn and grow from our mistakes. So, take it as a game, and only a game—an exciting one in which hardships are merely necessary challenges for us to level up. It is a game that we need to decide what's controllable and what's not, what we can learn from each trouble, and what's the best thing to do right now.

After all, no one can be successful without those difficult moments of hardships and adversities. I haven't seen one. Have you?

Eventually, nothing lasts forever. We can only stay young and vibrant for a certain stage of life. After that, we'll get old. We'll get sick. Each of us passes through various periods of life. We may stay intoxicated in love, lose ourselves in romance, build our family, and finally lose the one we love. Live and die. Life and death. We're all the same.

Remember, everyone will live, love, succeed, blunder, and eventually say goodbye. No exception. The important thing is, we can learn to embrace it all. We can learn to feel grateful for this chance to breathe and discover this world. We can then get excited and appreciate our privilege to participate in Life.

Indeed, if something lasts forever, it's not something special anymore. Death, as negative as it seems, is the exact thing that makes every living moment valuable.

Normally, it happens that we humans often desire superficial things. We want more. More. And more. The question is, why do we have to burden ourselves with so many desires? Isn't it better that we learn to accept, forgive, and embrace life as it is now? Many people can live happily without being rich, without having a family, falling in love or having an intact body.

So why can't we?

Indeed, the key for happiness is to genuinely appreciate what we're given while accepting that we cannot have everything in life. That's how we let ourselves be free and truly joyful.

After all, life is meant to give us challenges so that we can stumble, rise up, and then grow. Life is meant to be accepted and forgiven for whatever happened. Acceptance is not a weakness. Acceptance is power. Acceptance is the ultimate key to a happy and fulfilling life. Acceptance is what gives us a better future and a better opportunity.

Then inner peace will be within our hands.

Chapter 27
Habits That Guarantee Our Success in Life

I n life, there are habits that determine either your ability to fail or succeed at whatever you do. Your ability to master these habits will be significant to your success in every facet of your life. We shall explore some of those daily habits and routines as it applies to different goals and desires.

Health and Fitness an Important Habit for Success

There are two bits of the riddle with having an effect on everything to accomplish a perfect build. The first is physical exercise. The subsequent one is seemingly significant to keeping up the correct eating routine.

Both customary physical movement and a strong eating routine require a portion of the day to day discipline. When you follow these two habits every day, you'll manufacture an amazing wellspring of order, so you'll have the option to use it to accomplish different objectives throughout your life.

How about we start with self-discipline is a characteristic inspiration-physical movement. I won't give you a definite arrangement to follow. Much the same as there's no ideal arrangement when abstaining from excessive food intake, there's also no ideal arrangement for work out.

The main prerequisite is to present a schedule in your week after week timetable and stick to it. For example, you'll practice on normal an hour daily, and do it regardless of the differences that may pop up. Neither climate, apathy, nor your companions coming over for the end of the week will dissuade you from working out.

I'm inclined toward weightlifting and other anaerobic sorts of activity that can manufacture muscle and assist you with accomplishing a more grounded, gorgeous body.

Anaerobic exercise is described by brief length (up to two minutes), which is high force exercises that lead to expanded quality, speed, force, and bulk.

Great decisions here include:

Weightlifting—it's presumably the best decision for many people because of its capacity to build up your whole body in flawless style

Sprinting—especially slope dashes, which are more secure for joints, viable for fat misfortune, and more demanding than ordinary runs on level terrain

Swimming—when done properly, high-force explosions of movement rather than sixty minutes in length of long distances

Yoga—can be a strong method to fabricate a balanced slender body for the two sexes. Keeping up awkward postures is, in itself, an extraordinary order building exercise

Calisthenics (bodyweight works out)—can be an ideal trade for weightlifting if you continually progress to tedious activities

These methods bolster assembling a reasonable, strong, and sound body. Getting these outcomes is essential in building up a controlled lifestyle. Progress and rewards will fuel your endeavors to prop up misfortunes, however, the greater part of your inspiration should originate from inside, paying little heed to the outcomes.

Notwithstanding anaerobic movement, it's acceptable to acquaint some assortment with your exercises and play out some oxygen consuming exercises too.

I do them for the most part not for the medical advantages (which are still clearly significant), however, for the delight and the pressure lessening impact they give.

It's associated with discipline too—a relaxed individual faces less difficult opposing temptations and adheres to their arrangement rather than a stressed up and on the edge individual.

Here are a couple of thoughts for aerobics practices which are a great deal of fun and give you mind-blowing medical advantages:

Cycling—long rides can be demanding, yet intellectually, it makes for an ideal game for building self-discipline

Walking or Running—simple, modest, and a sprinter high feel better

Tennis—seemingly one of the most troublesome games requiring a great deal of self-discipline to ace even the nuts and bolts

Skating—an enjoyment practice that nearly doesn't feel like exercise

Swimming—when not done in short eruptions of high-force movement. Perhaps the best sort of exercises for large people

Martial Arts—a tremendous part of combative techniques is the mental improvement, which makes it an ideal all-encompassing activity

Secrets to Never Quit Your Fitness Program

The five most regular reasons why individuals quit their work out regimes (and in this way lose self-discipline) are:

1. An inappropriate source of inspiration

There are two sources of inspiration: inside and outside.

Denis Coon, top of the line creator in the field of brain research, characterizes inner inspiration (otherwise called inborn inspiration) as something that happens "when we act with no conspicuous outside remunerations. We simply appreciate an activity or consider it to be a chance to investigate, learn, and complete our potentials."

Outer inspiration, otherwise called extraneous inspiration, is characterized by sports therapists Peter Terry and Costas Karageorghis as inspiration that can come "all things considered, for example, the inspiration to win medals, get economic rewards, and stand out from in the media." This is known as outside, or extraneous, inspiration since it includes an interest in the sport for a prize that is external to the entire procedure of participation.

The kind of inspiration you have to adhere to your work out regime and construct your self-discipline is a characteristic inspiration. You shouldn't construct your self-discipline to intrigue someone, you shouldn't go to the exercise center simply because you figure somebody will adulate or respect you for it.

If it turns out you expect a specific prize and attract next to zero individual happiness or satisfaction by doing it, reexamine your inspiration.

You fabricate your self-discipline when you continue accomplishing something that encourages you to achieve your maximum capacity and not on the grounds that it will make you look great in the estimation of others or give you remunerates.

If you can't find inborn inspiration, attempt an alternate charming game that will urge you to investigate, learn, or realize your latent capacity. If you detest it, you won't do it in the long haul at any rate. Speaking of which the second explanation is...

2. Absence of pleasure

Having a ton of control is incredible, however, it doesn't mean you need to consistently pick things you don't care for.

In 1997, psychologists at the University of Rochester and the University of Southern Utah directed an investigation on natural inspiration and exercise adherence. One gathering of members took an interest in Taekwondo classes while the other gathering went to high impact exercise classes.

The primary group would do better than the second group since they concentrated on satisfaction, capability, and social cooperation. At the end of the day, they picked partaking in a wellness class they appreciated and not a class that was centered explicitly on helping them accomplish their wellness objectives.

The two decisions could have been similarly awkward for them if they weren't given to standard physical exercise, however, it was Taekwondo that they appreciated more, and that is a similar method you ought to follow at whatever point making changes become awkward.

If you loath your wellness plan, change it. Attempt to pick one of each sort of activity, anaerobic, and high-impact session. In the event that you go to the gym, no one says you need to utilize either machine. There are different methods for accomplishing similar objectives.

In the event prescribing high impact works out, it doesn't mean you need to go to a class at your neighborhood gym. Indeed, I'm against it since I can't imagine a more exhausting approach to practice than going through an hour in a room doing hopping jacks and other nightmarish activities, as I recall from my PE classes.

Have a fabulous time while moving. Play tennis with a companion. Run with your pooch. Go on a bicycle ride and peruse your environment. Have a kayaking trip with a group of buddies. The less it feels like exercise, the simpler it will be to make it a perpetual piece of your life.

3. Absence of help

It's incredible to have enough self-discipline to accomplish your objectives without the assistance of others. It doesn't mean that it's the most ideal method for getting things done. Truth be told, support from others can frequently represent the moment of truth for your goals.

An investigation directed by Brandon C. Irwin at the Michigan Stay University and his associates showed that practicing with an accomplice improves execution on oxygen consuming exercises. An alternate report led by similar scientists proposes that working out with a marginally better accomplice makes people more persistent.

It's because of the Kohler's effect, a wonder where an individual works harder than an individual within a gathering. In the event that you can work more diligently what's more than growing better in the discipline while working with a gathering, why not take advantage of it and get support?

4. Wrong desires

Ordinary physical movement improves your self-discipline by showing both of two things: how to hold fast to a particular arrangement and how to be understanding when hanging tight for the outcomes. In the event that you start your exercise plan with an inappropriate desire, it's presumable you'll stop before you improve your mental discipline.

Because of the marvel of the bogus expectation disorder, you're going to set ridiculous objectives and expect things that can't occur in a predefined time period. To maintain a strategic distance from debilitation, inquire about what sort of results you can expect and define them as your objectives. When building self-discipline, little successes are a higher priority than focusing on the stars and not in any event like the arrival on the moon.

5. An absence of time

An absence of time is the least genuine motivation to stop a workout regime since it covers an alternate class of an issue. In the event that you can't find time to deal with your body, at that point the issue isn't your absence of time, however, your absence of priorities. Not many individuals would differ that wellbeing is the most significant thing throughout everyday life, yet the lives of numerous individuals don't reflect it.

Right now, you need control to distinguish your qualities, and above all, plan your life so that it will reflect them. If wellbeing is one of your essential qualities throughout everyday life (and it ought to be since everything else matters except when you don't feel well), sacrifice your lesser qualities for it.

To give you a model from my life, I have a few principles with respect to the kinds of organizations I can run. For example, I deliberately abstain from enlisting full-time workers since the advantages of expanded income potential can't exceed the wellbeing that causes disadvantages (adding a great deal of worry to my life).

I could get more cash-flow contrary to my standards, however, my wellbeing is more essential to me than material riches, so I'm fine with this trade-off.

What sort of tradeoffs do you have in your life, and do they mirror your own qualities?

Do you esteem family and wellbeing over your vocation, yet go through sixty hours, seven days working with no genuine arrangement to decrease your outstanding task at hand? Maybe it's a great opportunity to make sense of how to change the work-family time.

In the event that you maintain a strategic distance from these five normal reasons, you'll have a simpler time adhering to your exercise schedule while building and enduring self-discipline. Remember that these issues are there to assist you with getting more control. You must make sense of them, not blame them whenever you feel like giving up.

Chapter 28
Your Attitude

Your attitude defines anything and everything that happens in your life. Have you seen those people that have the energy of a 20-year-old but the looks of a 40-year-old? Such people are endearing to every person that they meet, and they make it easy.

You will also come across a person that doesn't have the capacity to draw attention to them. They aren't happy and are always negative in everything that they do.

All this has to do with attitude.

The attitude that you adopt has a huge bearing on what you do with your lives. It influences how you see and interact with the world around you.

When you have a good attitude, your life will be full of happiness. As you know too well, good things happen to good people, and when you have a great attitude, then great things will happen to you as well. Negative attitudes turn into negative actions, and these result in negative results.

When you make that decision about your everyday attitude, you get to define the happiness in your lives. You will be able to define the quality of your life by just having the right attitude.

Attitude for People Close to You
Friends

Friends have a special place in our lives, and this is because they listen to us, encourage us, and support us. Well, this is what you need to expect from your friends.

The quality of friends that you have depends a lot on your attitude. When you have a certain attitude, you get to attract a certain type of people to be your friends based on the attitude. If you have a positive attitude, you will attract friends that are positive, and if you have a negative attitude, you will attract friends who are negative.

For instance, I had a negative outlook and low self-esteem, and I found it so hard to connect with people to have good relationships with them. When I discovered that the major problem as my attitude, I decided to change it and fast-forward a few years now, I am happy because I changed my attitude towards life. I did away with negative friends, and currently, I have a close group of friends. All the friends I have are armed with a great attitude, and I spend a lot of time with them.

Lover

Just the way it influences friendship, attitude also defines the people that you love. A positive attitude will make sure you attract a person that is suitable for your life. When you have a positive attitude, you get to build a relationship that is based on fun, passion, love, and happiness. A negative attitude, on the other hand, will build a relationship that is full of anger, mistrust, depression, and resentment.

As an example, before I met Carol, I had endured a lot of negative relationships that didn't do anything for me. I had been manipulated, cheated on, and even taken for granted. Well, the relationships had some great times, but overall, I would say that my past relationships had been awful. Then I decided to change my attitude, and then things started falling in place by themselves. I was able to love myself rather than focusing all my energies on people that weren't grateful. I started believing that I deserved something better, and that is exactly what I ended up with.

Work

When you join a company or any other place that you provide your services, your attitude matters a lot. Many people out there don't enjoy what they do; this is because they don't follow their passion; rather, they work just to pay their bills and then get on in life.

Instead of turning up to work when they are overjoyed, they turn up when they are already annoyed and looking for someone that they can take out their stress upon.

Early on in my life, I used to be at a position where I hated the work that I did. I never appreciated what I went through each day, and it made me lose my sake each and every day. The work was a lot and boring, to say the least, and I saw that everyone else was incompetent and had a negative attitude. The bosses didn't do anything to help the situation. Then I changed my attitude, I decided to look at the job in a positive light, and this made a lot of difference in my life.

Where Do Our Attitudes Come From?

Studies show that approximately 90 percent of our attitudes come from our childhoods. The first words that we learn when we are born are daddy, mommy, and no. We get to have a lot of no's in our early lives that when we get to our teens, we have turned the no into impossibilities.

As we move into adulthood, we believe that the no's become fears, and we can't do anything because we have grown up knowing that it doesn't work at all.

Types of Attitudes

In life, we have different attitudes that define your position in life. We shall not look at the positive or negative attitudes at this juncture; rather, we want to look at what point are you in life. Here is a lowdown on what to expect at any point in time:

The Poverty Attitude

This is an attitude of the people that are generally afraid and don't look for any opportunity that might help them generate any income for their livelihood.

Such people usually blame others for the failures in their lives, and they feel that they have a right to enjoy what happens for them without paying a single cent. This type of attitude usually encourages a sense of dependence, whereby the person feels that other people owe them something.

People that have this attitude usually have little or no money and will force you to pay their bills citing a lack of money.

Paycheck to Paycheck

This attitude is a step right above the poverty attitude. This person is looking for a job just to pay bills and will take very few risks. They don't focus so much on the reward; rather, they put their whole mind on the risk that they are up against.

Such people become bitter towards their friends who are successful, and they go through a lot of fear because they are in their comfort zone at all times. They have a lot of hate towards anything that might compromise their salary or wages.

Chapter 29
Strategies to Help Stop Procrastinating

Step 1: How Setting Priorities

Dwight D. Eisenhower was the 34th president of the United States, a five-star general, the founder of NASA and the first Supreme Commander of NATO. It would be an understatement to say that he was a driven man who knew some strategies for success and productivity. Eisenhower had a tool that he used to set his priorities and plan how to use his time efficiently. This is widely known as the Eisenhower Matrix. It looks like this:

Everything on Eisenhower's to-do list would fall into one of four categories:

1) Urgent and Important

2) Non-urgent and Important

3) Urgent and Unimportant

4) Non-urgent and Unimportant

Things that were Urgent and Important had to be dealt with first. These were things of high importance and value to Eisenhower that needed to be taken care of in a timely matter or that had a pressing deadline.

In daily life, this category might include your check engine light being on, a presentation at work two days from now that influences your success at work, or a sick child in need of medical attention. These would be listed in the "Quadrant One." Because these tasks need to be taken care of first. The three categories that often trip people up and have cause them to get bogged down working on things that are of little or no importance to themselves.

In the Second Quadrant, Eisenhower would list things that were Non-urgent and Important. This is the category that needs the most planning and attention. It is the category that will help you focus on what you value the most and help you achieve your long-term goals. In this category, would be things like exercise, time with family, home and vehicle maintenance, further studies, self-improvement, short-term and long-term planning, money management, volunteer work. These are the things that focus on self-improvement, relationship strengthening and planning for the future. These are the keys to our sense of fulfillment and success.

There are two main issues that may be preventing you from spending enough time in this category. One is simply not knowing what is important to you or what you want from life. If you decide what you want, you can work towards that goal. If you are unsure, you will end up simply "treading water" and not making progress in any specific direction. The other issue is being so caught up with urgent business (important and unimportant) that you have no time to work on what you value most. It is important to note that if one plans well, life will be less filled with urgent business and life will calm down. For example, good planning and budgeting will prevent the time—and energy-consuming stress of a personal financial crisis. Regular home and vehicle maintenance will help prevent an urgent repair need.

This brings us to the third quadrant, that which is Urgent and Unimportant. These are thrust upon us: a favor, an interruption, a trivial meeting, things that often distract from that which is important. This category must be trimmed wherever possible. Some things can be delegated to others. If a friend asks a favor that you are not suited for, perhaps you can point them in the direction of someone more able to help. Other tasks in this category can be delayed or even eliminated. Learning how to politely decline additional responsibilities that add no value to our lives can help immensely with urgent, unimportant tasks.

The final category of the Eisenhower Matrix is the fourth quadrant, which is Non-urgent and Unimportant. These tasks simply do not need to be done and can be eliminated or at the very least, pushed to the very bottom of the to-do list. This category would include notorious time-wasters and other traps that procrastinators often fall into.

Step 2: Eliminate Distraction

For a procrastinator it is particularly important to eliminate the distractions, for this it is useful to go further into this point. When we eliminate those things that are neither urgent nor important to us, we have more time to focus on the things we want and need to accomplish. I want you to picture a familiar scenario:

It has never been more imperative that we eliminate distractions that rob us of precious time! Specifically, we can be more aware of the time we are wasting on social media or web-browsing. There is even software that helps track and limit time spent online. If it is possible for your situation, you could unplug from the internet entirely while you tackle offline tasks.

As far as the smartphone goes, a small step that just about everyone can benefit from is to turn off notifications. These are almost never helpful, and they are a constant time waste. Another way to eliminate distraction is to work with your phone in flight mode and activate it only when you take a break. You could even your phone off for a time. 'Unplugging' is almost unheard of today, but it is both liberating and helpful in increasing our productivity.

A last form of distraction is an emotional distraction. There are some people in our lives that seem to bring nothing but drama and negativity. These "emotional vampires" tend to suck all of the positive energy out of our lives. If we can ward off these vampires, we keep our emotional energy in reserve and avoid being bogged down by unnecessary, distracting negativity.

Step 3: Completing Tasks

As a modern society, we have been told that multitasking is helpful to get things done. Your internet browser probably has multiple tabs open at any given time and your phone is most likely beside you and interrupting at intervals even as you read this. This has become the norm; it is how we live. But have you ever tried to text and drive at the same time? There is a reason it is dangerous. Doing multiple things at once means that nothing gets done well or efficiently. Learn to do one thing at a time and always carry it to completion. Do not start another task until the first has been completed. You can start by practicing small things like loading the dishwasher, cooking, writing emails, etc. Let the momentum and satisfaction of a task completed carry you onto bigger, more important tasks.

If at first you struggle to stay focused, chose a set timeframe or even set a timer. For example, you can work at a task for 10 minutes, take a break and then continue at the task at 10-minute intervals until the task is completed. As this becomes easier, you can train yourself to focus for longer periods of time.

Step 4: Planning (to Beat Procrastination and Increase Productivity)

Once you have used your Eisenhower Matrix to see which are the most urgent and useful tasks for you to focus on, you need to use this information to make a to-do list for each day. Before you go to bed, write a to-do list for the next day. You can start small and build. Write a basic list of what you need to accomplish the next day. At the end of the day, evaluate your list. If you did not complete a task write down why it wasn't done and reschedule it. Strive to finish everything on your list. As you become more comfortable with the system you can write more detailed lists with specific time goals. (E.g. 10 AM–11 AM respond to emails, 11 AM–12 PM phone calls, etc.)

Find ways to make your life more efficient. If there are any aspects of your life in which you could save some time, it's about time you started doing it. Saving yourself some time in some areas will leave more time for you to attend to the other, more pressing matters. For example, if you were to invest 2 or 3 hours one day during the weekend to prepare your meals for the rest of the week, you'll save so much time during the rest of the week because you're not busy cooking your dinner or your lunch, which leaves you more time to attend to other matters. Look at all the tasks you have to attend to and see where you can group similar activities together so you can tackle them in one go. Increase your productivity by minimizing the time spent working on activities individually.

Chapter 30
When Procrastination Is Not the Problem – Other Issues Which Look Like Procrastination

It may happen that the typical dynamics of procrastination are not the cause of inaction.

Not Knowing Where to Start

In this case, instead of choosing instant gratification over a delayed reward, a person delays action because they are overwhelmed by possibilities and does not know how to begin. In this instance, you might continually research options without ever starting towards your goal. It can be extremely overwhelming and stressful when you feel like you're being faced with multiple choices, and you don't have the faintest idea where to begin. When dealing with important, life-changing decisions, it can be even more stressful, especially with the pressure of knowing you have to make the right choice.

Sometimes it is the excess of information that confuses the ideas: especially today that it is so easy to find any information online, it can be difficult to organize and choose which ones are suitable, at a certain moment, for us.

Perfectionism

Another exception to the general procrastination rule is perfectionism. A perfectionist has strong beliefs about how their work or project should look. The problem is that what he seeks, perfection does not exist in this world. The perfectionist then follows something he cannot get. The perfectionist is frozen by the inability to achieve his own lofty standard. According to some psychologists, the antidote is to question analyze your beliefs and replace them with rational ones. If you are a perfectionist unable to start a project, you can question yourself: "do I believe that there is only one right way to do this? Is this a true statement, or are there any possible acceptable ways to complete this task? What other results can be considered acceptable?"

Perfectionists can set unreachable goals for themselves sometimes, and then it hits them hard if they fail to accomplish those goals because of that high level of expectation they set for themselves. Aiming too high, especially when the expectations are unrealistic, is a surefire way to set yourself up for failure. When you spend far too much time planning for perfection, you come up with all sorts of excuses to procrastinate and delay your plan because it will never be perfect enough to be executed in time. Sometimes you just need to look at things realistically, see the facts in front of you and accept that nothing can ever be as perfect as you want 100% of the time.

Inner conflict

The third case is that of the inner conflict. Each person has a system of internal rules that they on a subconscious level. These rules help them to determine which actions they should take. These rules also shape the perception that they have of themselves. For example, Person A has an image of themselves as someone who is enterprising and successful. Person A would never put themselves in a position as that of a regular employee, for example, because it would conflict with the subconscious idea and perception which they have already formed of themselves. We may not realize it, but every action that we take often passes through the scrutiny of our internal rule system. If the decision agrees with our internal rules, we have no problems executing it. However, if it disagrees, that is when internal conflict happens. This is what procrastination looks like. An internal conflict which is happening within you. One half of you wants to do it, but the other half is tempted not to. It is useful to reflect and think about our internal dynamics to help us make full use of the Happiness Formula. This formula makes it easier to determine which values are a priority, and which are not.

Chapter 31
The Principle of Cause and Effect and How It Controls Everything

The law of cause and effect (also known as "the iron law of the universe") plays a powerful role on your path to self-discipline. The law states that every effect has a precise and expectable cause. Every action or cause has a precise and expectable effect. For every effect in our lives, there is a specific cause.

This means that whatever you own in life is an effect brought about by a certain cause. In other words, to be become disciplined in a habit, you must be ready to take action (cause) and manifest that habit (effect) in your life.

The causes are the decisions you make and the actions you take every day. It does not matter if this decision seems trivial or unimportant, or major and important, every decision and action you have taken in your life is responsible for what you are currently experiencing in your life.

To find success in anything, the law claims, you must be prepared to perform specific actions. By being mindful of the things you do, and how they can push you to your goals, only then can you walk that path of self-discipline.

Life is all about making the right decisions and taking the right actions at the right time. You can become disciplined in your studies, diet, relationships, finance, and so on if you become mindful of those right actions and decisions. If you know what you want and know how to get there, then success can be yours.

First, examine the lives of the disciplined people (or people who are self-disciplined in the area you desire). Check out their actions, behavior, emotions, values, beliefs, habits, and decisions to attract similar success into your life.

There are no accidents

There are no accidents in life because everything happens for a reason, the natural rule of cause and effect also states. This means that our universe is orderly. Like a game of chess, every move you make is a choice, and that choice is the cause, that cause comes with an effect.

Negativity gives birth to negativity. Violence gives birth to more violence. It is that simple. When you think positively and take the right positive action to complement your thought, chances are you will find yourself in a positive place.

Doing the same thing over and over again will get you the same result— the law of cause and effect establishes this. You cannot put in bad work and expect a good outcome.

Whenever I look back on my experiences in life, I could easily see the specific causes of my failure and success. The same thing goes for fitness and health, for contentment and misery.

For instance, I am fit right now because I have been going to the gym for a couple of months now. But if I halt my workout for two months, I will not be as healthy and fit and healthy.

Looking back on my past relationships, I can pinpoint at least two toxic relationships and how they had caused me misery. Therefore, going forward with any intimate relationship now, I would know the toxic traits to avoid in a person that might drive me to that same path of misery. The cause of my toxic relationships is my choice. And the effect is the toxicity.

The same things go for my work life. There certain things that have brought me to attain more of my potential. From communication to organization skills—things I had adopted from successful people. Likewise, there are also certain things that in my work life that would negatively affect my general happiness. Appreciating the law of cause and effect has taught me to make better choices as I strive to become more self-disciplined.

Be mindfulness of your choices

The law of cause and effect hinges on being aware of your choices. This means you have to see your emotional state, feelings, and thoughts for what they really are, and how they affect your life and decisions you make.

By being mindful of your choices, you can objectively take better control of your life and consequently make better choices.

Your thoughts are powerful: they can either make or destroy your life. Being mindful of positive thoughts is the easiest way to stay away from negativity. A positive frame of mind is a disciplined frame of mind. What you think is what you get. Every good thing you want to achieve in life is based on the kind of feelings, emotions, and thoughts you are mindful of.

While there are some things in life outside of your control, the law of cause and effects says you will often reap what you sow. Hard work will likely bring success than failure. Working out would likely bring fitness instead of obesity. If you embrace the darkness, darkness will continue to follow you. If you choose the light, your path will also be clear.

One of the best things I have ever done in my life is freeing myself from the hold of negative thoughts. Letting go of thoughts that would infect my space and feelings—thoughts that were driving me closer to more negative actions and more negative people, leaving me unhappy as I was unable to reach my full potential.

By freeing myself, I stopped making excuses and blaming others for my lack of discipline. I began to take full responsibility for my actions. Instead of remaining in a cycle of unease, frustration, and unhappiness, I applied the law of cause and effect and invested time in examining the choices that I have made and what I could have done better, and what positives I can take from the situation. In addition, I identified what actions I can take now to make my future a better one.

Give what you get

Agreeing to Sir Isaac Newton's Third Law of Movement, "For each activity, there's a rise to & inverse reaction." This a logical clarification of the law of cause and impact.

The law of cause and effect has changed my life. Every one of my actions and inactions has brought me to where I am now. My poor health can be traced to my poor nutrition and diet. My mounting debt can be traced to my uncontrolled spending habits. Failure is not an accident. Success is not an accident. Every action I took (consciously or unconsciously) had consequences and produced specific results in my life.

In my personal relationships, the more honesty, compassion, love and respect (cause) I gave out, the more solid relationships—which lead to peace of mind, happiness, and fulfillment (effect).

If you want to be more disciplined in your life, identify the specific things you will need to do to become disciplined. Then take action! Making the first move to better is the hardest part; however, when you set things in motion, nothing can stop you. Then keep persevering. Rome was not built in a day. Success takes time. Success may not come immediately, but if you stay focused and continue to do the right things and fix where needs, you will eventually get the result you want.

Chapter 32
Change Your Action

You can't always rely on your unconscious habits (whether good or bad) to do all the work for you. Sometimes, you have to make deliberate thoughts, decisions, and actions to help move you forward in life. Until now, it is likely that many of the actions you have taken in your life are backed by pesky little habits like negative self-talk, poor self-confidence, or your commitment to staying comfortable. However, not every single action you make is a habit and so, when you arrive at new decisions, you need to know how to consciously take action in your life and move forward intentionally and successfully in the right direction. I'm going to show you how I was able to stop making weak decisions at every turn and start taking bold, confident, and focused action in my life.

Here We Go Again

If you have been trapped in a habit loop that has kept you making the same terrible decisions over and over again, it's time for you to take responsibility for your choices and make a change. In other words, you need to skip over your habits and start making decisions to take new action. It's time for you to learn your lesson and move on so that you can stop being dragged down by the same nonsense that has kept you down for so long already.

For me, the guilty pleasure that constantly kept me down was my diet. Hanging out on the couch watching Netflix and lounging my life away wasn't really conducive to positive eating decisions. I would consistently munch on unhealthy processed snacks, eat takeout, and skip over meals in favor of sitting down and staying comfortable instead. But in a way, I wasn't actually comfortable at all. I started gaining weight, I never actually felt good, and I was struggling to really make any significant changes in my life. My increasing weight and decreasing stamina left me feeling embarrassed, especially since I struggled to do basic things like walk and talk without feeling winded. Truth be told, I was at my lowest point when it came to health at the time and I was feeling really bad about myself. I knew I needed to make a change, but I couldn't seem to keep motivated or feel disciplined enough to actually stick to those changes or even make the first step. Lounging around and eating pizza or Chinese food was just so much easier than looking up a healthy recipe, going to the grocery store to get ingredients, and then cooking to make a healthy meal for myself. So, I stayed uncomfortable, unhealthy, and unhappy as I just repeated the loop over and over again.

Look In the Mirror

Have you ever looked at the people in your life as mirrors? Have you ever considered the people in your life as reflections of yourself? The relationships that you have in your life could very well directly reflect the relationship you have with yourself, giving you a clear look into who you are and how you truly feel about the person that you have become in your life. If you are like I was a few years back that may completely terrify you when you notice that the relationships in your life are toxic, meaningless, or completely non-existent. In fact, you may even do as I did and completely reject this reality until one day you are looking in the mirror and you make the connection by realizing that your relationship with yourself really sucks.

The closer you are with people in your life, the more they will reflect you to yourself and give you a clearer picture of how you truly feel about yourself and the relationship you share with you. If you lack any close, intimate relationships in your life or if the ones you do have are in shambles, chances are you don't feel too hot about yourself, and the relationship you share with yourself is not a positive one. You may find yourself avoiding close relationships or rejecting them because somewhere deep inside you realize that these people expose you to yourself in ways that you do not like. Or, you may find yourself clinging to them and wishing for them to work out while allowing these relationships to become damaging or destructive and tear you down from any success you may stand to achieve.

Chill Out, Bro

People who desire to be resilient and possess more mental strength probably want to do so because they ultimately want to get to work on becoming something bigger and better than they already are. After all, you don't need mental strength and confidence to just remain the same. But, as much as jumping into action and getting to work is necessary when it comes to changing your life, you also need to know how to slow down and engage in complete and total relaxation on a regular basis. Balance, people, balance.

In fact, one of the leading problems that result in people remaining unwilling or unable to move forward in life is burnout or total mental exhaustion from having to balance or think about far too many things at once. Has your head ever hurt from just thinking too hard? I remember right before I said, "screw it" and took my horizontal hiatus, my people-pleasing, lack of self-confidence, and apparent inability to do anything right despite repeated attempts resulted in me feeling extremely burnt out and unwilling to do anything more. I wasn't making progress in my life because at that time, I couldn't. Over time, the "I couldn't" became "I wouldn't" and I refused to move forward or do anything because I realized it was much easier to keep myself out from under serious pressure than it was to expose myself to it again and risk another serious burnout.

What On Earth Do You Mean?

Some people believe that every single person is born with their own divine purpose that they have been put on Earth to fulfill. Others believe that we create purpose in our lives by choosing something meaningful to us and fully engaging in it in a meaningful and heart-filled manner. Whichever side of the coin you're on doesn't mean anything and doesn't matter, but just know that you do need to land on one side or the other, rather than bumbling around in your life aimlessly with no purpose.

That's the most surefire way to end up being a weak-minded quitter because you have nothing driving you forward and no real, strong enough reason to keep going. People who attempt to go through life without any purpose or meaning end up depressed and haggard. They are either doing nothing at all, or constantly half-ass pursuing a better life but never have anything really pushing them along and mentally helping them achieve that "better" life that they dream of having. Without this driving force, it's impossible to be resilient and remain mentally strong in tough times. Staying devoted to any one thing is virtually impossible when everything you attempt to devote yourself is so wildly out of alignment with who you are and what you desire to achieve in your life. If you haven't already figured it out, you need to discover why you're here on this Earth and how you plan on making an impact with this one life that you have been given.

You're a Joke

When was the last time you laughed? And I mean a good, deep from the pit of your belly, so loud that you're embarrassed, stomach hurts, head hurts laugh? I am going to go out on a limb here (for the sake of making my point) and say that for you, it's been a while. In fact, you may even be willing to secretly admit to yourself that it has been years since you laughed so hard that you thought you might pee your pants because it was just that deep and genuine. You may think that laughter is for the weak, for the people who don't take things seriously enough. I mean, it kind of makes sense. Laughing is sort of the opposite of being serious. When we think of mental toughness and resilience and strength and confidence, it usually conjures up images of Marines, the military, frowns, stoic faces, furrowed brows, abnormally and uncomfortably erect posture, and yelling whilst making pretty much no facial expression. But, you may be surprised to know that laughter is a wonderful form of medicine that is actually known to increase your mental toughness and resiliency so that you can continue moving forward in life without taking everything so personally or allowing everything to keep you down.

Getting a good laugh in on a regular basis is not only enjoyable, but it will actually provide you with proven mental health benefits that will help you break through a rut and get into a new phase in your life. According to my good friends Dr. Lee Berk and Dr. Stanley Tan at Loma Linda University in California (okay, they're not actually my good friends, but they are doctors), laughing is known to reduce your stress hormone levels and support you in ditching feelings of anxiety. This may be why your body subconsciously responds with out-of-place laughter when you are experiencing extreme levels of fear or anxiety in your life. Ever laughed at a funeral, anyone? Just me? Getting laughter into your daily routine, or at least getting a good laugh at once or twice a week, can help you reduce the amount of stress you feel in your body and help you feel happier overall.

Who's To Blame?

When things aren't going your way and your life doesn't look how you want it to look, it's easy to blame everyone around you. But are they really the reason you are where you are? Are they really the reason why you are not taking action towards achieving your goals right now? For me, I was constantly blaming everyone and everything for why I was unable to do anything to get myself out of my rut and I was hell-bent on defending why nothing was ever my fault. I blamed my Mom for not teaching me better when I was growing up, my neighbor for being too loud so I couldn't sleep, my boss for being too mean so I couldn't perform, and my friend for being too needy so I couldn't take time to work on myself. I blamed my dog for needing to go to the bathroom and requiring time and attention from me, and I blamed the weather for why I couldn't be bothered to dress nicely. Literally, anything I could blame to excuse myself from having to take responsibility for my shit life, I did. I was constantly playing the blame game as a way to avoid the fact that there was only one reason why I was not doing better than I was in my life, and that reason was little old me.

Chapter 33
How to Take Your Practice Skills into the Big Game

Many times, your young athlete will feel very comfortable in practice and do well, but when it comes to the big game, the practice performance doesn't carry over very well. The trick is if you want to see consistency with the practice and game time, treat practice as though it were the big game.

Don't show up to practice and have the attitude of "Let me just get this over with." You want to show up to practice in competitive mode. You want to use practice time to develop confidence in the competition of the game time.

Examples:

- If you are practicing free throws, have some teammates try to distract you.

- If you are hitting in the cage, try to hit more off of your team pitchers to get a competition feel.

- If you're playing football, try to engage in more scrimmages than just drills.

- If you're a golfer, you can't leave until you make 20 putts in a row. Knowing you will have to start all over again if you miss the last one is a lot of pressure. What skills are you teaching yourself here? Discipline and concentration.

- If you're a basketball player, pick a spot to shoot from and get a certain amount of shots in or you have to start over. You can make friendly competitions so that the loser has to run laps, pushups, or design something for yourself if your teammates aren't into it.

How do you deal with all the distractions at game time? The comments from the home team crowd, the other opposing players, trash talk, bad calls by umps? What can you do? You prepare in practice. Put these distractions right into your practice so when it happens during the competition, you're ready. You've trained your reactions. You've controlled your emotions Have your coach yell at you or your teammate's right when you're trying to make a play or practice a drill. Try to distract each other making free throws if you're practicing at home, get family members to provide some distraction as you're working on things. The more you do this at practice, the more you'll be prepared for things that can happen at the game. You want to practice with the mindset that you want to be challenged, that you love pressure; bring it on! You love being the person people count on. You want to be put in difficult situations. Ask your coach to push you a little harder in practice one day. This will prepare you for the competition. Make every practice an exercise in building your mental toughness. You need to bring this into practice. The mental toughness comes from being in tough situations and then recovering from them. The mind grows stronger after every time you make it work harder.

Start to change your mindset that CHALLENGE IS GOOD. The only way to escape fear is to crush it beneath your feet. Don't let fear eat you.

You need to look at practice as a golden opportunity to build mental toughness.

Developing New Behaviors

Have your child think of some behavior they would like to change and decide on a new behavior to replace it.

Have them choose a role model, doing the skill they'd love to do. It could be their favorite athlete doing something they would love to emulate.

Have them close their eyes and visualize their role model doing the skill. Have them watch it like they were sitting in the movies watching a big screen in their mind. Have them see how their role model looks, how they use their body. Notice how they carry their posture. Notice their attitude, their confidence, and their actions.

Up to this point, you were having your child watching their role model in action. Now have your child remove their role model from the movie and visualize playing in the starring role. They're now visualizing acting just like their role model.

Have them visualize doing exactly as their role model did, displaying the new behavior they want. They should keep watching until they're happy with how it looks and feels. It should feel like being featured in a highlight reel of awesome plays.

Have them switch from watching to doing. Instead of watching from a distance, they're now inside the movie looking through their own eyes. They're now doing this new behavior just like they did when they were watching. Have them answer the questions: How does your body feel? How do you carry yourself?

Imagine you're in a future game and you're going to perform this new behavior. Look through your own eyes. You're the star and you are performing your new behavior in a new way. Everything is working for you. See it; feel it!

Have them open their eyes and have them imagine that they now possess this new behavior. Have them walk around with confidence and talk about how it feels. Do this exercise often, especially before practice and games!

"Success is where preparation and opportunity meet."

Bobby Unser.

Chapter 33
Train the Brain

To become mentally tough, you need to develop an unbeatable mind, the mind that always says to him or her, I'm the greatest and I can achieve anything, and nothing can stop me. That is an unbeatable mind. Many people in the world today have problems with their jobs, career, business, education, and projects, simply because they lack the unbeatable mind. Let me share from experience one man who constantly claimed to be the greatest, when he started and when he usually makes such bold claim "I am the greatest!" people thought that he was joking, but he eventually was, as many years passed, his track records in the world boxing is still a point of reference. He is no other than the late "Mohammed Ali." He had such a mindset that stubbornly claimed that he was the greatest, he was able to defeat so many opponents and even the ones he lost to, he came back to beat them.

The unbeatable mindset doesn't believe that someone can beat him or her, an unbeatable mindset always and constantly makes bold claim statement by being convinced that nothing can stop him or hold him back, when you get to that level you will definitely be mentally tough and actually nothing will pull you down. These are some of the characteristics of someone with an unbeatable mindset which you should know and begin to put in practice:

"Yes, I can"—Unbeatable Mindset

There are many people in the world today who have difficulty in telling themselves that they can do something. The majority of this category of people are not always achieving anything in life because they never have the conviction that they can do what other people who are successful are doing to get to the top. Once you are unable to have the constant conviction that "yes I can" you'll be where you are until you begin to believe you actually can do something.

I have been in the position where I sampled out a lot of people, and there was a particular thing I needed to be done for me, as I went around looking for someone to help me out, majority of the people I came across were always telling me "no I can't do it" am not talking about doing something negative, no! It was a simple task that needed to be done. But surprisingly only one boy who was about 15 years old accepted to do it and he did what even a 25-year-old said he couldn't do. You see, that's the problem with many people in the world today, they just don't believe that they can do something. Whether it is, in business, education, career, sports, and other areas of human endeavors, they aren't just bold enough to have that mentality of "yes, I can." The unbeatable mindset will not be complete without accepting and believing in the "yes, I can."

I want to tell you today that "yes, you can," I want to let you know that you can make it to the top, I want to tell today that I believe anyone can rise and get to the pinnacle of his or her career, but if I say "yes you can" and you refuse to say "yes I can" there is nothing anyone can do about it because you've not gotten that conviction. So, I need you to say it to yourself as many times as possible "yes I can," say it every ten minutes and every time and you will see the impact. There you go; you will begin to develop an unbeatable mindset.

Use what you have to your advantage

For you to have an unbeatable mindset there is something important I'll like to let you know and that is, using what you have at a greater advantage to achieve what you want. You are a unique person and there are no two persons other than you and there are no other you but you. What this means is that everyone has a talent and that can be used to great advantage against any opponent or contemporary. Therefore, use it to your advantage, if you refuse to use your talent or what you have better, someone else will use his or hers to better advance. So, you have to find a way to succeed in the survival of the fittest and one of the finest ways to become mentally tough is by having an unbeatable mindset, to use what you have as an advantage to your own benefit. Cristiano Ronaldo, Lionel Messi, Michael Jordan, Magic Johnson, Late Michael Jackson, Late Michael Faraday, etc. all these great people did not just exist without using their talent to great advantage.

They started by discovering their talents and they began to develop it by constantly using it and making it becoming relevant and they did that every day and today they have successfully stamped their history and authority in the sands of time. Michael Jackson was discovered alongside his brothers, he was gifted, he had a special kind of talent, which included his ability to sing, dance and also drew a lot of attention from the audience. When he discovered himself, he began to practice and he had a different kind of personality which was a result of developing an unbeatable mindset. He stayed on top of his game and he won so many awards, broke so many records. So, to have an unbeatable mindset, use everything that you have got, your talent and your biggest advantage is when you are able to make use of what you have got.

Remember the parable of the talents, each of them were given different talents of different values, some use their talents and multiplied, and they receive more rewards and praises by their masters, some went to hide theirs, and even the little they had was taken away from them and given to someone who had more. That is a very big lesson that you have to learn about life, always make use of what you have got. Don't abandon your talent and start looking for a result somewhere else. The answer to your desires lies within you, seek it, find it, and use it.

Constant Practice

To have an unbeatable mindset, you have to engage yourself in the constant practice of what you know how to do. You are the only one who knows how you do your thing and you are the best at what you do, you are not the best at what someone else does for you, No! You are the best at what you are doing for yourself presently. This is the basis of what it takes to develop an unbeatable mindset; don't think someone else will make you be the best. Only teachers, coaches, and trainers will show you the basics and technical part of what you need to know, but you still have to do it yourself in other to discover your abilities.

Constant practice can only be achieved when you are ready or prepare your mind to get into it. Don't always act as if someone is forcing you to do something, let your mind be made up that this is what you want and it is possible only if I involve myself in constant practice.

Constant practice, therefore, makes the job easier and your gaining mastery and perfection can only be achieved when you continue to work on something continuously. It may take some time to achieve, it may not be easy in the first instance, but it's definitely worth it when you start, don't look back and make sure you put the right facilities that will help you succeed. For instance, you want to start a career in football, you don't need a ping pong ball, you need a football, you need to play basketball, what you need is basketball and a basketball court where you can practice, etc.

Again, talent may not be enough, but constant practice will go a long way to further develop your talent, if you want to be the best, you need to develop your talent through constant practice. I have seen superstars in football learn and practice how to take free kicks, for instance, David Beckham, one of the English footballers was a free-kick specialist, I've seen him take three free-kicks in a match and he scored all three. It couldn't have been possible without constant practice. Hence, constant practice is the key to developing an unbeatable mindset because he believed in his ability to score free kicks even from long range and it was so for him.

Whatever you need, whatever you want to achieve, you need to get into the practice of that thing from the armature level and move on to the professional which is your next level.

Be Excited

You really want to make it to the top, you have to be very excited, developing a mindset is not when you are sad or neutral, if you are not excited about what you are doing or feeling too much pressure you may not get what you want. Hence, I'll advise that you stay excited, always see that there is something great coming out of what you are doing. Excitement brings out the best in you because your level of adrenalin will always be high. When you know the potential and chances behind what you are doing, you will always feel the need to always get things done to a level that you will become satisfied. The move, the plan and everything that you are doing must involve excitement, without excitement you will not stay afresh. Excitement makes you look fresh, putting a smile on your face will make you feel good, simply because you are excited about what you are doing, again excitement brings the feeling of goodness, being pleased with yourself when you discovered that you are making progress before the competition starts or during preparation for an event makes it possible for you to build up an unbeatable mindset. Excitement doesn't bring discouragement when you are excited you will always be encouraged to do more and become successful at what you are doing. Today, I encourage you to be excited no matter what you are going through and you will be prepared to face the biggest challenge and defeat it.

Whenever you discover that you are down or discouraged, try to raise your excitement level, because that is just the tonic you need. Feeling disappointed about something that didn't go as you expected is a common phenomenon that most people go through. But when it happens to you, don't feel bad about it; all you need to do is raise your excitement level. Look into the future and see yourself already where you want to be, smile and laugh at any disappointment, feel happy that you have already won the battle, don't let disappointments bring you down, and you will be glad that you are always feeling excited about your project or career.

Conclusion

N ow, you have learned a lot of very useful strategies for you to not just set your goals but make them happen. As you practice with these principles I've laid out in this, you will find yourself accomplishing a lot more over the months to come than most people ever get done in a whole lifetime.

If you are going to succeed, you can't just read this. Read it again. More importantly, put it into practice. Take action, every chance you get. The more you take action, the quicker you can learn what works for you and what doesn't, so that you can succeed. People who accomplish things in life don't just sit around doing nothing, or just making little moves here and there. They are always on the go.

So, get started on taking back your life. Your potential is limitless. There's always room for improvement. You don't have to make a quantum leap in a day. You only need a few steps each day to get you to your goal. You are the one who is responsible for what happens in your life. You can no longer claim to be ignorant of this fact. Blame your failures and setbacks on other people or the environment if you want, but deep down, you will always know that you and you alone are responsible. So, act like you're in charge, and move confidently in the direction of your dreams.

Don't just apply these principles to your work life. Use them in every aspect of your life. Apply them to your finances. Go through your financial life with a fine-tooth comb, and then make up your mind how much it is you would like to be making within the next couple of years. Don't just let the chips fall where they may. Decide where they fall... If they even fall.

Work on your relationships, as well. Make it a priority to have productivity shine through not just when it comes to work, but in your relationship with your family, friends, and significant other. People matter. People are the reason you will move forward in life. So do invest in your relationships. Invest in expanding your network. You know that clichéd but true saying: Your network equals your net worth. Also, there's no point finally achieving your dreams, only to end up sad and empty because there's no one with whom you can celebrate. What would be the point??

Your health is just as important. So, make sure you decide and commit to a life that is healthy and full of energy. Make fitness a goal. Decide what fitness means to you and work out a plan to make it happen. Remember, baby steps. We're not trying to build Rome in a day.

One thing I must mention before I completely wrap up this, that you've got to use your subconscious mind to your advantage. Your subconscious mind is responsible for all the functions of your mind that you do not consciously handle. It's where innovative ideas come from. It's where the willpower comes from, too. You just have to mold it in such a way that it serves you. Your subconscious mind is amazing because it has unspeakable power. Power to bring you every single thing you've ever hoped for or dreamed of. So always enlist the help of your subconscious.

CPSIA information can be obtained
at www.ICGtesting.com
Printed in the USA
LVHW011046191220
674520LV00002B/108